LESLIE MARMON SILKO'S
Ceremony

PETER LANG
New York • Washington, D.C./Baltimore • Bern
Frankfurt am Main • Berlin • Brussels • Vienna • Oxford

Robert M. Nelson

LESLIE MARMON SILKO'S
Ceremony

The Recovery of Tradition

PETER LANG
New York • Washington, D.C./Baltimore • Bern
Frankfurt am Main • Berlin • Brussels • Vienna • Oxford

Library of Congress Cataloging-in-Publication Data

Nelson, Robert M.
Leslie Marmon Silko's Ceremony: the recovery of tradition /
Robert M. Nelson.
p. cm.
Includes bibliographical references and index.
1. Silko, Leslie, 1948– Ceremony. 2. Laguna Indians in literature.
3. Oral tradition in literature. 4. Intertextuality. I. Title.
PS3569.I44C437   813'.54—dc22   2008006035
ISBN 978-1-4331-0361-2 (hardcover)
ISBN 978-1-4331-0205-9 (paperback)

Bibliographic information published by **Die Deutsche Bibliothek**.
Die Deutsche Bibliothek lists this publication in the "Deutsche
Nationalbibliografie"; detailed bibliographic data is available
on the Internet at http://dnb.ddb.de/.

Cover photo by Robert M. Nelson

© 2008 Peter Lang Publishing, Inc., New York
29 Broadway, 18th floor, New York, NY 10006
www.peterlang.com

All rights reserved.
Reprint or reproduction, even partially, in all forms such as microfilm,
xerography, microfiche, microcard, and offset strictly prohibited.

For my daughters

Erin and Ellie

with much love

there never was a time
this was not so

TABLE OF CONTENTS

Acknowledgments xi

Chapter 1: Introduction 1
    About Silko 4

Chapter 2: Mapping the Embedded Texts 13

Chapter 3: Re-Fleshing the Backbone: Pretext and Prose Narrative in *Ceremony* 19

Chapter 4: Analogy vs. Homology: The Kaupata Motif 27
    Starstuff 31
    Clouds and Cattle: Life for the People 33

Chapter 5: The Hoop Series: The Spectrum of Storytelling Modes ... 39
    Whose Voice is This? 39
    Jumping through Hoops 50

Chapter 6: The Sunrise Series 57
    "Sunrise" 57
    "A song for the sunrise" 59
    "Sunrise, accept this offering" 61
    A Note on One Function of the Series as a Whole 62

Chapter 7: The Laguna Sisters 65
    Pretexts 65
    Tayo and Reed Woman 68
    Tayo and Corn Woman 68
    "Auntie" Thelma and "little sister" Laura 69
    Oral Tradition and Prose Narrative 71

Chapter 8: The Backbone Series I: Departure and Pacayanyi 75
    Pretexts for Segment 1 75
    Function of Segment 1 77

Tayo and Ma'see'wi 78
Tayo and Pa'caya'nyi 80

Chapter 9: The Backbone Series II: Recovery and Hummingbird 83
Pretexts for Segments 2 through 9 84
Function of Segments 2 through 9 84
Segment 2 (53–54) 85
Segment 3 (71–72) 86
Segment 4 (82) 88
Segment 5 (105–06) 90
Segment 6 (113) 91
Segment 7 (151–52) 93
Segment 8 (180) 94
Segment 9 (255–56) 95

Chapter 10: Scalp Ceremony 99
Pretexts 100
Function 103

Chapter 11: Betonie's Medicine: The Navajo Series 107
Bear and Coyote 107
Bear-Child Transformation 108
Coyote-Hunter Transformation 109
The Big Hoop Ceremony 114
Re-appropriating Whiteness 117

Chapter 12: The Witchery 121
Origin of the Gunnadeyah 123
"The lava rock hills" 124

Chapter 13: Arrowboy 127
Pretexts 127
Hoop/Transformation Motif and Vision 128
From Acoma to Laguna 133
"Estoy-eh-muut and the Kunideeyahs" 134

Contents

"Estoymuut and the Gunnadeyah" 135

Appendix A: Mapping the Embedded Texts 139
Appendix B: Laguna Sisters 143
Appendix C: Kaupata 145
Appendix D: Pacayanyi 147
Appendix E: Hummingbird 149
Appendix F: Arrowboy/Estoy-eh-muut 153
Appendix G: Navajo Pretexts 155
Notes 161
Works Cited 183
Index 187

ACKNOWLEDGMENTS

My gratitude to the following for permission to quote:

Franz Boas, *Keresan Texts*. New York: American Ethnological Society, 1928. Reprinted by permission of the publisher. All rights reserved.

Robert J. Conley, "We Wait." *The Remembered Earth: An Anthology of Contemporary American Indian Literature*. Albuquerque: U of New Mexico P, 1980. Reprinted by permission of the author.

Leslie Marmon Silko, *Ceremony*. Copyright ©1986 by Leslie Silko. Reprinted with permission of The Wylie Agency.

Leslie Marmon Silko, *Storyteller*. New York: Seaver, 1981. Reprinted by permission of the author.

Leland Wyman. *The Red Antway of the Navaho*. Santa Fe: Museum of Navajo Ceremonial Art, 1965. Reprinted with permission of the Wheelwright Museum of the American Indian.

A portion of chapter 1 of this book first appeared as "Leslie Marmon Silko: Storyteller" in Joy Porter and Kenneth Roemer's *The Cambridge Companion to Native American Literature* (Cambridge University Press, 2005). A portion of chapter 2 first appeared in an essay co-authored with Peter G. Beidler, "Grandma's Wicker Basket: Untangling the Narrative Threads in *Ceremony*," in *American Indian Culture and Research Journal* 28.1 (2004). Much of chapter 3 appeared as an essay entitled "Rewriting Ethnography: Embedded Texts in Leslie Silko's *Ceremony*" in *Telling the Stories: Essays on American Indian Literatures and Cultures* (Peter Lang, 2001). A slightly different version of chapter 4 of this book first appeared as "The Kaupata

Motif in Silko's *Ceremony*: A Study of a Literary Homology" in *SAIL, Studies in American Indian Literatures* 11.3 (Fall 1999). A version of chapter 6 first appeared as "Sunrise and *Ceremony*" in the online journal *Native Realities* 1.2 (Summer 2001). Much of chapter 12 first appeared as an article, "Settling for Vision in *Ceremony*: Sun Man, Arrowboy, and Tayo," in *American Indian Culture and Research Journal* 28.1 (2004).

My thanks to the University of Richmond's Faculty Research Committee for several summer research grants, to Deans David Leary and Andy Newcomb for their generous support of this project over a span of a dozen years, and to my colleagues in and out of the Department of English for their interest and encouragement during the period of this study's composition.

I have benefited enormously from all the encouragement and support I have received from my colleagues in the field of Native American literatures and especially those in ASAIL, the Association for the Study of American Indian Literatures, a true community of scholars ever generous in their criticism and advice. I love you all.

For more than decade now Heidi Burns, Peter Lang's Acquisitions Editor, has provided constant encouragement for my work in the field of American Indian literatures and especially the work that has resulted in this study. Thank, you, Heidi, for your faith in my work and your unhesitating support of this project.

I want to extend special thanks to my dear friends Lee and Kathy Marmon, who opened their home and hearts to me again and again during the past twenty years of my visits to Laguna, who made their home my home and allowed me to tangle my story in theirs. May nothing I say in this book offend you.

And finally, my thanks to Karen Anderson, who coaxed me into coming out of my retirement retreat long enough to see this project into publication. You are a blessing.

CHAPTER 1
Introduction

The recent trend in academe toward promoting multicultural literacy has created a demand for sensitive but accurate introductions to American masterpieces that in turn respect and reflect "minority" cultural traditions. Silko's *Ceremony* has emerged as such a masterpiece, generally regarded as one of the two or three most useful and widely used twentieth-century Native American texts; the novel has become part of the canon in mainstream American literature courses as well as in Women's Studies programs at both the graduate and undergraduate levels.[1]

The growing demand for critical background on Silko's work is reflected in the number of recent publications devoted to her work. These include two collections of interviews, Melody Graulich's 1993 *"Yellow Woman," Leslie Marmon Silko* and Ellen Arnold's 2000 *Conversations with Leslie Marmon Silko*; three overviews of her work, including Gregory Salyer's 1997 *Leslie Marmon Silko*, Helen Jaskoski's 1998 *Leslie Marmon Silko: A Study of the Short Fiction*, and Brewster Fitz's *Silko: Writing Storyteller and Medicine Woman* (2004); and two collections of critical essays, Louise Barnett and James Thorson's 1999 *Leslie Marmon Silko: A Collection of Critical Essays* and Allen Chavkin's 2002 *Leslie Marmon Silko's* Ceremony*: A Casebook*, each of which gathers together the work of fifteen Silko scholars. In the introduction to his casebook, Chavkin claims (I think correctly) that "For non-Indian readers both the source of greatest difficulty and the source of greatest originality is Silko's heavy reliance on Pueblo and Navajo cultures, traditions, and mythologies" (8). So far, however, no comprehensive study of the Pueblo and Navajo sources for this novel —nothing on the order of Susan Scarberry-García's groundbreaking *Landmarks of Healing*, a study of the documentable Navajo sources of Momaday's *House Made of Dawn*—has been attempted. This book is my attempt to provide one.

To date, most of the critical light shed on the sources of Silko's work, including *Ceremony*, has focused on its roots in oral tradition—"literature" encoded solely in the spoken word rather than in a written form. According to the current conventional wisdom (reinforced by what Silko herself has said in printed interviews about influences on her work), oral performances are the most immediate sources, or pretexts, of the traditional stories embedded in Silko's text; this proposition in turn invites us to read the text in question as a print version of an oral performance. While such an approach to the novel is certainly consistent with many Native American literary traditions, including the Keresan[2] tradition underlying Silko's novel, it also creates some problems. For one, many readers are made uneasy by the proposition that a familiarity with Keresan oral traditions is a prerequisite to understanding such a book on its own terms. Having no way to experience directly the living Keresan oral tradition, such readers may be further alienated from the novel's cultural origins by such an approach. Further, the methodology implicit in this approach is not necessarily appropriate to a text like *Ceremony*. Privileging the aesthetics of "oracy"[3] over those of "literacy" can work well when the work being addressed is a short piece (as for instance any single one of the embedded texts in the novel) or when the work is an ensemble of shorter pieces (such as *Storyteller*, the subject of some of the best source studies of Silko's artistry produced so far). In such cases, the text in question can legitimately be read as a print version of a traditional oral performance. However, one major problem with applying this approach to a carefully integrated novel like *Ceremony* is that *Ceremony is* a novel, created to function as a print text, albeit perhaps a print text "about," *inter alia*, oral performance; if so, the text is theoretically a product of, and thus a reflection of, both Native American oral and Western written literary and cultural traditions.

The work in this book is designed to supplement (not replace) oral approaches to the novel. I do not wish to ignore scholarship that wrestles with the problems of reading a text (such as Silko's *Ceremony*) with respect to the conventions of oral, as opposed to written, performance. However, the body of my project involves locating Silko's novel and creative vision with respect to other print texts—especially printed texts that not only lend themselves to an oral critical approach but also function as print pretexts for Silko's own text, the novel *Ceremony*. I hope that by providing an analysis of the novel's relation to other print texts, many of which demonstrably are direct pretexts for the most "traditional"-looking parts of Silko's novel, this book will provide a useful context for many readers—including, especially, potential teachers of the novel and novels like it.

I have been preoccupied for some time now with the embedded texts that speckle the pages of Leslie Silko's first novel *Ceremony*, many of which also show up among the pages of her remarkable scrapbook *Storyteller*. My own special interest in *Ceremony* generally, and the embedded texts in particular, grows out of a 1987 NEH Summer Seminar, the "Tucson Seminar" conducted by Larry Evers. Not unpredictably, interest in these embedded texts led me at first to thinking about how they relate to their oral traditional antecedents. And while that Protean relationship is good to think about and fun to talk about, I have concluded that because the only available corroboration is hearsay evidence, my own testimony about who said what to whom being irrelevant because I was not there, it is impossible for me as a critic to demonstrate the certainty of any particular relationship to the satisfaction of any decent skeptic—including myself. Gradually, then, I decided to focus instead on identifying the ethnographic print sources of these embedded texts and then to analyze how these embedded texts relate (on the one hand) to their ethnographic antecedents and (on the other) to the prose narrative in which they are embedded —and which they embed.[4]

I am suggesting, then, that Silko's novel can be treated as an example of postmodern intertextuality—a text in which two kinds of text, prose in narrative mode and embedded poetry in several modes, derive (or better yet, recover) a semblance of authority from a third, absent yet acknowledged, text: the ethnographic pretext. However, my own overriding feeling is that Silko's inclusion of those embedded texts in her first novel is not, as the above claim might imply, about privileging those ethnographic pretexts. Rather, I think including them is, to borrow the title of the militant essay she published around the same time as *Ceremony*, part of "an old-time Indian attack conducted in two parts"[5] on the body of assumptions underlying mainstream American cultural hegemony, assumptions that by the mid-seventies were already quivering from the assaults of nascent postmodernism and its agenda of deconstructive interrogation. On the one prong, her inclusion of these texts represents a strong nod of acknowledgment in the direction of Laguna life and oral tradition as a righteous source of contemporary American fiction. On the other prong, their inclusion is an early literary manifestation of the impulse that came to inform, for instance, NAGPRA in the field of American jurisprudence and the National Museum of the American Indian project in the field of institutionalized American culture. It is an impulse informed by motives of recovery, reclamation, reintegration, and reanimation, all with a view to healing.

This is the impulse attributed also to both Tayo and Sun Man in the Kaupata episode, in which they are both moved to locate and re-appropriate the "stolen rain."[6] For Sun Man, the stolen rain is the stormclouds, the *shiwanna* or Cloud People; for Tayo, it is the speckled cattle; for them both, and for Silko as a reclaiming Laguna storyteller, it is the stories and pieces of story designed and circulated originally to preserve the life of the people. To expand on Silko's own metaphor, some of these stories became separated from their original cultural contexts and purposes when they got rounded up during the frantic turn-of-the-century period of "salvage ethnography" and corralled in foreign, inaccessible places. I am thinking here of the analogy between the fenced-in top of Mount Taylor, where Tayo finds the stolen cattle, and the research libraries miles away from Laguna land where readers would have had to go looking for the scattered ethnographic transcriptions and translations of Laguna's oral tradition prior to Silko's novel. As I will argue in chapter 3, Silko's presentation of these same materials amounts to an act of repatriation; like Skeleton-Fixer in the old stories, Silko gathers those Laguna bones collected by the ethnographers and puts them back to their original use—to serve as backbone for a Laguna story about Laguna life in Laguna country. In this way, the embedded texts become a part of a "now'day" performance, revived within the narrative skin of a print text novel.

ABOUT SILKO

Storytelling comes naturally enough at places like Old Laguna. Each house, and each crumbling adobe shell of a house, has stories attached to it; every mesa, cerro, arroyo, and spring in the surrounding countryside is home to some recountable event, or waiting to become so. As a child, Leslie Marmon grew up attaching herself, in memory and imagination, to the village and then to the land around it; and because this is Laguna land, many of the stories she grew up with were stories from the Keresan oral tradition, the stories of her father's people and their shared history. In her art as in her life, Silko has continued to maintain her identity with the story of the people of *Kawaika*, the People of the Beautiful Lake. The story of Laguna, like the biography of Silko and the fictional lives of her novels' protagonists, has always been a story of contact, departure, and recovery.

Leslie Marmon Silko was born in Albuquerque, New Mexico on 5 March 1948. Her mother, Virginia, was originally from Montana; her father, Lee Howard Marmon, was at the time just out of the Army, beginning his career as a professional photographer and managing the Marmon Trading Post in the village of Old Laguna, about 50 miles west of Albuquerque. Along with her two younger sisters, Wendy and Gigi, Leslie was raised in one of the houses on the southeast edge of Old Laguna village. It was just a short walk away, even for a child, from the Rio San José that arcs below the village on its south and southeast sides, separating the village from—or, seen differently, connecting the village to—what is now Interstate 40 and before that was U.S. Route 66. In several of Silko's *Storyteller* pieces, particularly those featuring the Kochinninako/Yellow Woman motif, this part of the river figures as a contact zone,[7] where a female representing Laguna identity "within" meets a male who represents some other cultural or spiritual identity "out there."[8] This place is also the liminal zone in which the spirits of the Katsinas, passing through it from the direction of sunrise into the village in November, take on the corporeal form of the masked dancers, a transformative event recalled in *Ceremony*.[9] In the work of many writers, such places take shape as wastelands, deserts, lifeless and/or life-threatening expanses; in Silko's work as at Laguna, the site of such transformative contact events appears as a place of comfort and regenerative energy, a place characterized by the twin blessings of shade and moving water even throughout the long summer months. Silko's own affinity for this place reflects, perhaps, her own felt "position," occupying as she does a marginal site with respect to both Laguna "within" and the dominant Anglo mainstream "out there"—and as she depicts it, it is not a bad place to be.

This same sense of contact zone becoming meeting ground also characterizes the position of the family household with respect to its Keresan and non-Keresan surroundings. From the perspective of the east–west highway, the Marmon house stands below and in front of the rest of the village; most of the rest of the village's houses are built farther up on the domed, white gypsum mesa that looks over the river and the highway beyond it. On the top of the mesa at the northwest corner of the village is the gleaming whitewashed Mission San José, the setting for her first published short story, "The Man to Send Rain Clouds." Along the south and southeast edge of the mesa are the commercial buildings which during Silko's childhood included the Marmon Store, the U.S. Post Office, and the old railroad depot building that was later to become her father's house. During the 1940s and into the mid-1960s, the Marmon family's general store, located a house or two nearer the highway interchange than the house in which Leslie grew up, served not only residents of Laguna and the surrounding Laguna Pueblo villages—Paguate, Mesita, Encinal, Paraje, Seama, and Casablanca—but also cross-country automobilists and truckers.

Born and raised at this cultural intersection, Silko grew up becoming part of both Anglo and Keresan cultural traditions at once, as had most of her Marmon ancestors at Laguna. The first Marmons to come to Laguna, Ohioans Walter and his brother Robert, came as surveyors just after the Civil War, married Laguna women, and stayed on, Walter as a school teacher and Robert as a trader; both eventually were elected to serve as Governor of the Pueblo. Conversely, Silko's Keresan great-grandmother Marie Anaya Marmon (Robert's second wife), the "Grandma A'mooh" of *Storyteller*, left Laguna to attend the Carlisle Indian School in Pennsylvania, and Robert and Marie sent their son Henry, Silko's paternal grandfather, to the Sherman Institute in California. Another of the Laguna women among Silko's forebears, her great-aunt Susie (*nee* Susan Reyes, who was married to Henry's brother Walter), attended both the Carlisle Indian School and Dickinson College (also in Carlisle); upon returning to Laguna, she served the community as a schoolteacher and also as a Keresan cultural historian—a "storyteller" like Grandma A'mooh, in one of the most important senses of that term. Leslie's father, Lee, served as Tribal Council Treasurer during the time that uranium began to be mined at Laguna. Not surprisingly, given such a heritage, Leslie Marmon Silko grew up in a house full of books and stories, part of an extended family whose members have always been prominent in Laguna's history of contact with Euro-American social, political, economic, and educational forces. The story of the Marmon family at Laguna is a story of outsiders who became insiders and of insiders who became outsiders—a story about the arts of cultural mediation, from both sides of the imaginary borderline.

In *Storyteller* and elsewhere, Silko acknowledges the extended Marmon family of storytellers, including her aunt Susie, her grandma A'mooh, her grandfather Henry, and her father, as a powerful shaping influence on her own creative vision and storytelling repertoire.[10] However, as Silko has also pointed out, the extended landscape of her early years was shaping her vision and providing stories as well.[11] Beyond the village and the river to the east lay the red rocks of Mesita, patches of rich, wet grazing land, and the Cañoncito Navajo reservation on the other side of some lava flats; to the south there were sand hills, red and yellow mesas dotted with springs, cool clear water on the hottest summer days; to the west lay most of the other Laguna settlements, and Cubero and Budville, and the Malpais; to the northwest, looming over it all, high and blue in the distance, rose Mt. Taylor, the place for deer hunting, bear country; and due north, up the long hill where bulldozers and Cats would change the landscape forever while creating the Jackpile open-pit uranium mine in the 1950s, there was the conservative village of Paguate, where many of the old-timers lived, and beyond that Seboyeta, near the site of the original Laguna sipapu or emerging place in some of the Keresan origin stories. By the time she was a teenager, Silko knew something of these places and their stories:

> My father had wandered over all the hills and mesas around Laguna when he was a child, because the Indian School and the taunts of the other children did not sit well with him.... I started roaming those same mesas and hills when I was nine years old. At eleven I rode away on my horse, and explored places my father and uncle could not have reached on foot. I was never afraid or lonely—though I was high in the hills, many miles from home—because I carried with me the feeling I'd acquired from listening to the old stories, that the land all around me was teeming with creatures that were related to human beings and to me. ("Interior and Exterior Landscapes" 166)

In addition to the informal education she was receiving from the land and the storytellers in her extended family, Leslie attended the BIA school at Laguna through the fifth grade and then parochial schools in Albuquerque during her teenage school years. She spent her undergraduate years at the University of New Mexico, where she was enrolled in the general honors program, and received her

B.A. in English (with honors) in 1969, the year the Pulitzer Prize for fiction was awarded to Scott Momaday's *House Made of Dawn*. She then enrolled in the American Indian law program at the University of New Mexico Law School but later transferred into the creative writing M.A. program there.

Though her interest in writing predated her college years—she was already writing stories in elementary school—that interest blossomed during her years at the University of New Mexico, during which time she took several courses in creative writing and saw her first work published ("The Man to Send Rain Clouds" in *New Mexico Quarterly*, Winter–Spring 1969). By 1971 she had chosen writing, rather than the practice of law, as her vocation, and in 1974 (at the end of a two-year teaching stint at Navajo Community College) her career became effectively established with two publications: her collection of poetry *Laguna Woman* (Greenfield Review Press) and Kenneth Rosen's *The Man to Send Rain Clouds*, an anthology of 19 Native American short stories, seven of them (including the title story) by Silko. In that same year, another of Silko's short stories, "Lullaby," was published in *Chicago Review*, and Silko was awarded an NEA writing fellowship. She then moved to Ketchikan, Alaska for two years; there, supported partially by a Rosewater Foundation grant, she wrote most of what was to become the novel *Ceremony* (1977). The time she spent in Alaska at Ketchikan and the small community of Bethel strongly engaged her imagination—"Storyteller," the title story of her major collection of short works and the only piece not set at or near Laguna, is unmistakably Alaskan in setting and character. Even while living in Alaska, however, Silko's creative vision remained profoundly rooted in the landscape of her native Laguna: "When I was writing *Ceremony*," she wrote to poet James Wright in 1978, "I was so terribly devastated by being away from Laguna country that the writing was my way of re-making that place, the Laguna country, for myself" (*Delicacy* 27–28).

Returning to the Southwest from Alaska, Silko continued to write while holding academic appointments first at the University of New Mexico and then at the University of Arizona. In 1981, after her marriage to John Silko had been dissolved,[12] Seaver published her book *Storyteller*, which brought together much of her previously published poetry and short fiction, re-embedded in a webwork of family narrative accompanied by photographs of the sources of her storytelling identity—

photographs, that is, of the people and the settings to which those stories attach. In that same year, Silko was awarded a five-year, $176,000 MacArthur Foundation Prize Fellowship, allowing her to devote herself full time to her artistic pursuits, including writing the novel that over the course of the next ten years would become *Almanac of the Dead*.

A few years earlier Silko had been the subject of a short film, "Running on the Edge of the Rainbow" (1978), in which she played herself as a Laguna storyteller[13]; during this time Silko began to develop her own interest in the visual arts, in particular filmmaking, an interest encouraged earlier in several graduate courses as well as by her father's career as a professional photographer (arguably, the combination of verbal and photographic texture in *Storyteller* anticipates this phase of Silko's career). During the late 1970s and early 1980s, even while her written work was relocating itself in a much larger sociopolitical context with Tucson rather than Laguna at its center, Silko's filmmaking efforts remained anchored at Laguna. There, she founded the Laguna Film Project and, with some additional support from an NEH grant and with an eye to eventual PBS release, began filming and producing "Arrowboy and the Witches," a 60-minute video version of her story "Estoy-eh-moot and the Kunideeyahs" (*Storyteller* 140–54).[14]

As *Storyteller* does mainly in print and "Arrowboy and the Witches" does mainly in motion-picture form, much of Silko's non-fiction work of the past decade continues to integrate the conventional domains of visual and verbal art. In 1989, for instance, an essay entitled "The Fourth World" appeared in *Artforum*, a journal of the visual arts, and in 1995 her photoessay "An Essay on Rocks" appeared in a special issue of *Aperture* magazine. In these essays, as in her filmmaking, Silko's creative vision remains grounded in her years growing up at Laguna: in "The Fourth World," Silko speculates about the connections between the high teenage suicide rate around Laguna and the open Jackpile uranium mine, while in "An Essay on Rocks" her story about a boulder in a Tucson arroyo ends with an allusion to the story of a similar rock on Mt. Taylor that first appeared in *Storyteller* (77–78).

Leslie Silko lives today on a ranch in the mountains a few miles northwest of Tucson, Arizona, where she has been living since the publication of *Ceremony*. In her longest novel to date, *Almanac of the Dead* (1991), Silko portrays Tucson, the novel's apparent center of gravity and the setting for much of the story, as a hopelessly corrupt city "home to an assortment of speculators, confidence men, embezzlers, lawyers, judges, police and other criminals, as well as addicts and pushers" (frontispiece, *Almanac*), trembling on the edge of apocalyptic redemption because of its locus with respect to the Azteca migration motif. But even in *Almanac of the Dead*, Sterling, Silko's on-again-off-again protagonist, is a native of Laguna, and the novel can end only when the "Exile" of the novel's second chapter returns to Laguna in its final chapter, titled "Home":

> Sterling hiked over the little sand hills across the little valley to the sandstone cliffs where the family sheep camp was. The windmill was pumping lazily in the afternoon breeze, and Sterling washed his face and hands and drank. The taste of the water told him he was home. Even thinking the word made his eyes fill with tears. (757)

Like Tayo's in *Ceremony*, Sterling's personal history is a story of contact with attractive but dangerous non-Laguna forces, departure from Laguna, and eventual return to Laguna with the acquired knowledge of how to live with those forces—the "Yellow Woman" motif that Silko so strongly associates with the image of the river at Laguna.[15] In *Ceremony*, Tayo completes his return by crossing this river from southeast to northwest at sunrise (255); in *Almanac*, the water-spirit of Kawaika is presented in its alternate shape: in the open pit of the Jackpile uranium mine, the giant spirit snake Maahastryu, who formerly inhabited the lake after which the Laguna people were originally named, has reappeared, "looking south, in the direction from which the twin brothers and the people would come" (763) in fulfillment of a prophecy of which the Laguna story is but a small part.

Silko continues to explore the motif of departure and return in *Gardens in the Dunes* (1999). Set at the turn of the century, this quiet, elegant novel imitates the style of Victorian historical romance in the diction and narrative distance that characterize the telling of the story; ultimately, however, both plot and style work to give voice to Silko's persistently Laguna storytelling persona. Though the protagonist, Indigo, is from Arizona, one of the Sand Lizard clan, the fragile gardens of the title recall Silko's own description of the gardens near the Laguna village of Paguate that were all destroyed by the Jackpile uranium mining operations in the 1950s (*Yellow Woman* 44). From a Victorian perspective, the novel recounts the life and Pyrrhic liberation of protagonist Hattie Abbott, acquired at the cost of the demise of her photographer and botanist husband, Edward Palmer. Hattie and Edward are collectors of exotica, and one of their early acquisitions is the child Indigo, a runaway from the Sherman Indian Institute in Riverside, California. From the perspective of the Indian protagonist, the plot of the novel recapitulates the familiar Laguna motif of departure and recovery: Indigo, like her Laguna analog Kochinninako/Yellow Woman, is spirited away from her homeland by an alien force (here, the failing colonial *zeitgeist* informing the barren couple Hattie and Edward). After surviving this encounter through a complicated process of both resistance and assimilation, Indigo returns carrying new life for the people —in the form of her story; in the form of the child newly born to her older sister Salt; in the form of the new alliance between the sisters of the Sand Lizard people and the Laguna sisters Vedna and Maytha; and in the form of the new seeds (exotic gladiolus tubers, which the women plant next to native datura in the ancient Sand Lizard gardens in the dunes). Like the hybrid calves of the speckled Mexican cattle in *Ceremony*, all these new forms become, by the end of the novel, a part of the long story of the people.

To date, the criticism of Silko's work published in eight books and innumerable critical essays has been mostly positive, especially in the case of *Ceremony*.[16] Silko was recently named a Living Cultural Treasure by the New Mexico Humanities Council. In 1994 she also received the third Wordcraft Circle of Native Writers and Storytellers Lifetime Achievement award, an honor she now shares with, among others, N. Scott Momaday (1992), her Acoma neighbor and old friend Simon Ortiz (1993), and longtime Creek friend and co-actress (in "Running on the Edge of the Rainbow") Joy Harjo (1995). Honored by critics and creative writers alike, Leslie Marmon Silko has clearly earned her status as one of America's premiere storytellers.

CHAPTER 2

Mapping the Embedded Texts

From a formal critical perspective, one of the most intriguing things about *Ceremony* is the recurrent presence of embedded text—passages set apart from the surrounding prose narrative and typeset to look more like poetry than prose: center justified on the page, surrounded by white space, and oddly skeletal-looking in the context of the margin-to-margin prose preceding and succeeding them. Most of these parcels of embedded text are also in narrative mode, styled to read like old-time, traditional oral narrative—what at Laguna Pueblo they often call "hama-ha[h]" stories, long-ago far-away stories.[1] Formally, their presence evokes the question of their relation to Keresan oral tradition on the one side and to the prose narrative on the other. This question is located at the heart of the broader and equally intriguing question of how contemporary Native American poetry and fiction generally relate to the oral traditions from which they derive.

I'll have much to say about the ethnographic sources and the roles of each of these embedded texts in the coming chapters; for now, I'd like to "map" the embedded texts, as a body, with respect to the more familiar-looking prose narrative they work for, and with.

The first step in mapping the embedded texts is to locate and identify them. Extracting the embedded material from the prose narrative yields the following sequence of embedded texts, which are here enumerated and located with reference to the pagination of the (relatively accessible) Penguin edition of *Ceremony*:

1	(1)	(Ts'its'tsi'nako sets life in motion)
2	(2)	("Ceremony")
3	(3)	("*What she said*")
4	(4)	(sunrise)
5	(13–14)	(Reed Woman-Corn Woman argument)
6	(37–38)	(Kuoosh's preamble to Scalp Ceremony)
7	(46–49)	**(Pa'caya'nyi introduces Ck'o'yo medicine; Nau'ts'ity'i departs)**
8	(53–54)	**(Hummingbird appears)**
9	(71–72)	**(making Green Fly)**

10	(82)	**(Hummingbird and Green Fly travel to "fourth world/below")**
11	(105–06)	**(Nau'ts'ity'i steers Hummingbird and Green Fly to Buzzard)**
12	(113)	**(Buzzard demands tobacco)**
13	(128–30)	(boy → bear transformation)
14	(132–38)	(origins of witchery)
15	(139–41)	(hunter → coyote transformation)
16	(142)	([a] departure-side transformation chant)
17	(142)	([b] chant vocable)
18	(143–44)	([c] recovery-side transformation chant)
19	(151–52)	**(Nau'ts'ity'i steers Hummingbird and Green Fly to Caterpillar)**
20	(153)	([e] coyoteskin-witchery connection)
21	(170–76)	(Kaupata and Sun Man)
22	(180)	**(Caterpillar gives tobacco to Hummingbird and Green Fly)**
23	(182)	(sunrise song)
24	(206)	(hunter's deer song)
25	(247)	(Arrowboy spies on Ck'o'yo workers)
26	(255–56)	**(Buzzard purifies the town, Nau'ts'ity'i returns)**
27	(257)	(Elders' "A'moo'ooh" chant)
28	(258)	([f] unraveling the dead coyote skin)
29	(260–61)	([d] return chant for the witchery)
30	(262)	(sunrise)

Some of these portions of embedded text form distinct groups. The longest of these groups is the nine-part departure-and-recovery story, marked in boldface in this enumeration, featuring Pa'caya'nyi, Our Mother Nau'ts'ity'i, and Hummingbird; this group forms a formal and thematic "backbone" which the prose narrative fleshes out in twentieth-century time and space, functions I treat in chapters 3 and 7. There are also two distinct but shorter groups: a six-part Coyote transformation-and-recovery series (the items in this list identified with bracketed letters [a]–[f]) discussed in chapter 11 and a series of three sunrise pieces that are the subject of chapter 6. As I will argue in chapter 5, the four pieces that occupy the first four pages of the novel also warrant special treatment as a series designed to function as formal and thematic hoops connecting the world outside the novel to the worlds within.

Perhaps an even better way to imagine the formal structure of the novel, and especially the siting of embedded text with respect to the prose narrative, is to

Mapping the Embedded Texts

visualize a rather literal story "line" running continuously from the first to the last page of the novel, each page making up an equally long segment of this line, and above that line add another that delineates the range of each of the six major present-time plot motions of the novel. If we do this and then additionally locate the embedded texts precisely within the space thus created, the resulting map might look something like the diagram in Appendix A, reproduced in miniature below:

Looking at the embedded text this way, we can see the skeletal backbone structure discussed in chapter 3.[2] We can also see several other distinctive features in the formal landscape of the novel thus mapped. Again, the first four pages of the novel stand in special relationship to the rest, looking not so much embedded in the prose narrative as finial to it, perhaps like the warning end of a great snake,[3] but now we can see that this formal structure is reiterated at the other end of the novel in a similar cluster of four short fragments followed quickly by two final pieces, again located technically "outside" the prose narrative body of story. We can see, too, how literally central to the structure of the text is the story about the power of story even when—or perhaps especially when—deployed by witchery; indeed, that particular embedded text is literally enclosed within several layers of other embedded text, as though being kept under ceremonial control by both traditional story and the surrounding prose narrative in both directions, all of it required to keep this one piece of story from moving elsewhere. We can also see how, in at least three places, a piece of embedded text functions as a bridge or gateway connecting two of the major moments of the prose narrative. We can see, too, how the prose narrative seems to gather momentum from the impetus of infused embedded text, each succeeding prose moment spanning a shorter narrative length at about the same rate that the frequency of embedded text gradually slackens (before the crescendo of the final half-dozen or so pages).

Looking a little more closely at the prose narrative structure that is in part formally shaped and highlighted by embedded text, the plot emerges as a series of movements, and more specifically as a series of departures and recoveries:

1. [1–105]: in late May (11) Tayo moves from the sheep shack to the bar near Cubero and back to Laguna land at Casablanca;
2. [107–70]: later that summer (the allusions to the Gallup Ceremonials [116–17] suggest late July or early August) Tayo moves from Laguna Village to the Chuska Mountains via Gallup, then back via Mesita to Laguna Village;
3. [176–215]: in "late September" (178) Tayo moves from Laguna to the North Top of Mt. Taylor and back to Laguna;
4. [218–35]: again in late May (218) Tayo moves from Laguna Village to the sheep shack (where he is located at the outset of the narrative) to Dripping Springs for the summer;
5. [235–55]: again in late September (during the time of the Fall equinox) Tayo moves from Dripping Springs to just north of the Jackpile Mine, then back via the mine to Laguna Village;
6. [256–60]: Tayo spends two days sequestered in the kiva at Laguna Village telling his story to the old men there, then returns to Auntie and Grandma's house.

In fractal fashion, there are also patterns within patterns—within the story of Tayo's movement from the sheep shack to the bar at Cubero ("Tuesday nights are slow," 49) and back to Casablanca, for instance, we are given the fragmented story of Tayo's departure from Laguna to the Philippines during World War II and his return via Los Angeles and a stay of indeterminate time at the VA hospital there, as well as the story of the Night Swan's journey to, and eventual departure from, Lalo's Place in Cubero; the second major plot motion, Tayo's several-day departure via Gallup into the dark Chuska Mountains and his roundabout return to Mesita with Harley, Leroy, and Helen Jean via the Y bar, carries in its belly the story of Tayo's birth in, and eventual departure from, the Dantéesque cardboard city of lost souls on the edge of Gallup; and so on.

The rhythm of departure and recovery that informs the prose narrative, easy enough to overlook in the prose narrative taken alone, is amplified by the prose narrative's juxtaposition to the embedded texts, where this motif is more clearly shared by several of the pieces and groups of pieces, especially by the following:

1. **departure**: Reed Woman's fallout with her sister Corn Woman [13–14].
2. **departure**: Nau'ts'ity'i's fallout with Pa'caya'nyi [46–49];

>   **recovery**: Hummingbird and Green Fly on behalf of the People [53–54; 71–72; 82; 105–06; 113; 151-52; 180; 255–56].
> 3. **departure**: boy transforms into Bear [128–30].
> 4. **departure**: man transforms into Coyote [139–41];
>   **recovery**: Bear medicine ("Red Antway") ceremony performed [142–44; 153; 258].
> 5. **departure**: stormclouds captured by Kaup'a'ta the Gambler;
>   **recovery**: Sun Man (with help from Grandmother Spider) recovers them [170–76].

This departure-recovery motif characterizes much of Keresan (Laguna) ceremonial story; it is, for instance, a primary component of the body of stories involving Kochinninako/Yellow Woman, a figure from Laguna traditional story introduced to non-Indian critical circles by Laguna feminist Paula Gunn Allen in her 1986 essay "Kochinnenako in Academe" (*The Sacred Hoop* 222–44) and whom several critics have associated strongly with Silko and her work.[4] Several critics, myself included, have referred at one time or another to the element of circularity in the structure and plotting of Silko's work and in American Indian literatures generally, but I suspect it would be more accurate to conceive of this non-linear element, in *Ceremony* at least, as being more like an oscillation than a circle, closer to the motion produced by dilation and contraction than by maintaining equidistance from some central point.

Mapping the novel this way also highlights an intriguing, perhaps paradoxical, but certainly ironic feature of the relationship between Western-looking prose narrative and Native-looking embedded text that Silko imposes, I think conscientiously, upon the overall text of the novel. For as much as it may be appropriate to call these portions of story embedded text, in fact it is also the case that the prose narrative is emphatically embedded in—in the sense of enclosed by, and thus by extension and (to at least some degree) both formally and conceptually controlled by—story that in text and texture is Native rather than Western. This formal device raises, and I suspect is designed to raise, an important question: which of the literary traditions, Western or Native, is functioning as context for the text being read at any given moment? Are the fragments of embedded text to be read and understood within the context of the prose narrative, or is the prose narrative to be read within the context of (the embedded representatives of) Laguna story tradition?

Overlooking for the moment the suspect dualism of the question as I've posed it and anticipating an alternative way of accounting for the relationship between the elements of prose narrative and embedded text in this novel that will be introduced in the following chapter, I want to end with this question because I think that once we map the formal structure of the novel we can't help but see that, whatever else Silko may be up to, she has crafted a novel wordweb designed to privilege Native Laguna story and designed also to lure her reader into the world of Laguna text and texture. Just as Silko sees to it that Tayo's Laguna Grandma gets the last word of the prose narrative, she sees to it that there is no getting into, or out of, this text except through Native ground.

It is also, of course, both possible and extremely worthwhile to "map" the event(s) of the prose narrative with respect to the kind of map most of us think of when we hear that term, a pictorial geographic image of the places and connecting roads named in the novel—or better yet, in the case of *Ceremony*, a combination of a Rand McNally-type map and the kind of topographical relief map published by the U.S. Department of the Interior Geological Survey (see Appendix A for a simplified version of such a map). A map like this is enormously useful in helping to locate and to visualize the pattern of departures and recoveries which Tayo undergoes in the prose narrative; I do not, however, think it is of much immediate use in helping to locate or situate the novel's embedded texts, either with respect to one another or with respect to the prose narrative itself, and so I have chosen not to explore this kind of mapping closely in this study.[5] It is enough for now, I hope, to suggest that in Silko's novel the prose narrative and the narrative that emerges from the embedded texts move together, eventually and finally touching down at all four corners of, and like Old Buzzard in the embedded backbone story circumscribing and working to regenerate, both the literal and the spiritual landscape of Laguna.

CHAPTER 3

Re-Fleshing the Backbone: Pretext and Prose Narrative in *Ceremony*

It is no secret that Laguna oral traditions figure as both text and pretext in *Ceremony*. In interviews and elsewhere, Silko herself has often stated that the primary source of the traditional stories contained in her novel *Ceremony* is Laguna oral tradition, specifically stories she remembers hearing from her Aunt Susie and her Grandma A'mooh,[1] and most critics concede (as do I) that family tellings may well have served as source material for much of the "traditional" storytelling that shows up in the text of *Ceremony*. In fact, a few years ago another Laguna writer, Paula Gunn Allen, criticized Silko for using some of this oral traditional material, contending that by including a clan story in her novel *Ceremony* Silko has violated local conventions regarding proper dissemination of such stories. Gunn Allen claims, I think correctly, that some clan stories simply should not be told outside the clan, let alone outside the tribe. Furthermore, in her view, literary critics should not deal with these pretexts in print: "I could no more do (or sanction) the kind of ceremonial investigation of *Ceremony* done by some researchers than I could slit my mother's throat. Even seeing some of it published makes my skin crawl." Moving from a critique of the critics to Silko's own writing, Gunn Allen continues,

> The parts of the novel that set other pulses atremble largely escape me. The long poem text that runs through the center has always seemed to me to contribute little to the story or its understanding. Certainly the salvation of Laguna from drought is one of its themes, but the Tayo stories which, I surmise, form their own body of literature would have been a better choice if Silko's intention was to clarify or support her text with traditional materials. [...] but the story she lays alongside the novel is a clan story, and is not to be told outside of the clan. ("Special Problems" 382–83)

It may strike some readers as ironic that Paula Gunn Allen, who at the time of her critique of Silko had just published *Spider Woman's Granddaughters* and was about to publish the patently New Age *Grandmothers of the Light*, comes off in her argument as the defender of Laguna traditionalism and privacy against Leslie Silko's brazen affronts to them both. Irony notwithstanding, Allen raises a very serious question, one that goes to the heart of still timely issues of cultural appropriation, misappropriation, and expropriation. Were Allen correct in her contention that Silko exposes clan secrets, I for one would have equally serious qualms about undertaking to write about these pretexts.

Let me direct attention, then, to the traditional stories, or embedded texts, that do appear in Silko's novel *Ceremony*, some of which, for Allen, constitute evidence of improper publication of secret clan stories. I use the term "embedded" in part to acknowledge the way most of these portions of text are formally set within the matrix of the prose narrative, like bits of turquoise and coral in some kinds of Zuñi jewelry.[2] Here I read differently from Gunn Allen, who sees these passages as lying "alongside" the novel proper, because I think they are integral to both the novel's text and texture. There are (as I count them) 30 of these embedded texts in the novel, typically typeset as though they were passages of poetry, center-justified on the page and with lines of varying lengths.

As I have already conceded, Silko may well have heard and recalled the gist of any number of such stories prior to writing the novel. However, it is also demonstrably the case that Silko has recovered most of the embedded texts in *Ceremony* from preexisting ethnographic print texts, sometimes verbatim, rather than immediately from remembered oral performance.[3] Even if we agree, then, with Gunn Allen that the original performers and transcribers of these ethnographic works might be guilty of violations of clan secrets, the fact that such texts exist in print outside *Ceremony*, and existed well before Silko was even born, puts a very different spin on the question of cultural expropriation. It does, at least, for me: once we concede that the pretexts for Silko's embedded texts are *printed* texts, gathered and published by both professional and armchair ethnographers before her birth, then it makes more sense to claim that in an important way Silko is not revealing or even re-revealing clan secrets but rather repatriating Laguna "artifacts," working to rescue them from their deadening status as ethnographic museum pieces and to return them to living circulation as part(s) of an ongoing, living story.

For now, though, let me propose that perhaps Silko's use of such materials is better read, not as an exploitation or improper exposure of Keresan materials, but rather as a "re-appropriation" of these previously expropriated materials, and further as re-appropriation in the service of very traditional Keresan purposes. To illustrate this proposition, I will examine the function of the fragmented embedded text to which Gunn Allen refers when she writes of "the long poem text that runs through the [novel's] center [that] has always seemed to me to contribute little to the story or its understanding," the story entitled "One Time" in her 1981 book *Storyteller* (111–21). I want to show how Silko's version of this traditional Keresan story derives from ethnography but functions as a traditional Keresan storytelling trope, fulfilling the role of the "backbone" in a "body" (i.e., her novel) that preserves, by giving new life and voice to, the "long story of the People" (*Storyteller* 7).

First, let me try to "flesh out" a little what I mean, and what I think some traditional Laguna storytellers mean, when they talk about the "backbone" of a body of story. As many readers will already know, one of the recurring formal elements of storytelling in orally literate communities is the device of "framing" or "bracketing." Typically this device consists of two conventional phrases, one to mark the shift in discourse from ordinary mode to storytelling mode—as, for instance, the way the phrase "once upon a time" functions in English—and one to mark the other side of the storytelling performance, the shift from story back into normal discourse—as, for instance, the phrase "the end" functions in English.[4] "The end" still gets printed, on its own separate line and typographically center justified, at the end of many novels today; however, this and other verbal frame devices are actually superfluous in a print performance, because the two covers of the book demarcate the story "space" pretty unambiguously.[5] Such frame elements are still desirable, however, in non-print story performance, even though the exact phrases differ from community to community and even from kind of performance to kind of performance.

At Laguna, at least among the storytellers both Gunn Allen and Silko remember listening to, as well as among the informants who between 1919 and 1921 contributed the stories collected in Franz Boas's *Keresan Texts*,[6] the conventional initiator phrase of the framing pair is "hama-ha."[7] Boas's favorite translation of this phrase is "Long ago—eh!"; Elsie Clews Parsons, in her 1920 *Notes on Ceremonialism at Laguna*, translates the phrase as "*hame*, long ago, *ha*, so far" (98 n. 5).[8] In addition, although neither Gunn Allen nor Silko directly mentions it, a conventional closure or terminator phrase frequently recurs as well in Boas's transcriptions of turn-of-the-century oral performance.[9] In *Keresan Texts* this phrase is given as *to·me ts'itc̓*, translated by Boas as "that long it is," or (to give two typical extensions) *to·me ts'itc̓ᵃ s'ak'o·'ya k'ayo·tsecpi t'itsᶜ*, literally translated, "that long is my aunt's backbone," or *to·me ts'itc̓ᵃ s'ak'o·'ya k'cis·'na kʰayo·tsecpi v̓itsᶜ*, literally "that long is my Aunt Kachena's backbone."[10]

In Keresan tradition, the idea that there is an anatomical relationship between stories and their tellers is not just metaphor. Silko touches on this relationship early in *Ceremony*, when a male storyteller, explaining the role of stories in preserving both the life of the People and the ceremonies, gestures to his belly and says "I keep them here/Here, put your hand on it/See, it is moving./There is life here/for the people."[11] Like everything else that moves and has power, a story properly understood is a living thing and is thereby related to every other living thing, sometimes overtly and directly and sometimes less obviously. A story may not always have a form that is materially palpable, like a badger or a human being does, but (like any badger or human being) any story has both a life of its own and partakes of the life it shares with all other living things: it holds a kind of life within itself, and it is itself embedded within other life. What we might call the "gist" or "essence" of any particular story, Keresan storytellers are apt to visualize as the backbone of that story, and in so doing they claim that this gist or essence is actually more substantial—denser, longer lasting, and much less elastic—than the articulated form of this backbone, any particular verbal performance of it per se. It is also well to keep in mind, as this conventional Keresan closure phrase reminds an audience to do, that without a backbone there is nothing to hold a human being (or a story about being human) up straight, nothing to attach flesh to; on the other hand, given an intact backbone one can conceivably perform all sorts of cosmetic surgery on the surface version of the story that gets told, but the important thing is to work from the backbone out to the surface of things when constructing a story.

Returning now to Leslie Silko's novel and its responsibility to Keresan oral traditionalism, one might wonder that she doesn't end her written performance with a statement like "And that long is my Aunt Susie's [or my Grandma

A'mooh's] backbone." A similar statement does, however, occur at the very opening of the performance, when Silko's authorial voice claims that the story we are about to enter is a project of that mother of all Laguna aunties, Ts'its'tsi'nako/Thought Woman, and that the present storyteller is merely "telling you the story she is thinking" (1). Continuing to exercise the conventional Keresan backbone trope, working to assemble story in the way that Badger Old Man works for healing in the old stories,[12] Silko then lays out the embedded texts in her novel so that formally these "bits and pieces" of Laguna traditional story, far from being positioned peripherally with respect to the prose narrative of Tayo's adventures, rather represent the very backbone—the spinal column—of the novel, the skeleton of story that Tayo's story, the prose narrative, takes shape upon and fleshes out.[13]

I'd like to draw attention now to the thread, or rather column, of backbone material in Silko's text that Paula Gunn Allen singles out as particularly problematic for her, that "long poem text that runs through the center [that] has always seemed to me to contribute little to the story or its understanding," and again that "story she lays alongside the novel [that] is a clan story, and is not to be told outside the clan" (383). This is the departure/recovery story that features as antagonist Pa'caya'nyi, whose introduction of Ck'o'yo medicine into the lives of the People drives our Mother Nau'ts'ity'i out of the Fifth World and down below, and as protagonist Hummingbird, who along with his sidekick Green Fly works tirelessly on behalf of the People to help effect our Mother's return.[14] In Silko's book *Storyteller* this story, titled "One Time" in the table of contents, appears as one continuous tale; in *Ceremony*, it is cast as nine discontinuous segments, the first beginning on page 43 and the last appearing on page 256.

This nine-part performance is one of the more interesting examples of embedded text in the novel, both in terms of its ethnographic roots and in terms of its function with respect to the prose narrative. Like many of the embedded texts in the novel, this one is clearly a rewritten version of some classic early twentieth-century ethnography. Specifically, the text of Silko's departure/recovery tale follows closely three of Elsie Clews Parsons's transcriptions of part of the body of Laguna story published in Boas's *Keresan Texts*: "P'acaya´nyi," "The Hummingbird," and "Origin Legend."[15]

One of the first things worth noting about Silko's redaction of these pieces of story is the way she has reassembled the record published by Boas. Boas places the episode dealing with Hummingbird's recovery of Nautsityi prior to the episode that deals with Pacayanyi's visit,[16] carefully attributing each to a different informant and attributing each with its separate title. By reversing the order of these two stories and then splicing them together, Silko at once generates a story long and complex enough to serve as a backbone for the whole novel and also recovers the departure/recovery motif that Boas's ordering disrupts.

A second thing worth noting is that, although the text of Silko's performance closely follows Boas's, the texture is dramatically different. For one thing: instead of casting the text as end-wrapped prose the way Boas does, Silko "elevates" these performances to the richer-looking status of poetry, in the process adding or restoring markers of oral performance, such as line lengths consistent with phrase duration and authorial asides rendered in squared brackets. Here, as in her use of embedded texts generally, Silko is in effect working to liberate the Story of the People from the confines of Boas's rather stilted ethnographic prose. That is, she is working analogously to the way Betonie works to help free Tayo of the coyote skin in which he has been too long wrapped and trapped,[17] or to the way Sun Man works to free the storm clouds (which are not only Sun Man's "children" but also the *shiwanna* or ancestral spirits of the People) whom Kaupata keeps locked up for several years in the northwest room of his mountain abode.[18] Also noteworthy is the way she sequences the nine blocks of this text from one end of the body of the prose narrative to the other, like trail markers for the reader who needs periodic reassurance that the direction of Tayo's story is staying congruent with the story of Our Mother's ceremonial recovery that ontologically precedes it. Finally, of course, this retexturing of the Boas transcriptions also suggests the arrangement of the vertebrae of a backbone, embedded within and giving distinctively human form to the fleshed-out body of Tayo's prose narrative story. Just in case we miss the forest here, Silko sees to it that we can see the same point in each tree: each of the fragments, center-justified on the page but composed of lines of varying lengths, takes on a suggestively skeletal appearance. Lives within lives, backbones within backbones.

Perhaps the most telling difference between Boas's and Silko's presentations of Keresan oral traditional material, though, has to do with context. Boas presents the reader with, and I quote from his very short preface, "the following series of tales ... collected during the years 1919–1921." Boas sorts the very miscellaneous collection of oral performances into such categories as stories, story fragments, songs, prayers, speeches, and autobiographical remarks, and he also attempts to arrange the origin and migration stories and fragments into a plausible chronological order. The gist of his closing remarks on the materials is, "well, we have all this material now, what shall we do with it?" Laguna oral tradition is presented, that is, as a quantity of collectibles. For a collector during the 1920s, Keresan stories were becoming more valuable, because most white Americans, even the trained ethnographers among them, believed that Keresan storytellers were dying out and that this might well be the last generation of "authentic" storytellers from whom to gather information.[19] Like Ishi in his glass case at Berkeley, authentic Keresan texts, like their tellers, qualified as museum pieces, and Laguna was as much an archaeological as an ethnographic site. All that remains to be done now, Boas's critical apparatus in *Keresan Texts* tells us, is to pickle as many of these artifacts as we can still find in the preservative of print for future study. It is a telling comment, then, that the Boas book is out of print, impossible to come by except through special interlibrary loan. One is reminded of the boxes and boxes of human bones and "artifacts" in a museum warehouse somewhere, waiting to be sorted and displayed in the museum—or, in the preferred scenario, repatriated back to Indian Country.

This, it seems to me, is what Silko's presentation of these same materials amounts to: an act of repatriation, putting those Laguna bones collected by the ethnographers back to their original use—to serve as backbone for a Laguna story about Laguna life in Laguna country. Properly speaking, in the structure of *Ceremony* the context for Laguna story is Laguna story: the "traditional" story involving Pacayanyi and Hummingbird Man traditionalizes the "now'day" story of Emo and Tayo while simultaneously the prose narrative context revives the backbone of embedded text. In this way, the embedded texts become part of a "now'day" performance, in the process becoming as *au courant* and contemporary as the narrative skin they are in.

I want to conclude this chapter by readdressing Paula Gunn Allen's comments regarding the propriety of telling clan stories to non-clan members. While I'm sure clan stories exist, I do not think that the story that appears in *Ceremony* as "the long poem text that runs through the center" is, properly speaking, just a clan story anymore. If it ever was limitedly a clan story, rather than a story common to the repertoire of accomplished storytellers of several clans, it ceased to be exclusively a clan story when, over 80 years ago, a man named Ko´Tʸɛ, along with a man named Gʸi´mi, along with a man named Pedro Martin, shared it with Elsie Clews Parsons, who was certainly not a clan sister to any of them. Perhaps there is still a version of that story that gets told only among the members of Side Corn clan Kawaika; if there is, I strongly suspect no non-clan member will ever hear it told, much less ever see it in print. At any rate, the version of the story of Pacayanyi and Hummingbird Man that appears in *Ceremony* is not about revealing clan secrets but rather is about re-quickening the spirit of storytelling that, until Silko wrote the novel, lay misplaced and, I would say, misrepresented in the form of the ethnographic record.

CHAPTER 4
Analogy versus Homology: The Kaupata Motif

In one of the longest of the embedded texts in the novel, Silko (or her invisible but omniscient narrative persona) re-tells the story of Sun Man's encounter with the evil katsina of the north mountain, Kaupata the Gambler. Silko's re-telling of this story is a particularly interesting example of how she relates her novel not only to Laguna oral tradition but also to the ethnographic record of that tradition.

I say "re-telling of this story" for several reasons. For one, we know from Ruth Benedict that the Kaupata story was still being commemorated annually during the winter solstice ceremonies at Acoma and Laguna at least as late as 1930,[1] indicating that the story was still an important episode in the ceremonial life of the people, and we have no reason to believe the story wasn't still in circulation for Silko to hear one generation later. For another, Silko has spoken and written frequently about the novel's indebtedness to Laguna oral tradition, particularly as those traditional materials were told to her by the storytelling men and women on the paternal side of her family tree,[2] and I have no doubt that much of the texture, and also much of the text, of the novel derives directly from oral tradition the way Silko says it does.

However, the performance of *Ceremony* involves not only the "re-telling" but also, in a more familiar mode for many readers, the re-*writing* of Laguna story, and the novel contains clear tracks of print-text precedents as well as the textural echoes of those remembered live voices. When Silko wrote *Ceremony*, she had not only Laguna oral tradition but also a substantial ethnographic print tradition to draw upon, and it isn't difficult to establish the presence of this written ethnographic tradition in Silko's novel generally or in her version of the Kaupata story in particular. Several instances of Silko's indebtedness to the ethnographic record, one involving Leland Wyman's edition of the Navajo Red Antway ceremony and the other involving Franz Boas's Pacayanyi and Hummingbird Man stories, have already been demonstrated,[3] and a similar case can be made for the origins of Silko's Kaupata story. At least three written-in-English versions of the story of Sun

Man and Kaupata predate Silko's version in *Ceremony* and the virtually identical version published in her 1981 collection *Storyteller* under the title "Up North." The earliest of these three ethnographic versions is titled "Ko-pot Ka-nat" in John Gunn's 1917 collection *Schat-chen*, subtitled "History, Traditions and Narratives of the Queres Indians of Laguna and Acoma"; the second is "Kaup`a·t´a," published in 1928 in the English translation volume of Franz Boas's *Keresan Texts*; and finally there is Ruth Benedict's "Kaupat´a," one of the "Eight Stories from Acoma" published in the 1930 volume of *Journal of American Folklore*.[4] A partial study of the similarities and differences among these three texts, and of their relation to the Kaupata story titled "Up North" in *Storyteller*, has already been published.[5] The text of "Up North" and the text of the Kaupata story published as part of *Ceremony* are virtually identical, and anyone who has read both Boas's version and either "Up North" or the Kaupata story in Silko's *Ceremony* will have noticed the strong similarity, and in several passages the word-for-word identity, of these two texts.[6]

I will have more to say later about what I think we should make of such intertextual identities; first, though, a word about Silko's own two print versions of the Kaupata story is appropriate. As others have already pointed out,[7] in Native American literary traditions, context largely determines meaning. We should keep this in mind when considering the relationship between the Kaupata story that appears under the title "Up North" in Silko's 1981 *Storyteller* and the version that appears in her 1977 *Ceremony*. Considered purely as texts, the two versions differ by only a few words and one or two typefont variations. Their literary contexts, however, are very different. In *Storyteller*, the Kaupata story is one of 66 typeset pieces and 26 photographs comprising a delicately structured scrapbook of Laguna story tradition in most of its many genres. Practically speaking (and consistent with Laguna aesthetics) the context for each piece in *Storyteller* is all the other pieces in *Storyteller*, all of which together are in turn, as Silko puts it, just a "portion" of "the whole story/the long story of the people" (*Storyteller* 7): the proper context for any *part* of the "long story of the people" is the entire Laguna oral tradition. In *Ceremony*, however, the Kaupata story (like each of the other embedded stories or story fragments) appears formally as one of several islands in an otherwise seamless stream of prose narrative: formally, the immediate context for each of these embedded hama-ha stories in the novel is the prose narrative in which it is embedded.

In the novel, this formal relationship between text and context implies a functional relationship as well. Let me turn attention, then, to one of the important ways Silko's 1977 version of the Kaupata story is working within the novel, particularly with respect to the Mt. Taylor episode it formally precedes. Like each and all of the novel's other embedded texts, the Kaupata story's presence proposes an extra dimension of authority to the prose narrative. This extra authority lies not so much in either the accuracy of Silko's portrait of post-World War II Laguna life or the presumed authenticity of the embedded text, either of which might be sufficient to guarantee the novel's place in the canon of American literature.[8] Rather, it lies in the novel's ceremonial texture, a byproduct of what I want to call the *homological* relationship that Silko proposes between prose narrative and embedded text(s). I say "homological" rather than "analogical" partly because an analogy might always be a product of chance or individual (or even idiosyncratic) perception, whereas a homology, in the biological sense of that term at least, exists only where two or more analogous entities are derivatives of some preceding entity, the way that for instance siblings are related and share some characteristics because they have a parent (or two) in common. An analysis of the relationship between prose narrative and embedded text which presumes homology rather than merely analogy as the basis of their similarities would go a long way toward accounting for the recurring sense that Tayo's experience on Mt. Taylor, like most of the other prose narrative episodes, is a ceremonial event by virtue of being a *re-happening* of that "long story of the People" of which he is, and is constantly becoming, a part. This "long story," that is, can be understood as the author, the genitor, of both the embedded texts and the prose narrative, both of which texts re-embody that older, more "original" pretext. This genesis gives rise to the authority of homology.

This homology exists along at least four axes of Silko's literary performance. There is first of all the homology of character. On this axis, Tayo and Sun Man are homologues, as are the spotted cattle and the stormclouds, Texan Floyd Lee and Kaupata, the two redneck fence riders and Kaupata's guard ducks, and of course Ts'eh and Ts'its'tsi'nako (Spider Grandmother).

There is then the homology of function. By this I mean the more or less allegorical correspondence between the two plots. I say "more or less" because classical allegory presupposes that one level of such a correspondence is more real, or more significant, or more in control of the structure than the other. In the case of the relationship between embedded stories and episodes of the prose narrative in *Ceremony*, though, neither member of the homological pair governs or generates the other; rather, both versions are embodiments of their shared "backbone" story.[9] The functional homology between the Kaupata story and Tayo's Mt. Taylor episode is rather straightforward: **x** [Sun Man or Tayo] goes to recover **y** [stormclouds or spotted cattle] from the mountain stronghold of **z** [Kaupata or Floyd Lee], first obtaining a template story from **α** [Spider Grandmother or Ts'eh] that maps in accurate detail the sequence of imagery and event to come; aided by this previewing story, **x** is enabled to see what his would-be deceiver sees and then some. What gives the protagonist that margin of vision, of course, is the story **x** comes to this encounter with compliments of Ts'its'tsi'nako, the Mother of All Storytellers and ultimately the origin of all homologies.

Third, there is the homology of cultural context. By this I mean to suggest that all of the various versions of the Kaupata story, in voice and in print, are all, equivalently, fleshings out of a single vertebra of the spirit backbone of story—that "long story of the People" of which Silko speaks in *Storyteller*. From this perspective, the portion of the prose narrative in which Tayo re-happens that story is properly read as one more equivalent version of that backbone story. As a source of the stories' authority, this homological principle of cultural context, which is also a principle of synchronicity, should, I believe, displace the more familiar, but diachronic, principle that chronological precedence bestows authority. For instance, and to the point: diachronically, the identical wording of several passages in Boas's Kaupata text and Silko's embedded story begs us to read Silko's version as indebted to Boas's *and not vice versa*. However, it is also the case—and I am saying we should accord this point critical primacy over the former one—that they both derive from the same source. This homological dimension is an inevitable, and indeed necessary, aspect of literary traditions in the oral mode: it behooves one always to keep in mind that sometimes subtle distinction between the story performance and the story that is being performed, and look to the preservation of the latter over the celebration of the former. There is no other way to imagine the value of continuity—or of recovery.

The final axis of homology I want to point to is the homology of motif. It is in the nature of narrative that imagery indicates event; all literary allusion depends upon our ability and willingness to recognize that when, for instance, Ken Kesey dresses McMurphy in boxer shorts covered with white whales, he is invoking Melville's novel as pretext, if only for the purpose of generating a low-grade pun about a Moby-Dick. In allusion, though, authority and meaning are transferred *from* the pretext *to* the present text; in a homological relationship, authority and meaning derive from the backbone story which two or more "retellings" are re-tellings *of*. Of course, many readers come to Silko's novel never having heard or read any version of the backbone story implicated in both the seven-page embedded Kaupata story and the Mt. Taylor episode which immediately follows it in the text of the novel. My point here is that Silko keeps faith with the long body of Laguna tradition in her novel by creating a homological relation between the two, even though this homological relation can easily be read as a merely allusive one in which the authority and meaning of the Mt. Taylor episode are derived from the embedded Kaupata story which immediately precedes it in the text.

The following are two extended working examples of this homological relationship between embedded text and prose narrative in the novel.

STARSTUFF

One of the homologies of motif that Silko uses to weave the Tayo narrative in with the Kaupata story has to do with the star patterns that appear in both the pretext tradition, including Silko's retelling of it, and in the prose narrative. Near the end of the story, as Tayo is completing the fourth phase of the ceremony just as "the sun was crossing the zenith to a winter place in the sky" (247), he comes to understand that "The stars had always been with [the people], existing beyond memory, and they were all held together there" (254); but Silko shows him *coming* to that understanding already in the second phase, the Mt. Taylor phase of his ceremony of recovery (176–215). Survival for both Sun Man and Tayo, first in the Mt. Taylor episode and then again in the Jackpile Mine episode, depends at least in part upon knowing how the constellations in the early night sky are configured at the time of the autumnal equinox.

In the prose narrative, one of the four signs that it is time for Tayo to undertake the second phase of the novel's postwar recovery ceremony is the star pattern that Betonie draws for Tayo, the "Big Star" pattern, appearing in the north sky. In the prose narrative, Tayo finally sees this constellation appearing "in the north" behind Mt. Taylor in "late September" (178), that is, at the time of the autumnal equinox. From Tayo's perspective, this constellation visually "frames" Mt. Taylor, which looms to the northwest of Laguna village both within and without the novel; likewise it is an image that formally frames the Mt. Taylor episode in the text. This is the pattern to which Ts'eh directs Tayo's and the reader's attention at the beginning of the Mt. Taylor episode by saying "The sky is clear. You can see the stars tonight" (178); it is also the pattern that Tayo perceives painted, in white on black, on the war shield hanging on the north wall of the otherwise deserted hunting cabin when he returns with Robert to collect his cattle at the end of the episode (214).

In Boas's Kaupata as in Silko's, the constellations that Grandmother Spider tells Sun Man to look for are the Pleiades and Orion rather than the Big Star pattern. However, even without Grandmother Spider's preview to prompt him, at the time of the autumnal equinox Sun Man would be able to solve Kaupata's life-or-death star riddle just by being able to "see through" the leather pouches hanging to the east and the south on the wall of Kaupata's high mountain abode.[10] At that time of year, in these latitudes, the Pleiades and Orion appear to emerge in the east and travel upwards to the south, Orion following behind the motion of the Pleiades.

I suspect it is no coincidence that when we merge the orienting star imagery from the prose narrative with that of the Kaupata pretext, we get a sketch of the autumn equinoctial sky in both directions, as it appears looking to the north and west and as it appears to the south and east. The "vision" encoded in the one story complements and completes the vision of the other. In the traditional Kaupata story, this vision motif gets expanded one more step: in the final phase of his encounter with Kaupata, and this time without a prompt from Spider Grandmother's story, Sun Man has to "see" that Kaupata's final ruse is to trick Sun Man into using the yellow flint knife to cut out Kaupata's heart. What makes Kaupata's offer a trick is that spirit, like energy in the First Law of Thermodynamics, cannot be destroyed but only transformed. That is why Kaupata cannot destroy the shiwanna (rainclouds) but only take them out of circulation. Thus, the proper gesture of triumph over Kaupata's trickery is to appropriate Kaupata's vision, as it were, and add it to the eternal "picture" by making his eyes the "horizon stars of autumn" (176), low in the south sky at the time of the autumnal equinox. In the prose narrative, Tayo never directly encounters the absentee Texan Floyd Lee who has fenced in the North Top of Mt. Taylor to keep the stolen cattle in and coyotes and Indians out, but then again he doesn't need to. He need only discover, in himself and in the world, the "heart" of Ck'o'yo witchery—to be able to see how it works by taking life *out of circulation*—in order to become one who is capable also of re-embedding that motive in the larger pattern of eternal verities represented by the stars in both the prose narrative and the Kaupata tradition that informs it.[11]

My other working example has to do with those spotted cattle, the ones whose instinctive internal compasses always point them southward rather than north.

CLOUDS AND CATTLE: LIFE FOR THE PEOPLE

One of the defter image transpositions Silko makes to "update" the traditional Kaupata stories is her substitution of speckled (or spotted) cattle for stormclouds. In either case, the missing element clearly represents ongoing life for the People. However, a herd of cattle seems infinitely more realistic, to a reading audience, as an object of recovery than a family of Cloud People. This image of the cattle also provides Silko with an opportunity to weave the image of her hero more clearly into identity with the object of his quest.

As Silko crafts it, both Tayo and the cattle are hybrids of a variety new to Laguna: the speckled cattle are originally Mexican, continually described as a virtual cross between cattle and desert antelope, characterized by the brown-and-white pattern of their hide, while Tayo is apparently originally Gallup-born, a cross between Indian and Anglo, "brown" and "white." The visual identity of Tayo with the cattle he is destined to recover is sealed, a page or two before Tayo returns to Gallup to visit with Betonie, when Tayo returns to Cubero to visit the abandoned Lalo's place. His memory full of the story of his prewar encounter with the Night Swan here, Tayo absentmindedly stripes the back of one hand with white gypsum adobe plaster; what appears on the back of his hand is "a spotted pattern" (104), white on brown. This is, of course, the color pattern appearing on the hides of the Mexican cattle. It is also a brown-and-white preview of the black-and-white pattern of night sky and stars on the war shield that will commemorate his recovery of the spotted cattle at the end of the Mt. Taylor episode. It is also the pattern in the finger-sketched sand painting that Betonie makes for Tayo to see at the end of the Mt. Chuska episode (152), a star pattern that is part of a perceptual map that, come the autumnal equinox, will guide Tayo to Mt. Taylor, where he will discover the stolen cattle and effect their recovery, along with his own, back onto Laguna land and back into the mainstream of Laguna life.

Silko reinforces the homological identity between the stormclouds and the cattle by attributing to both an identical motion with respect to the topography of the mountain. When Tayo liberates the cattle they move, as Ts'eh points out, the way both deer and water move when their motion carries them toward Laguna during the onset of the Koshare season in the Fall: "They went just like the run-off goes after a rainstorm, running right down the middle of the arroyo" (210), following the gullies and arroyos streaking down the southeast side of the mountain in the direction of Laguna village.

The cattles' adherence to the topography of the Laguna landscape is probably even more homologically driven than I have suggested above. As mentioned previously, both the stormclouds of Keresan oral tradition and those to which both the spotted cattle and Tayo are homologically related in the prose narrative should be recognized as the traditional Cloud People, the *shiwanna*. According to both Boas and Swan,[12] the Keresan shiwanna come in differing forms associated with each of the cardinal directions (four in Boas, six in Swan); one of these forms, strongly associated with the north or northwest at both Laguna and Acoma, is *heyaashi*, the kind of airborne moisture most people would call fog or mist—that is, the cloud form that is most proximate to the land itself and most likely to replicate in its motion the shape of the land over which it moves.[13] We may recall that earlier in the novel one of the symptoms of Tayo's shellshock is that he imagines himself as unself-conscious "white smoke" that conforms its shape to the walls of the Veterans Hospital cubicle to which he is confined (14–16), and most readers initially will probably agree with the Army doctors that Tayo's felt identity with *heyaashi*-like physical texture is an indication of mental illness. Silko makes it easier to see, in the Mt. Taylor episode, how this same felt identity is a very positive step in Tayo's recovery of Laguna identity when Tayo, convinced he is transforming into an "unsubstantial" state such that anyone looking "would see him only as a shadow" (195), sees his powerful spirit ally moving in exactly the same way:

> Relentless motion was the [mountain] lion's greatest beauty, moving like mountain clouds with the wind, changing substance and color in rhythm with the contours of the mountain peaks…. (196)

Other appearances of the shiwanna in the prose narrative that are strongly associated with the motion of overall recovery include those "delicate" white egg sacs carried by the [grand-]mother spider Tayo sees at the spring prior to World War II (94), the pattern of cumulus-shaped spots carried on the back of the snake Tayo encounters on his way to Dripping Springs and his rendezvous with Ts'eh late in the novel (221), and of course (and most obviously) the "clouds with round heavy bellies" in the west and south who gather at dawn to follow Tayo as he crosses the river at sunrise to rejoin the People, an image that reiterates the motion of Sun Man's children (who are also the ancestors of, and still live for, the People) following him down the mountain after his showdown with Kaupata.

I want to end this chapter by drawing attention again to the issue of homology of motif, this time as it applies to the relationship between Silko's novel, the version of the Kaupata story she gives in that novel, and the several ethnographic versions of the Kaupata story mentioned above. In *Ceremony*, Silko's embedded Kaupata story ends with Sun Man tossing Kaupata's eyes into the southern night sky and liberating his children, the four varieties of shiwanna or rainclouds, from the four rooms of Kaupata's mountain abode. Homologically, the following prose narrative episode ends with Tayo liberating his wards, the spotted cattle, from their captivity on the North Top of Mt. Taylor. Silko also reactivates the last phases of the Kaupata motif when Tayo confronts the Ck'o'yo medicine for the fourth time in the novel, this time in the person of Emo, at the Jackpile Mine. Like Kaupata in the pretext story, Emo invites his opponent to kill him, and like Sun Man Tayo somehow knows that opening a Ck'o'yo medicine man's skull with a steel screwdriver (252), or his belly with a broken beer bottle (63), is like cutting out his heart with his own flint knife—a temptation that must be resisted if life in the Fifth World is to continue. However, there is at least one very significant difference between the ethnographic versions and Silko's version of the Kaupata story, and consequently of her version of Laguna oral tradition insofar as the prose narrative stands as a twentieth-century re-happening of "the long story of the people." The difference is that in all of the preceding print-text versions, the Kaupata story does not end so happily for the People. In Gunn's version, in which Kaupata takes form as two brothers each of whom loses an eye to the protagonist, the enraged brothers split open the mountain they inhabit, setting off catastrophic flooding that eventually results in the annihilation of the People; in Boas's and Benedict's versions, the blinded and equally enraged Kaupata lets loose rivers of fire that behave like volcanic lava, destroying everything in their path until the fires are eventually extinguished by the recently liberated stormclouds.[14] It would seem, then, that in her novel Silko takes a major liberty with the body of Laguna oral tradition in order to contrive a graceful ending to her prose narrative.

I think, though, that there is a better way to read this disparity. We may just as easily view the prose narrative of *Ceremony* the same way we are invited to view each and all of the embedded texts contained in it and containing it—as only a "portion," as she puts it, of the "long story of the People." Perhaps this unfinished homology of motif is not, after all, unfinished, then: perhaps Silko was merely saving this part of that story for later—a possibility at least remotely encoded in the penultimate portion of embedded text in the novel: "It is dead for now./It is dead for now./It is dead for now./It is dead for now" (261). "For now": in that case, perhaps we should be looking beyond *Ceremony* for the rest of the backbone Kaupata story. Perhaps, having articulated and set in motion once again the spirit backbone informing the several Kaupata stories by writing *Ceremony*, Leslie Silko was in a sense obliging herself, in keeping with her fidelity to the backbone of Laguna oral tradition, to write her second novel, *Almanac of the Dead*, as a natural extension of *Ceremony*—a novel addressing the darker side of the story that in *Ceremony* is cast so as to begin, and end, with the blessing of sunrise.

CHAPTER 5

The Hoop Series: The Spectrum of Storytelling Modes

The first four passages of poetic text in the novel, each occupying a different one of the first four pages, warrant treatment as a closely related but somewhat anomalous group of embedded texts. What makes them anomalous is that they all —taken individually or as a group—beg the definition of "embedded text," since formally they occur before there is any prose narrative for them to be embedded in. Setting this apparent anomaly aside for a moment, I want to propose that, taken as a series of narrative units arrayed purposefully by some storyteller, these four pieces introduce a pattern of four-phase transformation that is one of the major recurring motifs of this novel, as it is also of Keresan traditional storytelling both on and off the ethnographic record. But let me withhold any elaboration on either of these two claims until after I present several distinctive characteristics of each of these pieces relative to the others in the set.

WHOSE VOICE IS THIS?
The first three of these four pieces, and arguably the fourth one as well, are designed to invoke and evoke a sense of oral performance. Together they also suggest a range of oral performance, running from the relatively formal style and traditional content of the first piece to the more casual brevity of the third and fourth pieces. Somewhat paradoxically, at least within the context of print-text conventions, the aura of oralcy is enhanced by the omission of quotation marks: Silko jettisons the conventional typographical distinction between written performance and "dialog" in these pieces. Instead, with the aid of differential pronouns and typographical cues, Silko cues only distinctions between narrators and auditors and between storytelling domains. These domains belong to what I want to call "embedded" and "embedding" voices. In the first piece, for instance, we apprehend the presence of the mother of all life and story, Ts'its'tsi'nako/Thought Woman, who is the "subject" of this narrative about the origin of all narrative; but we also apprehend—and are finally formally introduced to—another narrative presence that

is part of this performance, an "I" who is "telling you" the story that Ts'its'tsi'nako, within that story, puts into motion. Here, the voice and presence of Ts'its'tsi'nako is embedded within the narrative performed by "I," who in turn functions as the embedding voice of this piece. In the second piece, we apprehend the presence of a narrator, an "I" who is telling his audience ("you") "something about stories"; so far, this is conventional, unremarkable first-person narrative. However, when Silko introduces the bracketed interjection "[he said]"in the second line and again 17 lines later, she not only foregrounds the proposition that this text is to be understood as (a written record of) an oral performance but also introduces a second narrative presence, and a second domain of narrative performance: the narrating "I" and his narrative become embedded in the performance of the implied, embedding narrator who utters or writes the repeated bracketed interjection. In summary, the embedding voices in the first three pieces are the voices behind the statements "[He said]," "I'm telling you the story/she is thinking," and "*What She Said?*" while the embedded narrators in those same pieces are "She," "I," and "I."

Ts'its'tsi'nako (p. 1)

As I've suggested above, the first page of Silko's text presents a problem or two for an ordinary reader unfamiliar with Keresan traditional storytelling in either its oral forms or its ethnographic ones. First impressions are always important, and Silko's choice to make the first word of her text "Ts'its'tsi'nako" is calculated both phonetically and orthographically to position the reader in an etic (or "outsider") relationship to this text. As though anticipating such a reader's first impulse to skip over this page, and perhaps the next three as well, in order to locate and settle into more familiar prose narrative typographical space, Silko's text violates yet another standing convention of Western typesetting by numbering the first page,[1] formally insisting that readers take account of this piece of text.

The figure of Thought Woman or Spider Grandmother is probably, along with trickster Coyote and Kokopelli the humpbacked flautist, one of the most popularized (some might say most ruthlessly misappropriated) figures from Southwestern storytelling traditions,[2] and of the four pieces under discussion here, this story of Ts'its'tsi'nako, the Spider Woman who sets life in motion, keeps clearest company with ethnographic records of Laguna oral tradition. Silko's Ts'its'tsi'nako is in homological identity with John Gunn's Sitch-tche-na-ko, "the feminine form for thought or reason" who is "the creator of all, and to her they offer their most devout prayers" (89), and she bears the same relationship to Boas's Ts'its'tsc'i·'na·'k'o (as given by informants Ko'tʸe in 1921 [7] and José in 1919 [22]), whom Boas goes on to identify with a figure reported by Mathilda Coxe Stevenson from Zia (one of the Keresan-speaking Rio Grande pueblos located some 70 miles to the northeast of Laguna) as "Thought-Woman, the Spider, [who] lives alone in the lower world" (228). In the section subtitled "Cosmology" of her report on *The Sia*, published in the Eleventh Annual Report of the Bureau of Ethnology in 1893, Stevenson's first sentence after the introductory paragraph reads: "In the beginning there was but one being in the lower world, Sûs´sĭstinnako, a spider" (26).[3] Both Gunn and Boas understand her to be, and Stevenson's story transcription makes her out to be, the ur-creator, or rather creatrix, figure of the Keresan pantheon.

These four accounts are also in loose agreement that the first, or at least one of the first, creations this creatrix brings about is a pair of sisters, Silko's Nau'ts'ity'i and I'tcts'ity'i, to help her with the subsequent stages of generating "the Universe/this world/and the four worlds below." In Stevenson's Zia version, "The two women first created were the mothers of all; the one created on the east side of the line of meal, Sûs´sĭstinnako named Ût´sēt, and she was the mother of all Indians; he called the other Now´ûtsēt, she being the mother of other nations" (27). Curiously, Gunn includes no parallel story among his "traditions and narratives"; however, two of Boas's informants, Ko'tʸe and Gʸi'mi, give several stories[4] about the activities of "our mother Nau'ts'itʸ'i and our father I'tc'ts'itʸ'i" while two others, José and Pedro Martín, also mention these two figures.

The gender discrepancies in these several versions bear noting. In the Zia version given by Stevenson, both children of Thought Woman are definitively female, and both become mothers; in all of the stories from Laguna gathered in Boas, however, Nau'ts'itʸ'i is always female but I'tc'ts'itʸ'i is always male. In his attempt to extrapolate an essential origin story from the extant Laguna, Acoma, Zia, and Cochiti ethnography, Boas addresses this apparent discrepancy:

> The most prominent feature of the Laguna account is the transformation of the two creator sisters Nau´ts'itᵘ'i and Ï´tc'ts'itᵘ'i into a sister and brother. All my informants ... agreed in regard to this statement. In Mrs. Marmon's Laguna account, given by Dr. Parsons (APAMNH 19: 114) they appear as sisters but this is the only record of this type from Laguna. In all the other versions Ï´tc'ts'itᵘ'i appears as a man. Undoubtedly this is a new development due to Catholic influence. Ï´tc'ts'itᵘ'i is now the father of the Whites. In Sia the creators are women and this conforms to the general pueblo form of thought. It is also important to note that in the Laguna texts Nau´ts'itᵘ'i and Ï´tc'ts'itᵘ'i call each other Gaau´-na; a word presumably related to ĸaau´, sister, woman speaking. (221)

The "Mrs. Marmon" to whom Boas alludes was the Laguna-born widow of Walter G. Marmon, who was the brother of Silko's father's grandfather Robert Marmon (who also married a Laguna woman)[5]; one of her brothers was a Laguna *cheani*, a keeper of stories and ceremonies,[6] and in his old age she served as his prompter during the ceremonies until her own death during the influenza epidemic of 1918.[7] In the version she gave Parsons, originally there are four "sisters" named Iyetiku, Tsichinnaku, Naustiti, and Ūshstiti (Parsons, *Notes* 114); the story focuses on the relationship between "the *chakwena ma'sewi*"[8] and "his mother *iyetiku*," though, and of these "sisters" only Iyetiku is mentioned again, but it's clear enough that Parsons' "Tsichinnaku," "Naustiti," and "Ūshstiti" are identical to Boas's "Ts'its'tsc'i·´na·´k'o," "Nau´ts'itᵘ'i," and "Ï´tc'ts'itᵘ'i" and also to Silko's "Ts'its'tsi'nako," "Nau'ts'ity'i," and "I'tcts'ity'i."[9]

It is possible, then, that the genders given in Silko's version of this story are based on—and also designed to pay respect to—family tradition rather than on a broader community consensus.[10] If that is the case, then the three generations of storyteller it takes to get from Ts'its'tsi'nako to "I" in this fragment may be congruent with the three generations connecting Leslie Marmon Silko, the "I" who is "telling you the story she is thinking," to "Mrs. Marmon," the "she" whose voice and story are in *Keresan Texts* reduced to a bibliographical note. In both cases, the relationship is that of grandmother to granddaughter,[11] which with respect to the story is also a relationship of sister to sister: both stand in homological identity to the story they share, even though one may have preceded the other by several generations. The fourth, completing generation of story is the audience "you" in this piece, the audience who in the oral traditional dynamic must produce the next storyteller if the story (and by inference Ts'its'tsi'nako's project) is to continue in the Fifth World.

One other important function of this fragment is to introduce the Laguna concept of multiple worlds: "She thought of her sisters,/Nau'ts'ity'i and I'tcts'ity'i,/and together they created the Universe/this world/and the four worlds below." "This world," often also called the Fifth World, is the one the storytelling "I" and the audience "you" co-occupy; four other worlds are understood to precede in time, and exist below or "within" in space, the empirical world of which we are a part. Although these worlds can be enumerated and located with respect to one another,[12] they should not be thought of as separated from one another either in time or in space but rather as phases of a fundamentally singular event. In the First World, Ts'its'tsi'nako is thinking a story; in the Fifth World, someone is telling us that story; in between, "her sisters" (who are also her "daughters") Nau'ts'ity'i and I'tcts'ity'i are working to transform the story into the more material realities that the storyteller's Fifth World words will refer to. Note, too, that Silko could have labeled Nau'ts'ity'i and I'tcts'ity'i "her [Ts'its'tsi'nako's] daughters" or, alternatively, "my [i.e., the storyteller's] ancestors"; by selecting "sisters" Silko in effect collapses the distance we might imagine to be separating different generations and instead privileges the connection that is also always between them.

Finally, in this opening fragment Silko introduces one of the most formally important of all the novel's motifs, namely the motif of phase transformation. Here, Ts'its'tsi'nako's project becomes the shared project of the next phase/generation(s) in the form of Nau'ts'ity'i and I'tcts'ity'i, which in turn (but also, on another, time-independent, axis, *simultaneously*) becomes the project of the storytelling "I." From this perspective, "I," who was a daughter in her role as audience or recipient of her forbears' project, in the process of generating the text of page 1 becomes a "sister"of all those who have told this story, in any and all of its variations and versions, all the way "back" or "down" to Grandmother Spider, Ts'its'tsi'nako. Here too we can begin to see the phased transformation of a "story" from conception (Ts'its'tsi'nako's function) through realization (the function of "her sisters" Nau'ts'ity'i and I'tcts'ity'i) through verbal (spoken and/or written) articulation ("I"'s function); not to be overlooked in this process is the role of the audience, the listener/reader who completes the circuit of the story's becoming.

"Ceremony" (p. 2)

In this portion, once again Silko presents a narrative about narrative: the male narrator, the "he" referred to in the two bracketed asides ("[he said]"), will "tell you something about stories." In this piece, however, an additional third level of narrative is generated by the bracketed asides, since formally they predicate a narrative presence who is either creating or reporting (or both) the speaker, i.e., the "he" who is directly addressing the implied auditor "you" during most of the passage. This tri-level packing of narrative and narrators formally complements the three levels or realms of motion apparently required to make ceremony—(1) "his belly," which "you" can "see ... is moving"; (2) the stories, the "them" that "I keep ... here" in his belly, the otherwise invisible and intangible life informing the visible and tangible motion of the storyteller's belly; and (3), "in the belly of this story" (one, or one part, of "the stories" of the people that must be protected from, so as to protect the people from, "them" and "their evil"), the "rituals and the ceremony" that "are still growing."

Who is this narrator whose role is to articulate this special relationship between "ceremony," "rituals," "stories," and the life and welfare of the people? One thing for certain, thanks to the two bracketed asides, is that the narrator is to be understood as male, in contrast (or in complement) to the female (Thought-) Woman who "thinks" and "name[s]" things into being in the first piece. Just as some readers will be taken aback by Silko's female gendering of primordial creative power in the first piece, the image of life for the people being carried in a male's belly may take most first-time non-Indian readers aback. Perhaps what we are to understand, taking the first two pieces together, is that creative power occurs where gender is liminalized: to know the whole story is to know both the male and the female aspects of the story. Gender is an articulation of life, but the life being articulated, i.e., taking form, could go either way and, in a wholly realized universe, does go both ways.

Silko takes care to make this first male presence in the novel a counterpart to the first and fourth female presences in the preceding embedded text. The primary voice in this second piece is that of a generic storyteller and storykeeper, one who knows the stories and also knows how to talk about the stories, a distinction of skills that Dennis Tedlock uses to locate an important bridge between sacred and secular storytelling modes in Zuñi tradition.[13] Given that the title of the novel (*Ceremony*), the apparent title of this second piece ("Ceremony"), and the core of the narrative performance in this piece ("the ceremony") are all the same term, it seems fair to infer that "this story" (that is, the one that this storyteller says he is carrying in his belly and that is carrying, in *its* belly, "the ceremony") is the prose narrative that finally begins to emerge and take shape "outside" as the story of Tayo. The story of Tayo is, in turn, the story of one Laguna male's transformation from lost to found, from departed to recovered, from fragmented to whole, from motherless child to he who carries Our Mother within him as memory and story. It makes sense, then, to think of the narrator in this piece as the storyteller Tayo is to become—the product of the ensuing prose narrative.

The identity of "you" is in this piece remains, I think, purposefully and invitingly ambiguous. When the narrator is read as generic storyteller, the "you" being addressed could be either the reader (being addressed directly) or some embedded-within-the-narrative but otherwise invisible (because voiceless) novice being initiated by some master into the mysteries of oral tradition. This configuration foreshadows, of course, the relationship of Tayo to the old men Ku'oosh, the Laguna *cheani*, and Betonie, the Navajo *hataali*, in the forthcoming prose narrative. Alternately, when the narrator is read as Tayo-to-be, "you" could again be the reader, being offered a definitively Laguna context within which to frame the forthcoming prose narrative, or "you" could be some anonymous member of a next generation of the people, perhaps a generation reaching its majority at the historical time of the publication of the novel, for whom the events of the novel will have taken place a generation or two ago.

"*What She Said*:" (p. 3)

Typographically, this piece is distinguished from the other three in two ways. First, it is printed in two typefaces, the first line in italic and the other four in roman typefont. Second, except for the first line, the text is not centered on the page but instead indented a regular distance from the left margin. These typographical differences invite analysis.

Again as in the preceding piece, the first line bears an ambiguous relationship to the rest of the text, reading as either the title of the piece or as its first line. Typographical cues—the difference in typeface, the white space between this line and the others, and especially the capitalization—would seem to imply it is to be read as a title; but read as a transcript of oral performance, other cues—particularly the center justification and the colon, signaling that these words are part of a statement that will be completed by what comes next—invite us to read the first line as the utterance of the embedding voice, and the following four lines as the embedded voice, of that two-domain narrative Silko creates in the first two pieces. From this perspective, again one of the functions of the embedding voice is to establish the female gender (but, as in the second piece, significantly not the precise identity) of the embedded narrative "I" who equates ceremony with cure in the piece; one effect of gendering the embedding voice thus is to formally bracket the male storyteller of the second piece between female voices—or to put it differently, to embed the male storyteller within the context of female-gendered narrative space. Further, the "unusual" positioning of the un-italicized four lines might be taken as a cue that this portion of story occupies less formally "centered" space, even though the subject is still ceremony.

One final observation on the voicing in this short piece: stripped of typographical coding, the first and last three words of this piece are identical, which creates at least a phonological identity between the two narrators and the two narratives referred to by the "that" and the "she" of the two statements. Indeed, one might even argue that on the basis of this grammatical identity the first and last lines are to be read as uttered by the same storyteller, the final "that's what she said" being a repetition for emphasis of the original "*What She Said.*" However, it is equally valid, and I think more consistent with the polyvocality of the previous two pieces, to read the difference in typography as indicative of difference in narrative positioning. This reading is warranted in part because, absent quotation marks, Silko uses typography this way in the long witchery narrative at the center of the novel (see chapter 12) as well as throughout the poetically cast hama-ha pieces in her *Storyteller* collection.[14] Read this way, both the overall syntax of the piece and the differences in typography invite us to distinguish between not just two but at least three voices:

1. the embedding narrator who delivers the first line;
2. the embedded narrator who "said" the last line as a means of attributing the three bracketed lines to
3. some third narrator who, we discover only when we read the last line, is the "I" of the central line.

Thus, the statement "The only cure/I know/is a good ceremony" is produced by no fewer than three narrators, all three present within the narrative space of these five lines but having uttered the statement in three different generations of time: (1) someone claims that (2) *She Said* that (3) she said that the only cure I know is a good ceremony. To further the ambiguity of number: it is not clear whether we are to identify the implied, embedding narrator with Silko as author or whether we are to understand that Silko (like Ts'its'tsi'nako, sitting in her room somewhere sometime thinking) is here composing a "sister" self, a second generation of the storyteller urge, who in turn will utter a third generation (the "*She*" referred to in the first line), who speaks the words of, and then in the final line attributes those words to, a fourth generation of the story's telling.[15] However one chooses to count the narrative presences, though, this five-line tour-de-force in narrative ambiguity shares with the previous two pieces one important cue to understanding the narrative structure of the novel: the source of ambiguity and the resolution of ambiguity lie equally in coming to terms with the delicate webwork of multiple narrative presences in the text.

The question raised by the first two pieces arises again at the end of this one: who *is* the "I" who identifies herself in the center of the piece? When the piece is read as an isolated fragment, there is no good answer to this question; all we are given intratextually is the claim that at least one of the narrators is female. When read as an extension of the narrative project set in motion by Ts'its'tsi'nako and her helpers, however, it becomes very tempting to infer that the embedding narrator of this piece, the one who thinks or speaks the first line in italics, is identical with the "I" who emerges as the embedding narrator at the end of the first piece. If so, then it is equally tempting to infer that "the story" Ts'its'tsi'nako is thinking, the same story her daughter-sisters are composing out of time and space and the same story their agent, the storyteller, is composing in words, is a story that, we are being told here in the third piece, can be reduced to the proposition that ceremony is not only about defense (as the male narrator of the second piece claims) but also about curing.

Read within the context of the prose narrative, the most likely referent of "I" is Tayo's ancient grandmother.[16] Early in the prose narrative, Tayo recalls his return to Laguna from the VA hospital in San Diego after World War II and those first months at home, feverish, bedridden, and constantly vomiting. Not unlike Spider Grandmother in the first piece of embedded text, Tayo's Grandma spends her days sitting by the stove and thinking, and occasionally speaking on behalf of life and regeneration. The first time she speaks in the text, it is to address Tayo's malaise:

> He looked at old Grandma sitting in her place beside the stove; he couldn't tell if she was sleeping or if she was only listening to the wind with her eyes closed.... He watched her get up slowly, with old bones that were stems of thin glass she shuffled across the linoleum in her cloth slippers, moving cautiously as if she did not trust memory to take her to his bed. She sat down on the edge of the bed and she reached out for him. She held his head in her lap and she cried with him, saying "A'moo'oh, a'moo'ohh" over and over again.
>
> "I've been thinking," she said, wiping her eyes on the edge of her apron, "all this time, while I was sitting in my chair. Those white doctors haven't helped you at all. Maybe we had better send for someone else."
>
> When Auntie got back from the store, old Grandma told her, "That boy needs a medicine man." (33)

With these words, the process of curing Tayo's disease begins to be transferred from white doctors and their medicines to Indian "medicine men" and theirs— first old man Ku'oosh, a Laguna medicine man (*cheani*), and then, when Ku'oosh determines that his practice ("the Scalp Ceremony," 38) isn't the "good ceremony" needed to "cure" this case,[17] the Navajo medicine man (*hataali*) Betonie.

"Sunrise" (p. 4)

Standing as the shortest of all the embedded texts in the novel, the fourth member of this introductory series appears as the one-word sentence "Sunrise," centered high on verso page 4 of the novel and visually elevated above the first lines of the prose narrative that begins four-fifths of the way down the next, facing recto, page 5. In several ways this positioning suggests a transitional function for this fragment. For one: as mentioned earlier, according to Keresan origin traditions, life has emerged, and continues to emerge, sequentially through four worlds to take place in this, the Fifth, world. Seen in this context, page 4 and its one-word text stands as the fourth in a series of four pages of poetic pieces that precede page 5, where the prose narrative begins, thus paralleling the four-world emergence process that in Keresan tradition precedes the appearance of life in the Fifth World. Page 1 may be taken to represent the Keresan First World where Ts'its'tsi'nako, Thought-Woman, is always and forever sitting in her house, thinking Life into motion, aided down the line by the sisters she thinks into being to help her and, later, their children the storytellers—the "I" at the bottom of page 1 who is "telling you the story she is thinking"; the "he" who speaks on page 2; and the "she" who speaks on page 3. Page 4, then, can be taken as either the voice of a gender-anonymous fourth Laguna storyteller in this series or, and I think this comes closer to Silko's own creative vision, as a word that connects all the worlds before with the Fifth World of the prose narrative, a sort of verbal *sipapu* or Emergence Place in the geography and topography of the novel.

In any case, this positioning also allows the word to function as a setting for the prose narrative to come, locating the reading audience in time at the dawn of some unspecified day and waiting for the story proper to begin with the statement that "Tayo didn't sleep well that night." Seen from this perspective, "Sunrise" here functions as the first of a pair of formal brackets to the prose narrative, enclosing and contextualizing the story of Tayo within sacred time and space. The closing bracket, of course, would be the last page of the text of the novel, a space occupied exclusively by a short prayer to Sunrise to "accept this offering" of story. I'll provide a closer analysis of this function, and of the sunrise motif more generally, in chapter 6.

In part because of its brevity, which provides no internal indications of its origin or reference, and in part because of its location, this is possibly also the most ambiguous of all the embedded texts in the novel. Is it to be understood as the fourth member of an introductory series of statements, or is it more closely related, perhaps as a sort of stage direction, to the coming prose narrative? Adding to the uncertainty about its function is the question of whether it is to be read as narrative or not, and if so which of the several narrative voices introduced in the first three embedded texts is speaking here (or is some new voice being added to the growing chorus?). As I suspect I have been implying all along, my own sense is that the ambiguity is both intentional and functional: "sunrise" here marks the liminal zone of an event where (in space) and during which (in time) all possibilities gather in silence to become the source, or sipapu, of the coming story.

JUMPING THROUGH HOOPS

The "hoop" is one of several quickly recognized stock metaphorical images in the literary representations of Native American cultures. The *locus classicus* of Native American hoop imagery is a passage in Black Elk's "Great Vision" as translated and published in John Neihardt's 1932 *Black Elk Speaks*.[18] As a young man "seeing in a sacred manner," we are told,

> round about beneath me was the whole hoop of the world.... And I saw that the sacred hoop of my people was one of many hoops that made one circle, wide as daylight and as starlight, and in the center grew one mighty flowering tree to shelter all the children of one mother and one father. And I saw that it was holy. (43)

Perhaps even better known is another passage from the same book, this one the closing words of Black Elk's elegy for the 1890 massacre at Wounded Knee, in which the image of a broken hoop functions as vehicle for the idea of cultural disruption and annihilation: "... the nation's hoop is broken and scattered. There is no center any longer, and the sacred tree is dead" (276). Over half a century later, Paula Gunn Allen borrowed the image of the sacred hoop from *Black Elk Speaks* and made it the title of her own seminal book *The Sacred Hoop*,[19] in which the hoop comes to represent the idea of cultural survival and continuance. In their hoop imagery, then, Neihardt and Gunn Allen both privilege the connotation of wholeness, the spelled circle which contains and preserves.

However, while this may be the most popular tenor of hoop imagery in the field of American Indian literature and literary criticism, it is far from the only, or even the most frequently encountered, significance. For instance, the hoop also figures traditionally as a vehicle for the idea of transformation. Within this context, the hoop functions as a visible portal: to pass through a hoop is to pass through a "liminal zone," to move from one phase or stage of timespace to another. This is how Silko makes use of hoopwork in her novel *Ceremony*.

The first overt reference to hoops in *Ceremony* comes in the opening pages, right after Silko has narrated Tayo out of his bed in the shack on the remote southwest corner of Laguna land and out into the painful morning sunlight:

> The dry air shrank the wooden staves of the barrels; they pulled loose, and now the rusty steel hoops were scattered on the ground behind the corral in the crazy patterns of some flashy Kiowa hoop dancer at the Gallup Ceremonials, throwing his hoops along the ground where he would hook and flip them into the air again and they would skim over his head and shoulders down to his dancing feet, like magic. Tayo stepped inside one that was half buried in the reddish blow sand; he hooked an edge with the toe of his boot, and then let it slip into the sand again. (10)

Even without knowing anything about the ceremonial etiology of the hoop dance, most readers will know, given the prevailing etic lens of the mid-to-late twentieth century, how to read this image: Black Elk's sacred but broken hoop has become, in Tayo's post-World War II vision, a secular and inert one except when it is being manipulated as part of a tourist spectacle. Reading the hoop within the context of the popular Kiowa hoopdance, Tayo, we are to understand, is another victim of twentieth-century neurasthenia, a literary cousin of James Welch's Jim Loney, nostalgically aware that once upon a time to be Indian was to be alive in motion, but now those times are gone. Like the figure of the fancydancer in Kate Loney's paintings, Tayo seems to have come to the End of the Trail.[20]

I suspect that Silko is consciously teasing her reader when she deploys this familiar, even stereotypical, hoopdancer trope so early in the narrative. Like Tayo, who after all doesn't know a whole lot more about being "Indian" than a well-read non-Indian reader at this stage of his restorative ceremony, we understand that for the Indian protagonist the world has gone secular, that a hoop may be only a hoop, and that, even if it ever meant more than that, Tayo for one has no idea how to manipulate either the hoop or its potential meaning.

Easily the most dramatic use of traditional hoop imagery in the novel, though, occurs in the second major movement, featuring Tayo's departure to and eventual return from Gallup[21] and, beyond Gallup to the north and east, to and from the "dark mountains"—the Chuska Mountains—into the heart of which old Betonie conducts Tayo in order to reorient him ceremonially to his life and Laguna's. Here, the hoops are the ones Betonie and his helper Shush construct for the recovery ritual that Betonie sings over Tayo. However, Silko doesn't present this ritual use of hoops until after she returns, one more time, to an etically more familiar use of hoop imagery. After Tayo and Robert have arrived in Gallup, but before they meet up with Betonie, hoop imagery again appears, once again associated with "traditional" Indian hoopdancing. This time, though, Silko locates the image solidly within the etic context of commodification and appropriation of traditional Native identity:

> The Gallup Ceremonial had been an annual event for a long time. It was good for the tourist business coming through in the summertime on Highway 66. They liked to see Indians and Indian dances; they wanted a chance to buy Indian jewelry and Navajo rugs.... Dance groups from the Pueblos were paid to come; they got Plains hoop dancers, and flying-pole dancers from northern Mexico.

As Silko concludes the passage, ruefully, "The tourists got to see what they wanted" (116).

Juxtaposed with this very public, commercial display of Indianness is the very private and not-for-profit[22] hoopwork that Betonie performs. Formally, Betonie's hoop ritual[23] is set very near the center of the text, and perhaps this is a sign of its importance within the context of the novel as a whole.[24] As Betonie (and Silko) lay out this ritual, the hoops become transition zones made visible, a series of ritual *sipapus* or emergence places: by passing *through* a hoop made of one of five kinds of wood, Tayo passes *out of* one color-coded state of being *into* another. In the novel, the direction of transition is from the "back" of Betonie's hogan out through the door. If Betonie's ritual hogan is oriented conventionally by Navajo standards, this means Tayo is moving cartographically from west to east, the direction of sunrise and regeneration in both Navajo and Laguna tradition, as well as from "inside" to "outside." As laid out in the novel, Tayo starts from a sitting position at the back of the hogan, occupying the same space that is occupied by an image of the mythical Pollen Boy at the center of a "white corn sand painting," with the "rainbows crossed in the painting behind him" (141). Aided by Betonie on one side and by Betonie's bear-boy helper Shush on the other, we are told, "Betonie prayed him through each of the five hoops" (143), the last of which leads "through the doorway. It was dark and the sky was bright with stars."

"Five hoops." The Bear People who live at the summit of the Dark Mountain are very particular about the ingredients of the prescription required to bring the hunter back from coyote identity to human identity: "They said/Prepare hard oak/ scrub oak/piñon/juniper and wild rose twigs/Make hoops"; accordingly, "Betonie's helper scraped the sand away and buried the bottoms of the hoops in little trenches so that they were standing up and spaced apart, with the hard oak closest to him and the wild rose hoop in front of the door" (141). As Silko lays out the ritual in her novel, these five hoops in turn function to space the painted mountains and the pairs of footprints that mark the trail Tayo must walk in order to be restored—literally, to be returned through four ritual landscapes to the Fifth World that lies, as Betonie and Silko would have it, beyond the final, fifth hoop nearest the door leading out of ritual space.

These five hoops delimit four stretches of ground, zones of ritual identity—or six. Four if we see only the four sacred-colored mountain ranges and four sets of sand-painted footprints; but six if we see that these four ritual spaces (like the "big rainbow arching wide above all the mountain ranges," 142) are laid out for the purpose of transporting Tayo from a state of dis-ease to a state of relative *hozho*. To see this way is to see that the hoops also access, in one direction, the state Tayo is in prior to the first hoop and the four mountain ranges and, in the other direction, the state Tayo is in after the four mountain ranges and the fifth hoop. The ritual motion through the hoops thus connects pre-ritual time/space with post-ritual time/space. Through the hoop ritual, in other words, these two zones become part of the ceremony.

I shall return to the formal function of hoops and color coding in Betonie's ritual in chapter 11 of this book. I have discussed it at such length here only in order to direct attention to less obvious series of hoops that I think Silko has set at the entryway to her novel. Let me try now to suggest some ways of applying the structure of Betonie's ritual art to the structure of Silko's verbal art.

If we take our cues from Silko's text, rather than from our previous expectations of what constitutes a novel, we enter the prose narrative world of *Ceremony* in much the same way that Tayo is guided from the back of Betonie's ceremonial hogan into the Fifth World awaiting his return: by passing through four antecedent zones, conveniently located discretely on four separate but sequential pages. In Betonie's ritual, Tayo moves from a state of complete lost-ness to a state of complete [re-]centered-ness only by passing through four intermediate zones, color-coded white-yellow-blue-black. In Silko's ceremonialized and ceremonializing text, the opening structure moves a reader through zones of narrative; that is, to get from "outside" the novel "into" the prose narrative, the reader is obliged to migrate through four intermediate narrative zones. The structure of the text, then, brings a reader's experience under Silko's authorial control into homologous identity with Tayo's experience under Betonie's control. This homological identity of Silko with Betonie is recognized by several earlier critics who cast Silko in the role of *hataalii* or *curandera* and present the novel as Good Medicine for attentive readers.[25]

Having focused earlier in this chapter on four opening fragments of this novel, I now want to focus rather on the transition zones between these four performances and also on the transformation which I suspect these pieces have been designed and aligned to facilitate.

Understood as forms of narrative, the contents of the four opening pages of the novel represent four kinds of storytelling, four varieties of oral narrative. As many of us know from learning the hard way, subcategorizing the contents of the standard category "oral narrative" is risky and controversial business, but for the sake of purely literary distinction let me posit a *spectrum* of narrative performance, be it oral or written, ranging from the relatively sacred to the relatively secular and, drawing attention to a correlative quality of the same axis, from the relatively mythic or a-historical to the relatively mundane or "now-day." Seen this way, Silko's novel becomes five "zones" of oral narrative, ranging sequentially from the mythic story of Ts'its'tsi'nako, Thought Woman; through the initiatory explanation of the relationship of ceremony, story, and human life; past a four-line fragment of conversation; past the single word "Sunrise" occupying page 4; and finally, at the end of this series of one-pagers—or, seen another way, on the other side of this series—the prose narrative, the 250-page "body" of the novel.

Just as Betonie's hoop ritual allows Tayo to move as though his life subsequent to the ritual is also an extension of the ritual, Silko's opening formal hoop ritual allows a reader to read the prose narrative as though it were a novel but also an extension of the ritualized wordspace linking Ts'its'tsi'nako's project to the more familiar project of a twentieth-century author writing a novel. Yes, this is a print text; but it is also a storytelling performance, and the storytelling voice in this particular novel is more genuinely the initial subject of the novel than the story of Tayo, a story it takes care to introduce and also to embed within the traditions of healing oral narrative.

To home in on the element of "voice" here is to home in also on those invisible hoops I keep skirting. By analogy with Betonie's sandpainted mountain ranges and footprints, the texture of the text here in the first four pages of the novel transforms clearly enough, but how do we really get from one zone to the next?

To make the transition from "outside" to "inside" a ritual, we need a guide—in Tayo's case, Betonie; in this four-part series of transforming narrative, the storyteller Silko provides (the one who says "I am telling you the story she is thinking" at the bottom of page 1). Furthermore, we also (and finally I get to my point) need to see those protracted white spaces between these four portions of narrative as *narrative hoops*—spaces containing emptiness but at the same time spaces where transformation occurs, invisible but nonetheless functional liminal zones, narrative *sipapus*.

What transforms? First, as I have argued above, the narrative mode transforms, from one end of the narrative spectrum to the other. In addition (and this is where Silko's hoopwork is really located) the narrative voice, the storyteller, transforms, gradually, from what the non-Keresan reader might hear as the rather exotic, myth-inspired "I" of the first page—"I am telling you the story she is thinking," she says, referring to the mythical grandmother Spider Ts'its'tsi'nako, who in this four-page ritual occupies the space that Pollen Boy occupies in Betonie's—to the much more familiar-sounding narrator-storyteller who announces, with that quality of sympathetic detachment we have come to expect of a conventional novelist, that "Tayo didn't sleep well that night." Step by step, the storytelling voice transforms from being under the control of its subject ("I am [only] telling you the story she is thinking") to being in control of its subject. Simultaneously, the implied audience is invited to undergo a similar, reciprocal series of shifts, steps of a transformation leading from whatever subject position the reader might happen to occupy before beginning to read the novel to the subject position represented by the protagonist Tayo, or, more ambitiously, to the special narrative perspective being trained upon Tayo as protagonist.

I find it curious finding myself concluding that in this novel silence is a special kind of discourse, analogous to those hoops Tayo must pass through—be led through—in order to become oriented, or re-oriented, in the Fifth World.[26] However, I do hope I am not alone in surmising that each of the zones of white space demarcating the four sections of narrative at the beginning of Silko's novel functions as a narrative hoop, each hoop leading from more daunting and less familiar, to more familiar and less daunting, narrative ground.

CHAPTER 6
The Sunrise Series

One of the quietest, and in some ways the most interesting, of the several distinct groups of embedded texts in the novel is the three-part Sunrise series, the ones numbered 4, 23, and 30 in chapter 2.

First, let me offer some observations about these three embedded texts understood as elements of a series. They are the briefest of all the embedded texts in the novel, and, like most of those others, all three appear center-justified on the page. Unlike most of the others, however, the three pieces in this series are all non-narrative. Another unusual thing about this series is that the term *sunrise*, which unites them in series, undergoes a semantic metamorphosis each time it appears, transforming mode from frame signal, to traditional song when it (re-)appears two-thirds of the way through the novel, and finally to prayer on the last page of the book. The first time it occurs in the novel, the word *sunrise* reads like a descriptive statement, a word that provides the reader with a context of time and setting. The second member of the series, according to the prose explanation in which it is embedded, is the text of a brief ritual song associated with sacred, ceremonial occasions. The third and final element of the series functions as a supplicatory prayer addressed to Sunrise, understood as a living entity. I want to offer some notes and observations on each of these three embedded texts, followed by a final note on the function of the overall series with respect to the rest of the novel.

"SUNRISE"

As pointed out already in the preceding chapter, this first occurrence of Sunrise text in the novel fulfills several important functions when it is read as the fourth member of the opening series of embedded texts; I'd like to turn attention here to its function with respect to the prose narrative that follows. Earlier I pointed out that the peculiar positioning of this portion of embedded text allows the word to function as a setting for the prose narrative to come, locating the reading audience in time at the dawn of some unspecified day and waiting for the story proper to begin with the statement that "Tayo didn't sleep well that night." Seen from this perspective, "Sunrise" here functions as the first of a pair of formal brackets to the prose narrative (the closing bracket, of course, would be the "sunrise" that appears as the first and also the final word of the final statement on the final page of text in the novel), enclosing and contextualizing the story of Tayo within sacred time and space.

Silko's use of the term *sunrise* as a bracketing device is both rhetorically and semantically consistent with Laguna oral tradition. One of the conventions of formal storytelling in Laguna tradition is what I want to call the *initiating bracket*, a phrase that signals the beginning of the storytelling performance. Such initiating brackets, which function as the first of a pair of verbal brackets defining the storytelling "space," exist in many storytelling traditions. However, of course, the utterance that is used as that signal differs from culture to culture and, sometimes, from storyteller to storyteller within a given tradition.[1] In English storytelling tradition, perhaps the most common such bracket is "once upon a time." As I have argued already in chapter 3 in regard to the traditional Keresan backbone motif, in the conventions of Laguna traditional storytelling (to the extent that those conventions have survived translation from oral to written performance, and from Keresan to English) the most frequently used initiating bracket is the phrase *hama-ha*. Of the 47 early twentieth-century performances transcribed in Boas' *Keresan Texts*, 45 begin with this word or some variation of it, which Boas usually translates as "Long ago—eh."

Writing a few years earlier than Boas, John Gunn, a more casual student of Keresan oral literary tradition, notes,

> When a Queres Indian commences to tell a story he begins by saying Humma-ha; these words to him now have no particular signification, and are used merely as words of attention or introduction, as we would say "Once upon a time," but at one time they meant something more, as the words indicate, Humma, when, and ha, east, and were used to introduce a class of stories brought from an eastern country. (67)

Gunn's conclusion about the provenance of the stories thus introduced is suspect, as is his contention that the syllables "have no particular signification" to modern-day Laguna storytellers.[2] As Paula Gunn Allen, one of several published modern-day Laguna storytellers, notes in *The Sacred Hoop*,[3] for a Keresan-speaking audience the phrase not only cues the beginning of a storytelling performance, but it also locates the *event* of the coming story in the spatial and temporal vicinity of originality: "hama-ha" directs the Keresan audience's attention toward both a *time* (early) and a *place* (easterly) of beginnings, a vicinity of the time-space "tortilla"[4] associated with the daily event of sunrise. My point is that Silko's word *sunrise* not only functions in her text like the term *hama-ha* does in traditional Laguna oral performance but also may be read as a pretty good alternate, one-word translation of the Keresan phrase.

"A SONG FOR THE SUNRISE"

The second of the three pieces of Sunrise text, which appears on page 182 of the novel, is embedded in a gloss on the "traditional" function of the word. Tayo's memories provide a Keresan traditional context for the Sunrise motif—a context that illuminates not only the song Tayo recalls but also Silko's use of the term at both ends of the prose narrative it brackets. Just prior to the piece of embedded text, Tayo is at the foot of Mount Taylor at the time of the autumnal equinox, watching "the dawn spreading across the sky like yellow wings" and listening to the sound of his horse's steel bit, jingling as she grazes, a sound which reminds him "of the bells in late November" heard every year at Laguna:

> Before dawn, southeast of the village, the bells would announce their approach, the sound shimmering across the sand hills, followed by the clacking of turtleshell rattles—all these sounds gathering with the dawn. Coming closer to the river, faintly at first, faint as the pale yellow light emerging across the southeast horizon, the sounds gathered intensity from the swelling colors of dawn. And at the moment the sun came over the edge of the horizon, they suddenly appeared on the riverbank, the Ka't'sina approaching the river crossing.
> He stood up. He knew the people had a song for the sunrise.

We are then given the second embedded Sunrise text in its entirety:

> Sunrise!
> We come at sunrise

> to greet you.
> We call you
> at sunrise.
> Father of the clouds
> you are beautiful
> at sunrise.
> Sunrise!

At this place in the novel, then, the Sunrise motif becomes linked to two classes of Keresan supernatural spirit: the *ka'ts'ina* and the *kurena*. On one side of the song, we are told that sunrise is when the katsinas appear in the Fifth World, southeast of the village in late November, in order to visit with the People and renew their shared story during the winter months. On the other side, where the text is referred to as a "prayer" rather than a "song," we are told that Tayo

> repeated the words as he remembered them, not sure if they were the right ones,[5] but feeling they were right, feeling the instant of dawn was an event which in a single moment gathered all things together—the last stars, the mountaintops, the clouds, and the winds—celebrating this coming. Sunrise. He ended the prayer with "sunrise" because he knew the Dawn people began and ended all their words with "sunrise."

"The Dawn people." To understand what Tayo and Silko are thinking here, it helps to have in mind the Pueblo moiety system as it manifests in Laguna tradition. In brief, there are two moieties, the kurena moiety or "summer people," also known as the "dawn people," who are primarily responsible for the autumn ceremonies; and the kashare moiety or "winter people," who are primarily responsible for the rest of the Laguna ceremonial calendar.[6] Franz Boas, in *Keresan Texts*, has this to say about the kashare, the kurena, and sunrise:

> The kurena live in the northeast at i·'cak'a k`a´тcïtˈ.
> The kashare migrated from the Place of Emergence with the kindly supernatural beings (kopishtaya) to the house of the sun in the east (κoai´k`tc`). The kurena must also be closely associated with the sunrise for all of their songs end with the word "sunrise" (κo·aiκï·κai, poetic form for κoai´k`tc`). They migrated northeastward, leading a people called She-ken ... who carried flowers in their hands that withered and bloomed alternately. (293) ...

> These two societies alternate in their ceremonial activities. Only kashare songs are sung from the winter solstice to the corn harvest. Only kurena songs from the harvest until the beginning of the season of kashare songs. Members of all societies and those uninitiated may sing these songs. The kurena lead the people back from the harvest for the cacique, singing the following song: [There follows the text of the song printed in Keresan, along with an interlinear English translation; the last sentence of the song is the single word "KO·aiKï·kai·Kai," translated as "Sunrise!"] (294–95)[7]

Here, we get the Laguna word for sunrise that Tayo "knew the Dawn people began and ended all their words with": KO·aiKï·kai, poetic form for Koai´k`tc`. Although the orthographic spelling is quite different, I'm intrigued by the homophonic similarity of the kurena's word for sunrise, "Koai´k`tc`," and the Keresan word for Laguna, "kawaika." We can see here, too, how close the connotations of the term "hama-ha" are to those of the term "Koai´k`tc`." Finally, we can see how Silko contrives to make this song, and its key term "sunrise," the aural bridge her protagonist needs to link the two classes of supernatural helpers, the katsina on one side and the kurena on the other, to his own present task of recovering the stolen cattle.

"SUNRISE, ACCEPT THIS OFFERING"

Similar to the layout of page 4, the last page of the book (262) consists of a single brief, three-line sentence—"Sunrise,/accept this offering,/Sunrise"—again centered on the horizontal axis of the page, and this time also on the vertical axis. Structurally, the typography here calls final attention to the *centrality* of the sunrise motif in this work. We may recall here, for instance, that over and over again in the prose narrative sunrise, dawn, is presented as a time when the wholeness, the interrelatedness of all things is most apparent to Tayo. At the same time, the architecture of the text here may be taken to represent an essentialized template for any and all traditional Laguna story performances: an initiating bracket, a story which is also always a prayer, and a concluding bracket; if so, what's special about this recipe is that the opening and closing brackets are an identical utterance, "Sunrise," a term and a time strongly associated in this novel, as in the ethnographic record of Laguna traditions, with major Keresan spiritual forces including the katsina, the shiwanna, and the kurena. Finally, taken as a template for the novel as a whole, this final prayer to sunrise is a powerful reminder that the entire sunrise-bracketed narrative ("this offering," understood as the whole novel) is to be read, not only as a *series* of events (covering a space of 18 months of sunrises) but also, and as importantly, as a *single* event, a single sunrise, a single event of emergence and of re-emergence.[8] Retrospectively, this piece invites us to see that "Sunrise," which appears on page 4 to be simply part of the background setting for life, is also always becoming a part of—indeed, a source of—that life.

A NOTE ON ONE FUNCTION OF THE SERIES AS A WHOLE

One of the functions of these pretexts in the novel is to provide, for the prose narrative, an anchor in traditional Keresan motifs. I found it curious, then, that Silko presents a series of only three such fragments in this sunrise series: given the centrality and finality of this motif in the novel, as in Keresan tradition more broadly, I expected to find a fourth passage informed by the power of Sunrise. In fact, I expected it so strongly that I started looking for it. Being an unregenerate formalist at heart, and given the spacing of these three portions of Sunrise pretext (at the beginning of the novel, two-thirds of the way through the novel, and at the end) I looked for it to be about one-third of the way through the novel. There, about one-third of the way through the novel beginning at page 93, is this episode, one of a tangled skein of memories recalled by Tayo on his burro ride with Harley one late May morning. While the holy men from Acoma and Laguna are off on the mountaintops calling for clouds and thunder, Tayo recalls, "that last summer, before the war, he got up before dawn and rode the bay mare south to the spring in the narrow canyon." There, while "he waited for the sun to come over the hills," he climbs the narrow canyon to the spring there, dusting the surface of it with the pollen from "flowers with yellow long petals the color of the sunlight." In this passage, set at sunrise, Tayo witnesses four animal signs of rain emerge, but just as importantly recalls four pieces of traditional Laguna story, one associated with each creature—four drops, one might say, of that "stolen rain" mentioned earlier. In fact, to use Silko's words,

> Everywhere he looked, he saw a world made of stories, the long ago, time immemorial

stories, as old Grandma called them. It was a world alive, always changing and moving; and if you knew where to look, you could see it, sometimes almost imperceptible, like the motion of the stars across the sky. (95)

"A world made of stories, the long ago, time immemorial stories, as old Grandma called them"—*hama-ha* stories—if you know where to look. I am suggesting, in other words, that one important function of the Sunrise series is to call attention to this passage's signal importance as a step, and one of four sunrise steps, in the longer process of reintegrating Tayo's story with the backbone of *hama-ha* story tradition. More broadly, the term *sunrise* in the novel becomes a vehicle for bringing together, in a single word, energy from a broad spectrum of literary modes—song, narrative, oratory, and prayer—including energy recovered from ethnographic pretexts and repatriated to Laguna storyspace by Silko.

If all this is so, then I think we can see that there is indeed a distinct element of literary nationalism in Silko's use of ethnographic pretexts and that her successful incorporation of such materials in *Ceremony* is a very powerful testament to the ongoing adaptive capacity of Laguna cultural tradition.

Koai´k`tc`

CHAPTER 7

The Laguna Sisters

Within the context of the prose narrative, the first truly embedded fragment of traditional Laguna oral narrative (13–14) is the center-justified, skeletal-looking story of a falling-out between two sisters, Corn Woman and Iktoa'ak'o'ya-Reed Woman, that results in drought. When read without reference to the rest of the body of Laguna story, it is a somber tale of apparently irreparable loss—a tale consistent enough with the prose depiction of Tayo's state of mind in which this fragment is embedded. When read as part of the body of Laguna story, however, this fragment functions to sound the initial part of the departure-recovery motif that characterizes Laguna hama-ha stories.

PRETEXTS

A close homologue for this fragment of Silko's is the opening episode of "Ko-pot Ka-nat" in John Gunn's *Schat-chen*:

> I-ye-ti-ko and her sister, I-sto-a-ko-ya, lived in the Kush Kut-ret of the southwest. I-sto-a-ko-ya was in the habit of bathing in the big water. This she did almost continually, and it sorely tried the patience of her sister, so that one day I-ye-ti-ko scolded her because of it. This angered I-sto-a-ko-ya and she went back to Ship-op.
>
> Now it was because of the fact that I-sto-a-ko-ya was almost constantly in the water that the rain fell at Kush Kut-ret. When she had gone the rains stopped, everything became parched and dry and Kush Kut-ret was threatened with famine. I-ye-ti-ko, who divined the cause of the drouth, repenting of her harshness to her sister and fearful I-sto-a-ko-ya had been overcome by hunger and had died, sent a blue-bottle fly to find her. (115)

When Silko's and Gunn's texts are compared to each other, the homology between their two story lines puts Gunn's I-ye-ti-ko and I-sto-a-ko-ya into provisional identity with Silko's Corn Woman and Iktoa'ak'o'ya-Reed Woman, respectively. Sister pairs, including these two, figure prominently in the Laguna hama-ha stories, and in the embedded texts that Silko includes in the novel as well as in the Keresan ethnographic record preceding the novel's composition, the figures of Corn Woman and Reed Woman resonate strongly with those of Nautsityi and Ictsityi, the pair of sisters generated by Ts'its'tsi'nako/Thought Woman/Spider Grandmother in the opening lines of the novel and in the opening gambits of the emergence stories collected by Boas and Gunn (see chapter 5).

Unlike the last lines of Silko's version, the last sentence of Gunn's episode clearly signals that the story is not over yet. As Gunn's version goes on, the fly can find only the departed sister's footprints, which "led toward Ship-op, and ... everywhere that she had trodden the grass grew luxuriantly, while everywhere else it was dry and parched" (115). I-ye-ti-ko then commissions Stchi-mu-ne-moot, "a great runner and trailer," to recover the missing sister, which he eventually does[1]; "Upon her return the rains came back, giving new life to the dry earth and saving the people from famine" (116). Assuming that Silko's Corn Woman/Reed Woman story and Gunn's "Ko-pot Ka-nat" are homologically related thus invites us to regard Silko's embedded text as only a fragment—and, more specifically, as the departure segment of some longer, more complicated story of departure and recovery. In this sense, the fragment can also be understood as an alternate opening episode for the nine-part backbone story of departure and recovery: whether the people are suffering "because of that/Ck'o'yo magic/we were fooling with" (54) or because Corn Woman "scolded her sister/for bathing all day long" (13), the consequence (drought) and the cure (a ceremony of recovery) are the same.

Franz Boas's *Keresan Texts* provides another link between Silko's embedded text and this episode in Gunn's "Ko-pot Ka-nat." While *Keresan Texts* contains several stories featuring disaffected sisters, none of them overtly resembles Silko's Corn Woman/Reed Woman fragment the way Gunn's does. In a gloss on "The Emergence" (9–11) as told by Gyi´mi in 1919, a story which in turn is very similar in content to "The Hummingbird" (11–13) as told by Pedro Martin in the same year, Boas does however provide a précis of Gunn's story (237–38) . This précis contains a comment on Gunn's orthography in which Boas notes that Gunn's term for the sister who departs, I-sto-a-ko-ya, is "a word that looks like ιcτο·´a ικυ´yαnyi of the preceding story ["The Emergence"], although it may be ιcτο·´a k'o·´ya, arrow-woman, or ιcτoa·´a k'o·´ya, reed woman" (237). In this story, as in "The

Hummingbird" (as well as in Silko's 9-part backbone story in *Ceremony*), while the people were living at "the White-House" "there was starvation. Nobody did what our mother had told them"; when Hummingbird-Man then carries prayers and offerings to "our mother" below on behalf of the people, she tells him that this first offering is incomplete because something is missing: "'One thing more is not there. It will be very truly ιcτoa·´a.'" Hummingbird-Man then tells the people "She told me that one thing was not there, ιcτo·´a ikʋ´yɑnyi is its name" (10). In all three versions, as in Silko's backbone story, the missing ingredient turns out to be tobacco.

In the same gloss, Boas also identifies Gunn's I-ye-ti-ko as "Sacred-Ear-of-Corn-Woman" (237–38). In a separate gloss (on Gunn's "The Tradition of Shipop"), Boas identifies Gunn's "E-yet-e-co, the mother of all life" (110) with "Sacred-Ear-of-Corn-Woman (I´aτyik'ᵘ)" (230); Boas here presumes, I think correctly, that "E-yet-e-co" in the one story and "I-ye-ti-ko" in the other are variant phonetic spellings of the same name (Boas's I´aτyik'ᵘ). In yet another gloss—this one on a text collected by Elsie Clews Parsons (*Notes on Ceremonialism at Laguna* 115)—he asserts that her I´yaτyik'ᵘ is "probably equal to Nau´ts'ity'i" (234). If all these glosses are correct, and if all these texts are in homological relation to one another, then we are invited to see Silko's Corn Woman and Nau'ts'ity'i as homologues. Such an identity is readily apparent in the long nine-part backbone story of the novel, in which "our mother Nau'ts'ity'i" (48) departs after "nobody did what our mother told them"; in the Corn Woman/Reed Woman fragment, however, Nau'ts'ity'i/Corn Woman does not depart but rather causes her sister Reed Woman to depart.

One way to read this apparent contradiction is to conclude that, like the expansive narrator Whitman constructs in *Leaves of Grass*, the body of Laguna story contradicts itself, a sometimes disturbing but perhaps inevitable corollary effect of comprehensiveness. A different explanation—and probably a better one, because more consistent with Laguna thinking as spelled out by Silko at about this point in the novel (see below)—is that the "contradiction" is a contradiction only within the context of hegemonic *either-or/cause-effect* logic. In an either-or conceptual system, given two or more hypotheses regarding the cause of any effect, at most one of the hypotheses will be true and at least all but one of them will be false. From a non-causal perspective, though, finally it doesn't matter much *which* sister breaks with the other—if either does, the relationship between them both becomes dis-eased, and so both must suffer the diseasement.

TAYO AND REED WOMAN

Read in the context of the surrounding prose narrative, this portion of embedded text seems to propose an etiology for the drought that afflicts Laguna as the novel opens, in "late May" (11). Tellingly, this drought has been going on ever since Tayo's own departure from Laguna land: "They said it had been that way for the past six years while he was gone" (11). This identification of the drought with Tayo's absence suggests a provisional identity of Tayo with Iktoa'ak'o'ya-Reed Woman. Obviously this identity is not complete: although Tayo has returned, the drought has not broken. On the other hand, the alignment of the figure of Tayo with that of Reed Woman in the two story lines may serve to remind us that although Tayo may have returned physically, he is still not home in spirit.

TAYO AND CORN WOMAN

On another, equally warranted axis of interpretation, the conflict between the two sisters that triggers the drought in the embedded text may be taken to align with Tayo's own internal discord—so much so that Tayo bears as much resemblance to Corn Woman as to Reed Woman. This homological correspondence between the figure of Tayo and the other main character of the embedded text is highlighted formally by the content of the prose passages that immediately bracket the embedded story. Both passages call attention to Tayo's sense of his personal responsibility for this drought. Just prior to the embedded text, Tayo is recalling how, in a desperate attempt to keep his dying brother Rocky alive and an anonymous corporal on his feet during the death march, "he could hear his own voice praying against the rain" (12); the first words of the prose narrative following the fragment are "So he had prayed the rain away, and for the sixth year it was dry.... Wherever he looked, Tayo could see the consequences of his praying" (14). If we try to align the gist of the embedded text with the immediate prose narrative, then, we find

Tayo in provisional identity with Corn Woman, the earthbound one whose angry feelings and words trigger the departure of her waterspirit sister Reed Woman. By extension, then, Tayo's "brother" Rocky becomes aligned with the figure of Reed Woman, one of a sibling pair whose story is about unrecovered departure.

Of course Tayo makes no such connections in his own thinking. He only remembers praying for an end to the excessive rain (and the ubiquitous flies) that he saw destroying his cultural twin; he is not yet capable of realizing the subtle but all-important difference between praying against an excess of *rain* and praying against an *excess* of rain. Even so, Silko's alignment of Tayo with Corn Woman in the story via this strategic placement of embedded text adds a certain cachet to his sense that he is in some significant way responsible for the well-being of his kinsman. Silko's trick of aligning the figure of Tayo with both Reed Woman and Corn Woman allows the prose text to provide a reflexive comment on its own pretext: what is at issue, in the embedded text and perhaps in the prose narrative as well, is not the *cause* of the drought, but rather the *nature* of the drought. Applied to Tayo's case, the "moral" of the fragment is not about the relationship between his attitude toward rain and its disappearance, that (as Tayo sees it) one life-force causes the departure of the other. Rather, the fragment is a reminder that in traditional Laguna thinking the two forces of such a relationship are functionally interdependent. Properly understood, Corn Woman and Reed Woman are each and both only parts of the larger story of the people and the land; the "whole story" involves a realignment of the *relationship* between these two figures, and of the natural dimensions of the life of the land that they represent in the embedded story. In this episode, specifically they illustrate how "separation" and "departure" are but two symptoms of the same dis-ease, a break in harmony between two equally valid and necessary components of the life of the people and of the land. For Tayo, the need is to see beyond the apparent separations between himself and Rocky, between himself and the rain, between himself and the land, and between the White and the Indian in "himself."

"AUNTIE" THELMA AND "LITTLE SISTER" LAURA

Less immediately, this fragment highlighting the disrupted relationship between two sisters serves also as a template for reconfiguring the relationship between the two Laguna sisters who occupy the prose narrative, the two daughters of Tayo's blind old grandma. In this pair, homologically related not only to Corn Woman and Reed Woman but also to Ictsityi and Nautsityi, the older sister is Thelma, usually called "Auntie," while the younger is Laura, referred to variously in the text as "Sis" or "little sister."[2] Practically speaking, Tayo's life prior to World War II is a product of the diseased, diseasing relationship between these two sisters.

Histories of conflict, including family histories, are inevitably the versions told by the victors; in this case, the story is colored by Catholicized Auntie, who casts herself as the Corn Woman (the landowner, householder, institution-maker and -keeper) of the family and her younger sister Laura as the prodigal, libidinous, "free-spirited" Reed Woman. Rather than lolling in the river while her older sister works the land like her homolog Reed Woman, "Little Sister had started drinking wine and riding in cars with white men and Mexicans," and "The Catholic priest shook his finger at the drunkenness and lust" (68), as does Older Sister Thelma. Balanced against this Christian reading of Younger Sister's departure, however, is the older, pre-Christian Keresan understanding of how life moves, an "old sensitivity" that Thelma still possesses, in which "from before they were born and long after they died, the people shared the same consciousness" (68). The Catholic priest, representing Christianity, works to "separate the people from themselves" by condemning Laura, "but the people felt something deeper: they were losing her, they were losing part of themselves. The older sister had to act; she had to act for the people, to get this young girl back" (68). The phrasing here recalls Gunn's continuation of his I-ye-ti-ko and I-sto-a-ko-ya story, in which the Corn Woman figure eventually initiates the process of recovering the younger Reed Woman figure. Further, as Silko presents it, the conflict between land and water in the Corn Woman/Reed Woman embedded story re-emerges as the external conflict between old and new lifestyles in the life of twentieth-century Laguna, a conflict which in turn informs Thelma's own internal conflict between her Keresan and Christian understanding of things, her ambivalent feelings toward her Little Sister. Consistent with the prevailing motif of most of the embedded text in the novel, within the framework of the older, "deeper" understanding every departure is but the prelude to a recovery: "The people wanted her back. Her older sister must bring her back. For the people, it was that simple" (69).

Most readers who take their cues from the prose narrative alone are not going to see Auntie working *for* her younger sister's recovery; rather, Auntie seems fixated on dealing with Laura's life as an insult to family honor, effectively making shame and disgrace (rather than recovery and regeneration) the outcome of her sister's departure. In the story as Auntie tells it, young Tayo is simply the living evidence of Younger Sister's unredeemed profligacy, and apparently she succeeds pretty well in passing this story along to the next generation: as a child, we are told, Tayo himself is convinced that "without him there would not have been so much shame and disgrace for the family" (70).

ORAL TRADITION AND PROSE NARRATIVE

Silko's use of the sister motif to align traditional story and prose narrative here casts into new light an interesting episode in the novel that underscores the role of oral narrative in preserving and renewing the story (that is, the life) of the people. In this episode (69–71), Auntie takes young Tayo aside and, while Tayo is seated in the cool of the storage room on "a gunny sack full of the corn that Robert and Josiah had dried last year," she gives him the following story:

> "One morning," she said, "before you were born, I got up to go outside, right before sunrise. I knew she had been out all night because I never heard her come in. Anyway, I thought I would walk down toward the river. I just had a feeling, you know. I stood on that sandrock, above the big curve in the river, and there she was, coming down the trail on the other side." She looked at him closely. "I'm only telling you this because she was your mother, and you have to understand." She cleared her throat. "Right as the sun came up, she walked under that big cottonwood tree, and I could see her clearly: she had no clothes on. Nothing. She was completely naked except for her high-heel shoes. She dropped her purse under that tree. Later on some kids found it there and brought it back. It was empty except for a lipstick." (70)

Given only the prose narrative, it is hard to imagine what Auntie's motive would be for sharing this story with young Tayo. With an eye to Auntie's part in the larger Story of the People, however, this incident functions to confirm Silko's immediately previous explanation of how the old tribal feeling has survived even the psychocolonization of Christianity. Regardless of how impossible her acquired Christianity makes it for Auntie as an individual to effect the recovery of her little sister, her older Keresan self still knows that the missing sister must be recovered, and that the ceremony of recovery is always preserved in the form of the stories.

Young Tayo, a child of the twentieth century, still mourns the loss not only of his mother but of a particular image *of* her, the tin-framed photograph confiscated earlier by Auntie. Tayo's immediate response to the story is to ask obliquely about that photograph: "'Auntie,' he said softly, 'what did she look like before I was born?' ... That day in the storeroom, when he asked how his mother had looked before he was born, was the closest he'd ever come to mentioning the picture" (70–71). Though Auntie does not respond to Tayo's question in this episode, she does in effect replace the material (and therefore susceptible to physical manipulation) photographic image of the missing mother with an oral/aural image that reveals the spirit identity of the missing mother much more clearly than any photograph could. In the story that Auntie gives Tayo to remember his mother by, Little Sister is strongly associated with the river and thus with Reed Woman, while Auntie becomes the stay-at-home keeper of the corn and the Pueblo. This, according to Auntie, is what his mother—and the relationship between the two sisters—"looked like" before he was born; this, then, is the unresolved story that Tayo is born into.

Auntie's story is an important episode on a number of counts. In addition to its function as a bridge between the prose narrative and the oral and ethnographic pretexts of the novel, it serves as a nexus of important motifs—the timing ("right as the sun came up"), the "big cottonwood tree," the Yellow Woman identity, the river as natural liminal zone, and even the emptied purse[3]—that will be developed as the novel progresses. Further, as Tayo will come to recognize by the end of the novel, Auntie's anecdotal account positions Little Sister at precisely the correct location in time and space for ceremonial reentry into the life of the village[4]; this is precisely the spot where Tayo heads at the end of the prose narrative, on his way home from his final confrontation with the Ck'o'yo witchery, when "the transition was completed." Carefully positioning himself by the cottonwood on the bank of the river with the rising sun at his back, he waits until the first sunlight caught the tips of the leaves at the top of the old tree and made them bright gold.... He thought of her then; she had always loved him, she had never left him; she had always been there. He crossed the river at sunrise. (255)

At this point in the novel, Silko places the final piece of the nine-part backbone story (255–56) in which Our Mother materially returns to the Fifth world and the Laguna village, and "the storm clouds returned[5]/the grass and plants started growing again," thus formally conflating Tayo's return, Laura's return, and Our Mother Nautsityi's return with all the stories of Yellow Woman's return, usually carrying some form of new life for the People in much the same way that Laura, on her last return, brought Tayo. Completing the pattern, Tayo, at the end of the novel, returns to deliver the story/ceremony that has been gestating and incubating within him for eighteen months.

Finally, Silko sees to it that Auntie's story, itself fittingly an oral performance, functions to splice the two threads of missing-mother pretext into a single thread of recovery story. In both the traditional Reed Woman and Nautsityi stories, the turn from departure to recovery commences when someone—in the Gunn Reed Woman story, Stchi-mu-ne-moot, "a great runner and trailer"; in the Nautsityi story as given by Boas and Silko, Hummingbird Man—assures the People that he has seen the mother and knows where she is. In telling Tayo the story of Laura's earlier river visit, the Auntie who takes shape *within* the story becomes homologous with Corn Woman, but the Auntie who *tells* the story is homologous with Hummingbird and Stchi-mu-ne-moot, the crucial eyewitness to the missing mother's last known whereabouts. This momentary role transformation brought about by the act of storytelling signals the broader transformation, from focus on departure to focus on recovery, that the prose narrative is undergoing at this point. Silko underscores this transformation formally by placing, immediately after Auntie's story, the third portion of the nine-part backbone story, which begins by shifting from the question of where the source of regeneration is to the question of how to get back in touch with her:

"So that's where our mother went.
How can we get down there?"

The next lines also provide a nice explanation-by-homology of Auntie's otherwise missing motive for telling Tayo this story in the first place:

> Hummingbird looked at all the
> skinny people.
> He felt sorry for them.

In this way, Silko also dovetails the figure of Tayo not only with the twin culture heroes Ma'see'wi and Ou'yu'ye'wi of the nine-part backbone story[6] but also with the anonymous "thirsty" and "starving" victims of the fallout between the two sisters.

CHAPTER 8
The Backbone Series I: Departure and Pacayanyi

As noted in chapter 3, it is possible to regard Silko's backbone series as a spliced[1] version of two stories recorded separately (and in a different chronological order) in Franz Boas's *Keresan Texts*, one titled in Boas "P'acaya·´nʸi" and the other titled "The Hummingbird." Although these nine embedded texts may appear to many readers at first to be scattered almost randomly throughout the text of the novel, Silko herself invites us to read them also as one continuous story, and in the sequence in which they appear in the novel: in *Storyteller*, the text reappears (with a few typographical alterations[2]) on pages 111 to 121 as a poem titled "One time" in the table of contents. Reading this backbone series as a single story composed of several episodes also foregrounds the departure/recovery motif that informs both this backbone story and the surrounding prose narrative of the novel. The first segment, in which Pacayanyi's visit to Laguna results in "our Mother" Nautsityi's departure, picks up the departure theme of the novel's first completely embedded text, in which Reed Woman rather than Nautsityi embodies life for the people (see chapter 7). Silko then conjoins this departure motif to the balancing recovery motif played out in the ensuing eight segments, in which Hummingbird and Green Fly work for and with the children of Nautsityi to effect her return to the earth surface world.

PRETEXTS FOR SEGMENT 1

Several Keresan ethnographies contain the figure of a powerful medicine man who shows up among the people advocating ceremonial change. Mathilda Coxe Stevenson, in her account of the Zia origin and migration story in *The Sia* (1894), spends several pages (59–67) recounting the story of one "Po´shaiÿanne," a product of a virgin birth at Pecos pueblo who visits Zia during his career as a traveling shaman.[3] According to Stevenson's informants, Po´shaiÿanne is "the culture hero of the Sia," and Stevenson notes that he "bears a name similar to that of the corresponding prodigy among the Zuni" (66 n. 1); interestingly, her informants also valorize the Sko´yo (compare Silko's "Ck'o'yo") Chai´än, which she translates as "Giant Society."[4] Closer to home, Gunn (1917) also mentions "a character whom they call 'Po-chai-an-ny' [who] comes to them from the cane brakes of the north" and who "changes their medicine from the use of simple remedies to incantations and jugglery" (72–73); in Gunn's version, when Po-chi-an-ny[5] fails to cure the drought the people are experiencing, he flees from their village, but they pursue and catch him and "tying large stones to him they cast him into the deep water" (73), then relocate their village to the northwest of its previous site. Even closer to home, in *Notes on Ceremonialism at Laguna* (1920), Elsie Clews Parsons reports some "fragments of the myth" accompanying a winter solstice night chant told to her in 1917 by "the sister of the *shikani cheani*," the widowed Mrs. W. G. Marmon.[6] In this version, shortly after the people emerge into the fifth world of sunlight they are visited by "*bacheani*," who "came from the northwest," introduces a new mode of ceremonialism, and then runs away; a terrible drought ensues, and finally "Mother *iyetik* took pity on them and told *ma'sewi* [her son(s) the warrior twin(s)[7] to go after *bacheani* and find him and kill him"; as in Gunn's version, they track Bacheani/Pacayanyi/Po-chi-an-ny to the "big water" and drown him (115).[8]

However, as noted in chapter 3, the most immediate pretexts for Silko's version appear in Boas's *Keresan Texts*: "P'acaya·´nʸi" (13–16), given by Ko´ᴛʸe in 1920, and a shorter untitled fragment (223) given by José in 1919. As is readily apparent from even a cursory examination of the texts in question,[9] the similarities between Boas's text and Silko's are for a while so numerous and striking that they are in virtual homological identity. This identity collapses, however, once the Mother departs. In Silko's version, the return of our Mother Nau'ts'ity'i is effected through the intercessional motion of Hummingbird and Green Fly; in Boas's version, the twins themselves are set in motion (as punishment for aligning with P'acaya·´nʸi's Ck'o'yo practice), forced to run around the world four times[10] and to visit with "their sister K'oo·´ᴋo,"[11] before all is set right again. It is intriguing that in this version K'oo·´ᴋo lives "in the northwest region in Reed-Leaf-House" (16), because P'acaya·´nʸi also comes to the people from "the northwest region from Reed-Leaf-House" (14), as Silko's Pacayanyi "came in/from Reedleaf town/up north" (46).[12] Further, K'oo·´ᴋo's east-west transformation in the Boas version aligns homologically with P'acaya·ˊnʸi's Ck'o'yo version of bear medicine in both Boas and Silko.[13] One inference of these overlaps is that P'acaya·ˊnʸi is to be understood as closely related to "their sister" K'oo·ˊκo, and therefore related also the warrior twins—their northern cousin or brother, perhaps. I shall return to this issue of a family relationship between Corn Mother medicine and Ck'o'yo medicine below, because I think it operates strongly as an unstated pretext in Silko's own creative vision.

Another important motif that relates the Pacayanyi story both to other embedded texts in the novel and the novel's prose narrative is the motif of *seeing*, in the sense of physiological perception but also in the sense of recognition—and in Silko's novel, *re*-cognition, seeing again and seeing the relationship of identity between two perceptual events, is always an important kind of knowledge. In Boas's and Silko's Pacayanyi stories, the test of Pacayanyi's magic is what it *looks* like to the boys: "He said 'What does that look like?/Is that magical power?'/... 'Yes, it looks like magic all right,' Ma'see'wi said" (47–48). The culture hero Ma'see'wi's inability to see—or "see through"—Pacayanyi's trickery is balanced later by Sun Man's ability (thanks to Spider Grandmother's story) to see past the surface of Kaupata's handsome facade and hanging sacks to who he is and what they contain and, even later, to Arrowboy's disruption of Ck'o'yo witchery merely by watching it (247)[14]; the fourth and final homological reiteration of this motif in Silko's text is, of course, Tayo's acquired ability and willingness to watch and witness while Emo, Pinkie, and Leroy work the latest variety of homegrown Ck'o'yo medicine upon Harley (and, they hope, on Tayo) during the Jackpile Mine episode.

FUNCTION OF SEGMENT 1

Within the context of the prose narrative, the story of Pacayanyi's coming to the people and the subsequent departure of our Mother Nautsityi seems at first glance to function (much as the earlier Reed Woman/Corn Woman fragment did) to offer a traditional analog to the story of Tayo, who at this point in the prose narrative is, like the land, suffering from literal as well as spiritual drought. Once again, the narrative returns from its flashback wandering to the time and place that is the present tense of the prose narrative, in which Tayo is on his way to Cubero with

Harley and for the moment lying on the ground at the mouth of a canyon where he fell off his blind mule 15 pages earlier. Here, Tayo's attention is diverted from the illness that haunts his memory (fragments of imagery from his days in the Japanese prison camp, which Tayo associates with the sound of crushing made by Harley chewing wild grape seeds, associated in turn with the sound Tayo didn't hear while he saw the rifle butt crushing his brother's skull underneath the soggy blanket) by the sight and smell of the land he's lying on together with its promise of an alternative to drought conditions: "The canyon was the way he always remembered it; the beeweed plants made the air smell heavy and sweet like wild honey.... The people said that even in the driest years nobody could ever remember a time when the spring had dried up" (45). Tayo then recalls Josiah's pre-war commentary about the identity of the people with this place ("This is where we come from, see. This sand, this stone, these trees, the vines, all the wildflowers. This earth keeps us going," 45) and then drinks from the spring: "He tasted the deep heartrock of the earth, where the water came from, and he thought maybe this wasn't the end after all" (46). As always in Silko, the merger of land and story in personal vision is good medicine; in the novel, this process seems to create the condition which enables the embedded text to emerge, as though traditional story were, like water and personal identity in Josiah's healing vision, coming from this *sipapu* place.

TAYO AND MA'SEE'WI

Read this way, the story of the coming of Pa'caya'nyi functions most immediately as a diagnosis of the disease currently afflicting Laguna and Tayo, suggesting that the disease is of etic origin and warning about the potentially deleterious effects of contact from the outside. From this perspective, the children of Nau'ts'ity'i, Ma'see'wi and Ou'yu'ye'we, align with Tayo and Rocky while Pa'caya'nyi aligns roughly with the Army recruiter (64–65, 72) who, like Pa'caya'nyi, comes to Laguna seeking converts to his cause : "'Now I know you boys love America as much as we do, but this is your big chance to *show* it!' He stood up then, as he had rehearsed, and looked them in the eye sincerely" (64).[15] The opening gambit of the recruiter's speech—"'Anyone can fight for America,' he began, giving special emphasis to 'America,' 'even you boys. In a time of need, anyone can fight for her'" (64)—further aligns America with Kʻooˑʹko (and Ckʼoʼyo medicine) as the mother figure here vying with Nauʼtsʼityʼi (and corn medicine) for the attention and protection of the people. The inference is that Tayo and Rocky got distracted by the recruiter's promises of enhanced power— "'Sure, sure,' he said, 'you enlist now and you'll be eligible for everything—pilot training—everything'" (65)—in effect were seduced by the promise of America/Ckʼoʼyo instead of staying home and tending to Laguna affairs/the Mother Corn altar.

Within the context of twentieth-century American history, it is easy enough for contemporary readers to see that the recruiter's promises are "just a trick" to seduce Rocky (and, because they are brothers/*cütsʻ* who move together, Tayo as well) into leaving home: in the still-racist armed forces of 1942, neither of these boys was ever going to see the inside of a P-38 except to clean it out for the pilot, and neither would ever wear stars rather than stripes on his uniform. What is harder to see is what's wrong with Paʼcayaʼnyiʼs medicine within the context of the story in which he appears: although the narrative presence of the embedded text's storyteller insists that the twins are "fooled by" Paʼcayaʼnyi and that "it was all just a trick" (48), and although the people's adoption of Ckʼoʼyo ritual entails disastrous consequences, I suspect Paʼcayaʼnyiʼs medicine looks as good to most contemporary readers of the novel as we are told it looks to the people, even though the storytelling voice implies they should have known better than to adopt it. After all, in the world of the prose narrative present, the land and the people are suffering from drought, so what could be intrinsically wrong with the ability to make running water magically appear, as Paʼcayaʼnyi does? Later in the novel, we learn that Tayo's recovery depends in part on the efficacy of Betonie's bear medicine, in which the Bear People who live at the summit of Dark Mountain "have the power to restore the mind" (141); how, then, is Paʼcayaʼnyiʼs ability to make bear appear "just a trick"?

The answer to these questions lies in "seeing" not only water flowing and bear appearing but also the *motion* of which these elements are also manifestations. In the first place, what sets both water and bear energy in motion, in Paʼcayaʼnyiʼs Ckʼoʼyo practice, is violence, connected particularly with using "a piece of flint" to "strike" (that is, stab into[16]) a "wall," which would be a surface of the living land if the ritual is being performed in an underground kiva, the appropriate place to be practicing esoteric medicine in Pueblo tradition. In the second place, the *direction* of motion in Pa'caya'nyi's medicine is incompatible with the way life moves at Laguna. Pa'caya'nyi stabs the north wall, and the water that emerges from the wound flows "down/toward the south." The motion of Pa'caya'nyi's water is congruent with, say, the flow of the Rio Grande, but it is incongruent with the way water moves at Laguna: the San José River flows west to east along the south side of the village. In addition, while Pa'caya'nyi's first demonstration of Ck'o'yo energy is 90° at odds with the way life moves at Laguna, his second is diametrically opposed: Pa'caya'nyi's medicine causes Bear to appear "from the east wall"; however, in Laguna tradition (and also in the journey Tayo makes to acquire Bear medicine from Betonie in the Chuska Mountains), bear stands on the western, not the eastern, side of the circle of the people, making Pa'caya'nyi's bearwork 180° at odds with the Laguna way of things.

Of course, in the story behind the embedded text the brothers Ma'see'wi and Ou'yu'ye'wi have never before encountered Ck'o'yo (understood both as an absent sister of Nau'ts'ity'i and as a kind of medicine practiced to the relative north of where the people live), and so have yet to be sensitized either to it or to the particular and necessary motion of life at Laguna. In order to *become* the people who know and appreciate this story, they must live the event the story tells. This is approximately the position in which Tayo finds himself at this point in the prose narrative: he cannot yet sort out the poison from the balm in the magical events of his own life to date, but having "tasted the deep heartrock of the earth, where the water came from, he thought maybe this wasn't the end after all" (46). What follows for Tayo, and for the reader, is a fresh beginning, a different story in which the (for most readers, all-too-familiar) characteristic motion of beginnings that lead to endings is replaced by the motion of departure and recovery that is characteristic of both Laguna and Navajo healing story and ceremony.

TAYO AND PA'CAYA'NYI

As correct as it may be to read the story of Pa'caya'nyi homologically as a story about how Ck'o'yo medicine comes, in the form of its practitioners Pa'caya'nyi and the Army recruiter, to infect the body of the people and to see *cits'* Ma'see'wi and Tayo as two versions of the patient who undergoes recovery in the ensuing narrative, such a reading tends to mask an equally important homological lesson. In the memory flashback immediately preceding the appearance of this embedded text in the prose narrative body of the novel, Josiah reminds Tayo that "the wind and the dust, they are part of life too, like the sun and the sky. You don't swear at them. It's the people, see. They're the ones. The old people used to say that droughts happen when people forget, when people misbehave" (46). What is hard to see, for most readers at least, is that in the Pa'caya'nyi story the "people [who] misbehave" include not only Ma'see'wi and Ou'yu'ye'wi but also Pa'caya'nyi: Pa'caya'nyi is, whether the brothers recognize him or not, a relative, as much a part of the body of the people as, for instance, Tayo's mother Laura is part of Auntie's family or Iktoa'ak'o'ya-Reed Woman is part of Iyetiko/Corn Woman's, whether the older sisters behave accordingly or not—as much, we are finally to comprehend, as Emo is a part of the Laguna people in the novel's twentieth century.

The connection between Josiah's words and the subsequent story of Pa'caya'nyi's coming to town would probably not be apparent even to experienced readers, even after several readings of the novel. What might become apparent sooner, however, is the connection between Tayo's condition at this stage of the prose narrative and the condition of Pa'caya'nyi in the embedded story. In fact, once one gets beyond the apparent contradiction that Tayo is the protagonist of the story he appears in and Pa'caya'nyi is the antagonist of the story he appears in, one begins to be impressed by how much the two characters have in common, begins to see that Tayo and Pa'caya'nyi are in provisional homological identity. Neither knows who his father is; both come to the village from the anti-sunrise direction, Pa'caya'nyi from Reedleaf Town "up north" of the *kush-kutret* where Ma'see'wi and Ou'yu'ye'we live and Tayo from Gallup to the west and northwest of Laguna village where his "brother" Rocky is born and raised; both are carriers of a cultural virus, the diseasing Ck'o'yo trickery in Pa'caya'nyi's case and the contemporary strain that manifests as Anglo contamination (via Gallup and, later, World War II) in Tayo's; both move with Mountain Lion.[17]

I say *provisional* identity to draw attention to one of the major motifs informing both the backbone story as a whole and the prose narrative which Silko creates in order to flesh out that backbone. This is the transformation motif. In this backbone story, power—the power to direct the course of the life of the people—slowly transforms as the effects of Ck'o'yo medicine become the causes of the re-empowerment of the people, who by the end of the story are who they were prior to the coming of Pa'caya'nyi but who are, additionally now, in possession of the story of how to recover from that erstwhile near-fatal disease. Part of that story, in turn, is the coupling of the motion of departure with the motion of recovery; and in this story, as in most of the embedded texts as well as in the prose narrative, the process of recovery is a phased, four-step transformative process linking a state of disease to a state of wholeness and balance embodied in the reunification of the children with their mothers, daughters all of their common Grandmother.

CHAPTER 9

The Backbone Series II: Recovery and Hummingbird

In the backbone story, the apparent primary agents of recovery are, successively, the twin brothers, who in the second fragment (i.e., the first of the eight fragments comprising the recovery story) diagnose the disease whose primary symptom is drought and starvation; Hummingbird, who agrees out of pity to help recover their mother from the First World; the combination of Hummingbird and Green Fly, which comes about in the third and fourth episodes; our mother Nau'ts'ity'i herself, who provides direction to the flying duo in the fourth and sixth episodes; Caterpillar, who provides tobacco in the seventh episode; old Buzzard, who uses the tobacco to help purify the village in the eighth episode; and finally (and once again) our mother Nau'ts'ity'i, who brings rain and crops and baby animals with her when she (re-) emerges in the final episode. Between the brothers in the first episode and the mother of the people in the last, four "new" agents come into play during this process of recovery—a pattern that is nicely congruent with the hoop structure of Betonie's recovery ritual as well as with the overall episode structure of the prose narrative.[1] Read this way, the backbone story functions as a template similar in its drift to the biblical prodigal son story, inviting us to read the prose narrative as the story of a Pa'caya'nyi-like advocate of Ck'o'yo medicine who undergoes a gradual return to identity with the twin sons of mother Nau'ts'ity'i, of the transformation of Tayo from being a child of the Dark Mountain of Navajo lostness to being a child of the White House at Kawaika (for more on the Navajo dimension of this transformation see chapter 11).

Also important to note of the recovery portion as a whole is the element of directionality that is carefully spelled out throughout. The disease that requires curing enters the life of the people from "up north" (46); in order to re-establish balance or *hozho* in the recovery portion, Hummingbird and Green Fly import assistance specifically from the west 113, 255), the east (the 180), and, repeatedly as well as finally, from the south or "down below" (82, 151, 255). These directions are spelled out with equal frequency in the Boas pretext (see Appendix E). This pattern of directionality serves to remind us that the damage wrought by the introduction of the diseasing Ck'o'yo medicine cannot be cured by attacking the disease itself; rather, the cure lies in a process of metaphorical inoculation, a delicate process of *re*-introducing counterbalancing medicine from the other three directions. As I will argue at length in chapter 13, the process is not about destroying evil but rather about reconstellating the story of the people so as to locate and "fix" the evil as only one episode within the context of a larger, life-affirming story. Perhaps this is why Silko also changes the sequence of directions touched by Buzzard in his cleansing circular (hoop) motion, from south/east/north/west in the Boas pretext (13) to east/south/west/north in hers (255–56): resetting the medicines of the other three directions sets the stage for reintroducing, but this time under ceremonial control, the medicine of the fourth. The plurality of allies who come to the aid of the people is but another reminder of the need to bring the whole long story of the people to bear on any disruption of any part of it.

PRETEXTS FOR SEGMENTS 2 THROUGH 9

Silko's eight-part story of the people's recovery from Pa'caya'nyi's Ck'o'yo medicine has only one direct ethnographic antecedent[2]: the 1919 story given by Pedro Martin, augmented by a second version given by the same informant, entitled "Hummingbird" in Boas's *Keresan Texts* (11–12, 226). Readers wishing to see some sample comparisons of Silko's version with the two versions given by Pedro Martin are invited to consult Appendix E, "Hummingbird," of this book, but roughly speaking the degree of similarity (of storyline, of imageric detail) is approximately that of Silko's Pa'caya'nyi story to Boas's.

FUNCTION OF SEGMENTS 2 THROUGH 9

The embedded backbone story of recovery has several associated functions with respect to the prose narrative story of Tayo's recovery process. At times, a given segment functions to anticipate or preview the coming episode of the prose narrative; at others, a segment summarizes the preceding prose plot motion. Usually, however, the embedded segments of the recovery story contain elements of both summary and preview, so that they serve as segues or bridges between moments of the prose narrative's motion as well as well-timed reminders that the story of Tayo's life is at all points congruent with—a "fleshing out" of, to put it more than metaphorically—the "long story of the People."

SEGMENT 2 (53–54)

Formally, the first of the backbone story's recovery segments is separated from the departure segment by a little less than five pages—the closest to each other of any of the nine segments in the novel. This propinquity prepares even first-time readers to make the connection between two otherwise separated parts of a single segmented story and also invites a reader to allow that the white space at the end of this portion of embedded text may signal merely a pause in its telling rather than the end of the story.

The prose narrative between this segment and its predecessor consists mainly of Tayo's memory of a deer hunt he and Rocky undertook prior to World War II. This account emphasizes the growing difference between Rocky and Tayo with regard to traditional Laguna ways of doing things, a difference brought about by Rocky's commitment to adopting white American values in response to Auntie's dreams for her son: "She wanted him to be a success. She could see what white people wanted in an Indian, and she believed this way was his only chance" (51). However, the segment is also sandwiched between two batches of passages (totaling about ten pages) that develop the long-standing enmity between Tayo and another advocate of white ways, Emo. In this way, the positioning of the segment serves to align both Rocky and Emo with "that/Ck'o'yo magic/we were fooling with"—Rocky cast as a local boy seduced away from traditional Laguna ways by the magic, Emo as the one who will emerge in the prose narrative as one of the family of witches represented by Pacayanyi in the backbone story and elsewhere by Kaupata and by the anonymous witch who sets this new variety of witchery in motion in Betonie's story.[3]

How Tayo aligns with the figures of the story segment is less clear—or at least less pronounced. However, that seems appropriate considering where Tayo is in his own story: at this point he seems to intuit that something important is happening, but he (like most readers) cannot yet see a connection between the characteristically gentle deer spirit he loosely associates with Rocky and the potentially violent mountain lion energy that accompanies Pacayanyi in the backbone story and that Emo elicits in the passage closely following this segment of embedded text (see n. 18). All he is sure of is that the cause of the people's twentieth-century diseasement is bigger than World War II: as he recalls telling an Army psychiatrist a few lines before this segment of embedded text, "It's bigger than that. I can feel it. It's been going on for a long time.... I don't know what it is, but I can feel it around me" (53). The "it" Tayo senses is, of course, the ck'o'yo spirit loose in the world, and we should take it quite literally when Tayo tells the doctor, in the last sentence prior to this segment, "Emo was asking for it": as we see in the episode on pages 55 to 63 immediately following the segment, Emo quite literally evokes the capacity for violence inherent in Tayo. At this point in the novel Tayo aligns most gracefully not with the apparent protagonist of the segment, Hummingbird, but rather with the figure of "the people," who all know something is wrong and who suspect they are complicit in the drought and famine currently afflicting them, and who also know they need help, albeit not the kind Army psychiatrists can provide.

SEGMENT 3 (71–72)

In the third segment of the backbone story, Hummingbird tells the hungry people that they "need a messenger" (71) and provides them with the recipe for creating an ally who will turn out to be, in segment 4, Green Fly. Readers familiar with hama-ha tradition may find it curious that Hummingbird here seems to be telling them they need to *create* this messenger, since Hummingbird is a standard messenger figure in both Keresan and Navajo traditions.[4] Perhaps we are to understand that Hummingbird is modestly telling the people they need his assistance, in which case Green Fly comes about primarily to provide Hummingbird with a sidekick—or perhaps a trainee, one whose existence originates in response to this specific strain of the recurring disease and whose self-story originates as part of the story of the ceremony for healing ck'o'yo infection. Like the corn that is identified with Our Mother Nautsityi (who, we should recall, is "below" the earth surface—planted, as it were—for the duration of the ceremony of her recovery), Green Fly's life gestates in the combination of "black mountain dirt/some sweet corn flour/and a little water" contained within a "pottery jar/painted with parrots and big flowers" (71), a jar covered with a "new buckskin" like a drum but enlivened by speech and song rather than by being struck with a drumstick. The vessel of recovery, the jar itself, is to be decorated with images of regenerative energy—flowers that keep Hummingbird "fat and shiny" and parrots that represent the female energy associated with the south, from whence Our Mother returns whenever she returns in the stories.[5]

Within the context of the prose narrative, this segment functions both to link Tayo's history to the stories of the Laguna sisters (discussed in chapter 7) and to telegraph Tayo's homological identity with the speckled cattle and, by extension, the rainclouds which need to be located and escorted home, by Hummingbird in the backbone story and again by Sun Man in the Kaupata story (see chapter 4). The first line of the segment—"So that's where our mother went" (71)—can be read both as the people's response to Hummingbird's message at the end of the previous segment and as a response to the story of Tayo's mother Laura's departure from the circle of the people, and most immediately to the verbal image of Laura standing "under that big cottonwood tree" (70), which replaces the photo of her that was taken from Tayo as a child. That is, "our mother" can be read as either, or better as both, Nautsityi in the backbone story and younger sister Laura in the prose narrative. On the other side of this segment, the subject "our mother" becomes replaced by the subject "you," a pronoun referring to an as yet unformed, unrealized potential life form whose life will be (part of) the answer to the people's prayers. Readers already familiar with the story already know "you" will emerge as Green Fly; in the prose narrative, however, the composite life form that represents the answer to the prayers of the people (who are personified in the narrative at this point by Josiah, Tayo's traditionalist uncle) is the twenty Mexican cows Josiah has bought (in a deal brokered, we learn later, by the mysterious and ageless Mexican grandmother Night Swan). These spotted cattle, alluded to immediately and for the first time in the prose narrative following this segment, are like Tayo a "special breed" (75), a new (at least in the context of the Laguna story) life form evolved to provide life for the people in the face of the drought the people cannot otherwise hope to survive. Already emerging in the relationship between the backbone story and the prose narrative here is Tayo's homological identity with Green Fly—"In four days you *will* be alive" (emphasis mine): the event is already in motion even though, like the return of the departed mother, it is not yet manifest in the Fifth World of either the prose narrative or the backbone story.

SEGMENT 4 (82)

In segment 4, the chant-activated "big green fly/with yellow feelers on his head" (82) and Hummingbird set out on their mission on behalf of the people to plead with Our Mother for her return from "the fourth world below" to the earth surface world. In the paragraph immediately preceding this segment, Silko introduces the figure of the Night Swan, and the 20-odd pages of prose narrative between this segment and the next are devoted mainly to her story, first in relation to Josiah and then in relation to Tayo. Insofar as this segment foreshadows the narrative to come, it is clear enough that this woman is in homological identity with the mother of the people in the backbone story: Like Nautsityi her original home is "below," far to the south of Laguna; like the south and like Parrot in Laguna cosmogeny her color is blue; her strong affinity for Mt. Taylor further aligns her with both rain and deer, sources (like corn) of life for the people; even her name—"They *called* me the Night Swan" (84, emphasis mine)—might be heard as a rough Anglicization of the Keresan word Nautsityi.[6]

Given the Night Swan's provisional identity with the backbone story's Nautsityi, and in light of how her relationship first to Josiah and then to Tayo is presented in the following pages, it is tempting to go a step further and consider Josiah, the older of the two, to be in provisional identity with Hummingbird and Tayo with Fly, an identity already telegraphed in segment 3. And while I think this conclusion is certainly warranted, I also think that in the prose narrative following this segment we are given indications that Tayo is also growing into the role of Hummingbird—and not growing into Hummingbird *instead of* Fly but rather into Hummingbird *as well as* Fly. Following the story of Night Swan's liaison with Josiah (82–93) in which this segment is formally embedded, and after a formally isolated paragraph resounding the theme of the death/departure of Tayo's biological mother (93), the prose narrative shifts in time to "that last summer, before the war" (93) when Tayo prays for rain during the pre-war drought and is rewarded with a vision of "a bright green hummingbird" and its significance: "as long as the hummingbird had not abandoned the land, somewhere there were still flowers, and they would all go on" (96). When the rain returns a few days later, Tayo is enlisted by Josiah, one of the people preparing the fields to receive the coming rain, to take a note from him to the Night Swan, and like Hummingbird in the hama-ha stories Tayo becomes a messenger ("only delivering a message," 97) while at the same time Josiah ceases to be the go-between connecting the people's need for new life and the source of that new life (most obviously, the speckled cattle). The promise of our mother's return to the earth surface world is echoed in the song and the words emanating from the old Victrola in her back room ("*Y volveré*" = "I shall return"), and not only is it raining outside but also "[he] felt the sweat run down his ribs like rainwater" (97) as he delivers Josiah's note to the Night Swan, dressed all in "blue satin" (98) and smelling like "the ivory locust blossoms that hung down from the trees in the spring" (97). As though to seal Tayo's emerging identity with the messenger figure in the old stories, and more immediately the backbone story, Silko makes the Night Swan's last words to Tayo "Thank you for bringing the message" (100).

This segment can be taken as the referent for the homily on flies which Josiah delivers to Tayo before the war (101–02). Like Rocky Tayo has been paying attention to what his school teacher tells him about flies—"She said they are bad and carry sickness"—and so (like the Mexican bartender who has made a "serious business" of killing flies in the prose narrative's present tense) Tayo thinks nothing of killing them until Josiah counsels otherwise:

> "Well, I didn't go to school much, so I don't know about that but you see, long time ago back in the time immemorial, the mother of the people got angry at them for the way they were behaving. For all she cared, they could go to hell—starve to death. The animals disappeared, the plants disappeared, and no rain came for a long time. It was the greenbottle fly who went to her, asking forgiveness for the people. Since that time the people have been grateful for what the fly did for us." (101)

Josiah's gloss on the backbone story makes no mention of Hummingbird; but then, at the time Josiah gives this story to Tayo, Tayo is still young and clueless, like Fly is in this segment of embedded text, and Josiah's precis of this part of the story is intended to teach young Tayo only a small part of what he must come to know in order to become the fulfillment of the whole story.

SEGMENT 5 (105–06)

Within the context of the backbone story, segment 5 completes the first movement of the recovery story, as Hummingbird and Fly complete their first visit with Our Mother and then return to the people, and begins the second movement, their first visit with old Buzzard. Within the context of the prose narrative, this segment marks a similar transitional period in Tayo's journey of recovery. In the narrative present of the novel just prior to the segment's appearance, Tayo returns to the room above Lalo's place where before the war the Night Swan lived; though the place now stands deserted, the succor once offered by the Night Swan still awaits Tayo there ("The place felt good; he leaned back against the wall until its surface pushed against his backbone solidly" 104). After this visit to the white gypsum-plastered previous home of the lady in blue, we are told, Tayo walks to another white house, the village of Casa Blanca,[7] where "he slept all night without dreams" for the first time since the war. Immediately following this segment, Tayo begins the second phase of his own recovery journey, his trip to Gallup (site of his own diseasing childhood) and his appointment with the Navajo singer/*hataali* Betonie, the specialist in curing ceremony selected by Grandma and old man Ku'oosh on behalf of the other Laguna elders, occupying the role of "the people" in the backbone story. The transfer of healing authority in the backbone story from Our Mother to old Buzzard, then, is formally and thematically aligned here with the shift from the figure of the Night Swan in phase one of the prose narrative to Betonie in phase two as the primary figure of healing energy. Moreover, because it is Grandma and old Ku'oosh who in effect send Tayo to Betonie, we are invited by this segment to add Grandma and old Ku'oosh to the ensemble of characters who are doing the work of Our Mother in the prose narrative. Furthermore, the segment invites us also to add Robert, who brings Tayo the message that his healing is not complete and that there is more to do and who then drives Tayo to Gallup and his encounter with old Betonie, to the ensemble of characters in the prose narrative who at one time or another are in homological identity with Hummingbird of the backbone story. At this point in the convergence of backbone story with prose narrative, Tayo is still in homological identity with both Hummingbird and Green Fly, a dual identity which presents no difficulty for most readers after the first sentence of segment 5, in which Fly finally grows out of his selfishness ("Fly started sucking on/sweet things so/Hummingbird had to tell him/to wait," 105) and the two creatures begin, and continue for the rest of the story, to move and even speak ("[t]hey told the town people ..." 106) as one.

SEGMENT 6 (113)

In the sixth backbone segment, Hummingbird and Fly, after returning to the people's village to pick up "more pollen,/more beads, and more prayer sticks" (the same set of offerings presented on behalf of the people to Our Mother in the fifth segment), travel east to ask old Buzzard to purify the town in advance of the mother's return, only to find that an additional offering—tobacco—is required. In several other recovery pretexts in which the missing mother is Iktoa'ak'o'ya/ Reed Woman rather than Nautsityi/Corn Mother, it is clear that the people and their messengers have no knowledge of tobacco prior to this episode, and much is made of the near-identical phonological relationship between the Keresan word for "reed" and the word for "tobacco" (see chapter 7, pp. 66-67); here, Silko (in keeping with the Boas pretext given in Appendix E) makes little of the idea that tobacco becomes part of the people's ceremonial paraphernalia only subsequent to the mythic time of this story. I mention it here only because I find it interesting that in order to put things right again after the introduction of the (new, to the people) ck'o'yo medicine, at least two new life forms—Green Fly and tobacco—must be added to the long story of the people.

Formally, Silko embeds this segment in the story of Tayo's return with his uncle Robert to his own birthplace, Gallup, prior to being handed over to old Betonie; embedded within that story of return is the longish (108–13) description of a new way of life—life as it is lived by Indians from all around the area—"I saw

Navajos ... [t]here were Zunis and Hopis there too, even a few Lagunas" (107)—who have become trapped in Gallup, somewhat like the green flies stuck in the flypaper of the Mexican's bar a few pages earlier in the text (101). Out of this milieu emerges a new life form:

> They had been born in Gallup. They were the ones with light-colored hair or light eyes, bushy hair and thick lips—the ones the women were ashamed to send home for their families to raise. Those who did not die grew up by the river, watching their mothers leave at sundown. (108)

What follows in the prose narrative is a description of this new species' life as seen from the perspective of a very young anonymous child who spends most of the narrative waiting for the men to leave his mother or for his mother to return, and the episode ends with the child curled up in a clump of tamaric bushes in the arroyo, waiting for his mother to return, either confident of her return or else perhaps merely praying for it: "He would wait for her, and she would come back to him" (108). Silko places the sixth segment here, where it splices the image of the anonymous waif (who could be Tayo, and who could also be any of "those who did not die" but rather became, like Green Fly in the backbone story, a part of the life of the people during a time of traumatic change and eventual recovery) and the image of Tayo, standing with Robert on the bridge looking down into the same arroyo perhaps a quarter of a century later in narrative time.

Within this prose narrative context, then, the town that needs to be purified could as easily be Gallup as Laguna village, while Hummingbird and Fly still stand as analogs for Robert and Tayo. Otherwise, the segment functions only loosely as a template for reading the section of prose narrative in which it is embedded: in the prose narrative (as in geographical fact) Gallup lies west of Laguna, not east, while the arroyo where most of the action takes place in both the prose narrative present and the embedded narrative past runs along the north, not the east, side of Gallup.

However, the segment also telegraphs Robert and Tayo's interview with old Betonie, who still seems to be in homological identity with old Buzzard. With respect to Gallup rather than to Laguna, old Betonie does indeed live somewhat to the east of the heart of the city, "in the foothills north of the Ceremonial Grounds"

(116), where he has been monitoring the emergence and development of this newest variety of life for the people for some time:

> "People ask me why I live here," he said, in good English, "I tell them I want to keep track of the people." ... He turned and pointed to the city dump east of the Ceremonial Grounds and rodeo chutes. "They keep us on the north side of the railroad tracks, next to the river and their dump. Where none of them want to live." (117)

SEGMENT 7 (151–52)

Thematically, the seventh segment continues the messengers' search for tobacco, a search which leads from old Buzzard's place in the East back to the village, and from there "all the way back down/to the fourth world below" (151) for their second interview with Our Mother, who directs them to Caterpillar (who, we learn in the next segment, lives in "a place in the West," 180).

Formally, the sixth and seventh segments bracket Tayo's time with old Betonie, so that Tayo's time with Betonie—and the considerable instruction he receives from Betonie both on the edge of Gallup and then out in the Chuska Mountains—comes to occupy the narrative space that in the backbone story is covered by Fly and Hummingbird's first visit with old Buzzard and second interview with Our Mother, the two encounters linked by the messengers' need to find the location of the tobacco, the new fifth ingredient (in addition to blue and yellow pollen, turquoise beads, and prayer sticks) required by the ceremony of recovery. By extension, then, Betonie becomes homologically identified not only with old Buzzard but also with Our Mother—the one requiring the offering of tobacco, the other possessing the knowledge of what it is and where to find it.[8] Further, then, we might take old Buzzard's rather peremptory dismissal of the two emissaries of the people in the sixth backbone segment ("Oh. What do you want?"/ ... /"Well, look here. Your offering isn't/complete. Where's the tobacco?") as previewing the next-to-last words attributed to Betonie in the prose narrative, formally located immediately after the seventh embedded backbone segment and also at the end of the second of the novel's six major sections:

"One night or nine nights won't do it any more," the medicine man said; "the ceremony isn't finished yet." He was drawing in the dirt with his finger. "Remember these stars," he said. "I've seen them and I've seen the spotted cattle; I've seen a mountain and I've seen a woman" (152).

From this perspective, it is tempting to identify Buzzard's required tobacco with Ts'eh, the woman in the prose narrative who will guide Tayo through the second phase of his recovery (see chapter 4) and who will also come to replace both Our Mother Nautsityi and Iktoa'ak'o'ya/Reed Woman as the female principle incarnate for Tayo and the people in the postwar phase of Laguna life.

SEGMENT 8 (180)

In the eighth and penultimate segment of the backbone story, Hummingbird and Fly travel up from the First World, where they learn about tobacco from Our Mother in the previous segment, to "a place in the West" (180) where they acquire the necessary tobacco from Caterpillar. Formally, this segment is located early in the episode located on Mount Taylor, a "place in the West"[9] in the geography of the prose narrative, on a line between Laguna Village and the Chuska Mountains, where the events of the preceding section of the novel take place. Within the context of the prose narrative, this segment appears right after Tayo arrives at the foot of the mountain, eats the red chili prepared by Ts'eh, and contemplates the night sky including the star pattern sketched by Betonie near the end of the preceding section of the novel; immediately after this segment Tayo and Ts'eh make love, and subsequently he dreams of the cattle, the fourth element of the compound image (stars, cattle, mountain, woman [152]) that, like the story Spider Grandmother gives to Sun Man prior to his ascent of his mountain in search of the rainclouds, serves as a map of the second leg of Tayo's journey of recovery.

As noted earlier in this chapter, tobacco is homonymically closely related to the figure of both Iktoa'ak'o'ya-Reed Woman and, by homological extension, Nautsityi, and so it is tempting to identify the lady on the mountain with the tobacco sought by Hummingbird and Fly on behalf of the people. However, and in spite of the genders involved, it makes as much (if not more) sense to align the figure of the lady Ts'eh with the figure of Caterpillar in the backbone story. Both are associated strongly with plant life, and the provisional connection of the lady with tobacco is spelled out a few pages later when, while Tayo breakfasts on cold roast venison and coffee the morning after their lovemaking and before he heads up the mountain in search of the spotted cattle, she lays out a pattern of rocks and plants on the table; of the three plants that are named, the second or middle one is a "dark yellow plant from the rocky mesa top [that] smelled like wet tobacco" (184).[10] More generally, both in this third (Mount Taylor) section of the novel and the fourth (Dripping Springs) section that follows, Ts'eh (like Betonie in the earlier section) provides Tayo with ceremonial insights and prompts necessary, like the tobacco of the backbone story, to the space-clearing ceremony that allows for the return of the life for the people celebrated by the old men of the village in the return chant near the end of the novel: "'A'moo'ooh! A'moo'ooh!'/You have seen her/We will be blessed/again" (257).

SEGMENT 9 (255–56)

In the ninth and final segment of the backbone story, Fly and Hummingbird move from Caterpillar's home in the West to old Buzzard's in the East with their tobacco offering, whereupon Buzzard purifies the town, circling "first to the east/then to the south/then to the west/and finally to the north" (255–56), ending at the place where the ck'o'yo medicine first entered the village; the storm clouds return, vegetation begins to grow once again, the people have food and are happy again.

With respect to the other segments of backbone story, this one is formally located much more remotely (75 pages) from the previous segment than any other two segments. As though to offset that remoteness, however, it appears in the text as the first of a crescendo of five tightly packed portions of embedded text, the tail ends of five different strands of thematic web running through the novel. Further, it is located in the narrative gap between the fifth and sixth prose narrative segments: just prior to the segment, Tayo crosses the river at sunrise after resisting the night of witchery at the Jackpile Mine; immediately following the segment we find Tayo "[a]t the center of the kiva" (256) being debriefed by the old men of the village. Thus, this segment functions also and at the same time as the fifth hoop of the prose narrative structure (see chapter 5). Beyond this hoop we re-enter the

Fifth World of everyday prose reality, a zone in which life is lived like a story and in which there are no new stories, only new versions of the life that all the stories are about. As the old men put it once they have heard Tayo's narrative of his encounters with Our Mother in the form of Ts'eh, "You have seen her/We will be blessed/*again*" (257, emphasis mine). Or as old Grandma, who has the final words of the prose narrative, puts it, "It seems like I already heard these stories before.... Only thing is, the names sound different" (260).

The backbone story ends with the words of Our Mother Nautsityi, who is, of course, related to that other Grandmother Ts'its'tsi'nako, who occupies the very first word of the novel. Nautsityi's last words admonish the people to "Stay out of trouble/from now on" and to "Remember that/next time/some ck'o'yo magician/comes to town" (256), "that" being the complicated process of restoring balance after the ck'o'yo disruption. Formally, Nautsityi's words to the people echo Ts'eh's words to Tayo during their restoration of the she-elk shrine near the end of the novel: "as long as you remember what you have seen, then nothing is gone. As long as you remember, it is part of this story we have together" (231). Less immediately, Nautsityi's admonition also recalls the Night Swan's parting words to Tayo before the war—"remember this day. You will recognize it later" (100)—as well as Josiah's very last words of advice to Tayo in the course of the prose narrative, following his explanation of how green flies became important to the people: "Next time, just remember the story" (102). In this way, Nautsityi's last words in the backbone story also provide a context that invites readers to see the Night Swan and Josiah, delivering their similar messages to Tayo within two pages of each other, as a paired agent in much the same way that Betonie's grandfather Descheeny and the mysterious Mexican lady with bobcat eyes function as a pair in the Chuska Mountains section of the novel, that the lady and the Mountain Lion man function as a pair in the Mount Taylor section, and that, finally, Ts'eh and Tayo end up working together by the end of the third phase of Tayo's recovery near Pa'to'ch butte. Each of these male-female pairs works to perpetuate the project set in motion in the backbone story: the recovery of life for the people following the departure of its source in the face of antithetical medicine. The point being stressed in all these cases, as throughout the backbone story itself, is the interdependence of (and the benefits of cooperation between) differing, often complementary life forms. In the case of Descheeny and the Mexican slave girl, the major differences stressed in Betonie's telling are age ("she was only twelve or thirteen," 147) and nationality; on Mount Taylor, the difference is between hunter (of animals) and gatherer (of rocks and plants) and also between Mountain Lion as hunter and Deer as hunted ("Her eyes slanted up with her cheekbones like the face of an antelope dancer's mask," 177); by the time Tayo and Ts'eh begin to work together consciously, the differences seem to be reduced to gender and experience, the timeless female medicine woman teaching the time-bound male apprentice how to keep life in motion for the people. Read this way, one of the signs that Tayo is ready to proceed solo into the fourth and most dangerous phase of his own recovery is his willingness to take on the work of all those who have gone before:

> "There's only one more [plant] I need," she said, pointing her chin in the direction of the gunny sacks full of roots and plants. "It won't be ready for a while, but I'll show you which one it is, and maybe you can gather it for me, in case I have to go before it's ready."
> ..."I'll remember it," he said. "I'll gather it for you if you're not here." (226–27)

CHAPTER 10
Scalp Ceremony

The way
I heard it
was
in the old days
long time ago
they had this
Scalp Society
for warriors
who killed
or touched
dead enemies.

They had things
they must do
otherwise
K'oo'ko would haunt their dreams
with her great fangs and
everything would be endangered.
Maybe the rain wouldn't come
or the deer would go away.
That's why
they had things
they must do
The flute and dancing
blue cornmeal and
hair-washing.

All these things
they had to do.

This short fragment differs from most of the other embedded texts in the novel in that it is not so much a story as a narrative *about* a story, a narrative that alludes to the ceremony designed to re-happen that story. In this respect it is much like the hoop piece that occupies page 2 of the novel: a discourse offered by a male storytelling voice about the healing and preserving power of ceremony.

The immediate context of this piece invites us to attribute the statement of the text to old man Ku'oosh, who has been called in by Grandma to help Tayo. A few pages earlier, we are told in an echo of the opening line of the prose narrative ("Tayo didn't sleep well that night") that Tayo "woke up crying" (32), sweating and shaking and trying to tell old Grandma "they had to take him back to the hospital" (33); Grandma's response is to hold Tayo's head in her lap, "saying 'A'moo'oh, a'moo'ohh' over and over again."[1] The words she then speaks to Auntie—"That boy needs a medicine man"—echo the statement on page 3 of the opening hoop series, the one titled "*What She Said*": "The only cure/I know/is a good ceremony,/ that's what she said"; this textual and textural resonance with the hoop series invites us further to align this piece of embedded text with the narrative voice of page 2 in the hoop series, which in turn may be taken to be the voiced collective wisdom of the male elders and keepers of Laguna traditional knowledge, one avatar of whom is old Ku'oosh.

PRETEXTS

The "Scalp Society" mentioned in the piece probably refers to the "shamanistic society" (291) alluded to by one of Franz Boas's (female) informants in the 1920s. The members of this group (Boas was not sure it was a formal society) are called Opi (in Boas, $o \cdot p^{\epsilon}$ [289]; in Gunn, *Ope* [108]); both Gunn and Boas agree that Opi (as a group, or as any individual of that group) is in near homological identity with Masewi, one of the Warrior Twins, as a figure of the Warrior. Boas cites two Laguna sources, an unnamed female informant[2] and his frequent male informant Ko′ᴛʸe (207–10), for his account of Opi ritualism given in a section subtitled "Warriors" (289–90). According to Boas, the term *opi* referred to a warrior who had taken the scalp of an enemy in battle[3] and also to the scalp itself; any Laguna warrior who had killed and scalped an enemy was eligible to become, and indeed expected to become, Opi. The public part of the Opi ceremony, described in Boas as a dance, significantly features not only Masewi and Opi as main dancers, along with the scalp of the slain enemy displayed on a pole, but also K'oo'ko, a sister of the Warrior Twins who figures in some of the Pa'cayan'yi recovery stories (see chapter 8 n. 10 of this study). In Silko, "They had things/they must do/otherwise/ K'oo'ko would haunt their dreams/with her great fangs and/everything would be endangered" (37); according to Boas, "The warriors, after killing and scalping an enemy, must be continent for four days. If they do not do so the sister of the Twin Heroes, K'oo·´ko will appear to them in their dreams with large teeth, as she appeared to her brothers when they were running around the world" (289). Although the description of Opi ritualism in Boas nowhere relates failure of the ceremony to drought the way Silko's narrative does (Maybe the rain wouldn't come/or the deer would go away," 37), the items enumerated in Silko's version which signify "the things/they must do"—"The flute and dancing/blue cornmeal and/hair-washing"—appear also in Boas's account of preparations for the public dance:

> After the four days are over ... his head is washed and he may go out. The kurena shaman with his reed whistle leads him out.... [The warrior] wears a bandolier with a pouch in which sacred meal, ? ,[4] pollen, quills of turkey feathers and smoking tobacco are kept. (289, 290)

Neither Boas nor his informants volunteer the story (or "legend," as it would be called in Navajo ethnography) of the origin of the Opi ceremony or the Scalp Society composed of Opi initiates. But Matthew Stirling, in his 1942 B.A.E. report entitled *Origin Myth of Acoma and Other Records* (83–90), reports a close analog from Laguna's next-door neighbor Acoma. According to the version recorded by Stirling, near the end of the migrations the people are "lucky and happy because they had come to their permanent home" (83) at the foot of Haako (= Acu, the Acoma mesa), and "Masewi and Oyoyewi were active as usual, traveling in different countries, from which they brought back many scalps of people they killed" (83). However, "The rulers in the four directions" decide that the twins are becoming too arrogant, and so they enlist "Pishuni hachtsa [old man] (the evil spirit)" to punish them. Pishuni[5] waits for a very beautiful, virtuous Haaku girl to die, then disguises himself as her; she moves in with the twins and later crawls into bed between them. Then, "[w]hile Masewi and Oyoyewi slept the girl turned into corpse of horrible appearance. She fondled one of them and he awoke to see her as an emaciated hag" (83). "The twins were frightened and ran out of the house followed by Pishuna. The spirit was called Ko'oko, a haunt. Thus, if a man murders another, he is always haunted by Ko'oko at night" (84). Pishuna follows them—in effect, chases them—unrelentingly on a course which takes them past North Mountain, then past West Mountain, to "Gaukapuchume, the gambler of the South Mountain." Exhausted, the terrified twins beg his help; he chases Pishuna off with a bloody stickball made of a baby's head. Then Gaukapuchume tells them:

> "I am going to tell you why you have been punished. You have been killing people all over the country and have left their bodies scattered all over. That is the reason this Kooko was chasing you. From now on do not kill just for the purpose of sport and just because you think you are brave. Human beings are sacred (precious). They are not like animals." (85)

Gaukapuchume then instructs them how to perform "the ritual of washing and preparing scalps and the dances to do"; Stirling goes on to describe these rituals in great detail (86–89). Stirling concludes: "One who kills an enemy is known as Opi or Masewi, he always represents Masewi. The last of these, an old man, about 25 years ago, had scalps buried as there would be no one to feed them and care for them when he died, and he feared sickness or pests might come to the village as a result" (90). Boas also reports that the Scalp Society at Laguna was extinct: "The last o·p'i died in 1904. His last performance was in 1902" (290).

If, as Stirling and Boas both claim, the Opi or Scalp Society had died out at both Laguna and Acoma around the turn of the century, then old Ku'oosh (if indeed that is who is speaking the lines of this portion of embedded text) should probably be understood to be merely reminiscing about a time, prior to Tayo's birth, when there was a traditional cure for the kinds of bad dreams Tayo has been experiencing, and the drought that Laguna has been experiencing, since his return from World War II. Then again, though, this ceremony could not have done Tayo much good, because although he is a returned warrior he has taken no enemy scalp (indeed, he is fairly certain he has not "killed/or touched/dead enemies"—"I'm sick, but I never killed an enemy. I never even touched them" 36). Thus old

Ku'oosh's Scalp Ceremony, which requires *inter alia* an enemy scalp to display publicly and dispose of ritually, would be a suspect prescription for Tayo's disease. Silko reminds us, just a few lines before the appearance of the embedded text, of this problem:

> ... the old man shook his head and made a low humming sound in his throat. In the old way of warfare, you couldn't kill another human being in battle without knowing it, without seeing the result, because even a wounded deer that got up and ran again left great clots of lung blood or spilled guts on the ground. That way the hunter knew it would die. Human beings were no different. But the old man would not have believed white warfare —killing across great distances without knowing who or how many had died.... Not even oldtime witches killed like that. (36–37)

Silko's point here may be that, properly speaking, Tayo is not ill because he has touched an enemy or failed to bring an enemy's spirit under ceremonial control; he is ill because he has been touched *by* an inimical spirit, the latest strain of the Ck'o'yo disease which has mutated into existence during World War II and the violent inauguration of the nuclear age. What ails Tayo calls for a new variety of medicine, one that old Betonie, one of old Ku'oosh's intertribal colleagues, will help Tayo concoct out of Navajo antecedents.

FUNCTION

One immediate function of this short allusion to the Laguna "Scalp Society" is to relate World War II and its fallout to Laguna traditionalism—even though the relationship turns out to be less than clear-cut. The representative[6] of that traditionalism in the novel, old Ku'oosh, is clearly a good man, a Laguna *cheani* analogous to Betonie the Navajo *hataali*, a devoted keeper of the old stories and ways. However, the Laguna ceremonial repertoire Ku'oosh maintains contains no recovery medicine that works for the veterans of World War II. As even Tayo acknowledges sometime between Ku'oosh's visit and the departure for Gallup to see Betonie, "It isn't just me, Robert. The other guys, they're still messed up too. That ceremony didn't help them" (106). One of the functions of this particle of embedded text, then, is to delicately imply certain limitations associated with "traditionalism" and to open the door for an exploration of the possible benefits of a provisional pan-Indianism, that is, a more eclectic and opportunistic solution to the problem of aligning "now'day Indianness" with "old-fashioned" narrative empowerment. Thus the ritual later conducted by Betonie, which contains elements of both Enemyway and Red Antway traditional ritual, legend, and chant,[7] is also referred to as "[t]he Scalp Ceremony" (169), and works to Laguna as well as to Navajo ends: "it satisfied the female giant who fed on the dreams of warriors" (169).

Another function is to make it a little easier for readers to see how two other, more prominent embedded texts, and the departure/recovery motif they share, are relevant templates for the story of Tayo in post-World War II America. The common denominator of all three of these texts, a denominator they share also with Tayo's story, is drought. In the first of the novel's embedded texts, drought is one manifestation of the disharmony between the sisters Reed Woman and Corn Woman; in the third (which occurs almost immediately following old Ku'oosh's visit), drought is associated with the destabilization of Laguna life brought about by the introduction of Pa'caya'nyi's Ck'o'yo medicine. Here, old Ku'oosh claims that warriors who bring their war home with them also bring K'oo'ko, the mother of Ck'o'yo medicine men,[8] whose presence endangers "everything": "Maybe the rain wouldn't come/or the deer would go away." Tayo, we may recall, is at his point in the prose narrative still convinced that he is personally responsible for the postwar drought at Laguna because he "prayed the rain away" during the forced march when Rocky died (16). In this manner, Silko also works to bring a story of separated sisters into homological identity with a story of separated warrior brothers.

One final function of this portion of embedded text is to re-introduce the ceremonially potent connection between land and language, the connection between place and vision. Readers may recall that just prior to this passage, Ku'oosh speaks to Tayo in the "old dialect full of sentences that were convoluted with explanations of their own origins ... Tayo had to strain to catch the meaning, dense with place names he had never heard" (34). Ku'oosh's breakthrough comes when Tayo finally recognizes a *place* Ku'oosh refers to in his monolog: Tayo recalls "a cave, a deep lava cave northeast of Laguna where bats flew out on summer evenings" (34), a "wide round hole" that is "deeper than sound" where rattlesnakes gather in the early spring "to restore life to themselves" (35).[9] Silko continues:

> He nodded to the old man because he knew this place. People said back in the old days they took the scalps and threw them down there. Tayo knew what the old man had come for. (35)

This cave "northeast of Laguna" turns out to be the anchor not only of the ensuing conversation between Tayo and Ku'oosh, including the embedded fragment about the "Scalp Society," but also of the story of the witches' convention that Betonie gives Tayo (which also presents formally as a passage of embedded text) in the novel's next episode: "Way up in the lava rock hills/north of Cañoncito/... Up here/in these hills/[where] they will find the rocks,/rocks with veins of green and yellow and black" (133, 137) would in fact be the same place as "northeast of Laguna," and both would be located geographically right where Tayo finds himself near the end of the novel, on his roundabout way to his encounter with Emo and the others at the Jackpile Mine: "The country was dry, and the hills were covered with dark lava rock. The earth was eroded to gray clay, and deep arroyos cut through the length of the valley between the mesas. These were the hills northwest of Cañoncito ... this was their place, and he was vulnerable" (241, 243). The "they" referred to is an enemy older than the Japanese of World War II, older than the Navajos and Apaches of the nineteenth and eighteenth centuries, and (if we believe Betonie) older than white men or even Laguna traditionalism. Additionally, this cave associated with Laguna scalp ritualism is at least formally related to the one occupied by the Gunnedeyah in the Arrowboy story, and also to the space in which Pacayanyi performs his Ck'o'yo magic for the Warrior Twins (which has earthen walls to the north, west, and east [47]); perhaps counterbalancing these three sites of evil is the cave that Tayo sees during a brief moment of presque-vu at the end of the first episode, the "sandstone cave in the cliffs" (104) that will turn out to be where he and Ts'eh spend their summer together, at Dripping Springs.

CHAPTER 11
Betonie's Medicine: The Navajo Series

A quick glance at the "map" of the novel offered in chapter 2 (and again in Appendix A) shows that the text of the novel is formally centered on the second episode of the prose narrative (pp. 107–70). In this episode, Tayo travels from Laguna Village to Gallup,[1] where he lived with his wayward mother Laura (108–13) prior to being left on Auntie's doorstep at the age of four (65–66). There, Tayo becomes the patient of Betonie, the mixed-blood Navajo *hataali* (singer, "medicine man," healer); after first diagnosing Tayo's disease on a hill just north of Gallup, Betonie then takes Tayo out into the Chuska Mountains for a therapeutic "sing" involving ritual poetry, sandpainting, and directed physical motion as well as a variety of narrative performances ranging from mythical to familial to anecdotal. Following his time with Betonie, Tayo makes his way back via Mesita to Laguna village.

Centered within the prose narrative of this episode are a set of three embedded texts. The second, and formally centralmost, of these is the long story Betonie gives to Tayo about the origin of the ceremony to end all ceremonies, the story/ceremony about the creation of white people to serve as carriers of the disease that, in the Gunnedeyah version of the story, will end all life on earth (132–38); I will treat this story separately in chapter 12. This story is bracketed by two other embedded texts, both of them transformation stories. The first of these (128–30), which I'll call the bear-child story, tells of a child who wanders off from his family, transforms into a bear, and is subsequently called back to human identity; the second of these tells of a hunter who becomes a victim of Coyote's machinations, is transformed into coyote form, and is called back into human identity with the aid of bear medicine.

BEAR AND COYOTE

Taken as a pair, the bear-child story and the hunter-to-Coyote story relate to one another in much the same way that the earlier pair of departure-of-the-Mother stories do. The story of how Corn Woman effectively chases her sister Reed Woman away and the story of how Pacayanyi effectively alienates the warrior twins from their mother Nautsityi can (and probably should) be read as different "heads" —accounts of the origin of drought—either or both of which attach to the same "body"—the story of the process, or ceremony, designed to recover our Mother and re-insure life for the People.[2] Analogously in this central section of the novel, the story of how a child wanders across the liminal zone separating (and, as this and all transformation stories point out, also *connecting*) human identity and Bear Country is related to the story of how a hunter is tricked into identity with Coyote: both serve as heads to the same body, the ceremony of recovery originally taught to the (Navajo) People by the Bear People[3] and performed over Tayo by Betonie. Read homologically, the Reed Woman and bear-child fragments both model relatively accidental precipitations of alienation and dis-ease, whereas the Pacayanyi and Coyote episodes both model alienation and disease that are induced by malevolent medicine. Silko goes out of her way to underscore this distinction by strategically inserting the "NOTE ON BEAR PEOPLE AND WITCHES" right after the bear-child story but before the long story about the origin of the new strain of witchery that has become pandemic in the postwar years. Thus aligned, the connection between "Ck'o'yo" and "Coyote" developed throughout the novel, both within and outside of the embedded textual material, becomes easy to see and hear as well as to conceptualize.

BEAR-CHILD TRANSFORMATION

The first of these embedded transformation stories is in some ways also the most curious of the group. For all that it appears to be a version of some Navajo pretext, it is not. The most likely source of a Navajo pretext would be a transcript of Mountainway, in the backbone myth of which representatives of the Diné first encounter and acquire Bear medicine[4]; however, no story resembling Silko's appears in Leland Wyman's edition of *Mountainway*, the most obvious and accessible candidate pretext, and Katherine Spencer's exhaustive 1957 *An Analysis of Navaho Chantway Myths* mentions no such plotline. It is of course possible that the story of a child's transformation into identity with Bear recounts some Laguna pretext, but if so the pretext is transcribed in none of the published accounts of Laguna or Acoma traditional story.

Pretexts aside, Silko's personal fascination with Bear energy, like Momaday's, should not be overlooked. In *Storyteller* she recounts her memory of an episode in which she saw a bear, or just a rock, or both, on the slopes of Mt. Taylor (77–78), a story briefly reiterated at the conclusion of "An Essay on Rocks" in her essay collection *Yellow Woman and a Beauty of the Spirit* (191); in *Yellow Woman* she also recalls a children's book titled *Brownie the Bear* that becomes strongly associated with her storytelling Grandma A'mooh (160); and in *Storyteller* she offers her brilliant poem "Story From Bear Country" (204–07) in which the embedded narrator (which may well be the voice of Bear Country herself) insinuates that anyone, reader included, is susceptible to certain places on the land having the power to transform a personal vision of identity from human being to bear. It makes sense, I think, to allow that the bear-child story given in *Ceremony* is Silko's own contribution to the "long story of the people" (*Storyteller* 7), a Laguna story in the Navajo style designed to complement the Coyote transformation story appropriated from Navajo oral tradition and ethnography.[5]

COYOTE-HUNTER TRANSFORMATION

As Robert Bell has already demonstrated,[6] the prose descriptions of Betonie's ritual sandpaintings, along with the coyote-hunter transformation story and the ritual chants that accompany Betonie's performance in this part of the novel, derive (in places almost verbatim) from Father Berard Haile's 1934 transcription of a traditional Navajo curingway as told and sung by Son of the Late Tall Deschini,[7] subsequently published as part of Leland Wyman's 1965 book *The Red Antway of the Navaho*. To illustrate this claim, and at the risk of duplicating much of Bell's work, I offer facing passages from this portion of the novel and from Wyman's text in Appendix G ("Navajo Pretexts") of this study.

According to Wyman, part of the "myth" (or, roughly speaking, plotline) of Red Antway is a longish episode in which Coyote, who wishes to copulate with a hunter's wife, transforms the hunter into the appearance of a coyote, and himself into the appearance of the hunter, by covering the hunter in a coyote skin and taking on the guise of the hunter; once the deception has been discovered and the hunter-almost-coyote located, the hunter is eased back into his full humanity by means of a ceremony involving hoops, sandpaintings, ritual poetry, and his own participation in the (re-)enactment of the "myth" behind the coyote transformation rite, including the ritual removal of the coyote skin. In the novel, Silko casts Betonie in the role of *hataali* (and his helper, Shush, in the role of the Bear People's agent[8]), and, in turn, Betonie casts Tayo in the role of the hunter/patient; in his role of *hataali*, Betonie constructs a sandpainting, conducts a hoop ceremony, and chants the appropriate accompanying texts: a version of the "Bear's Prayer" (designed to restore the patient's bearings in sacred time and space) and of one of the "Thunder Prayers" (designed to restore the patient's hearing, or more precisely his ability to hear as a human being hears) as recorded in Wyman's English translation of these oral performances.

Narrative

It is possible, though not necessary, to presume that Betonie also narrates the embedded Coyote transformation story (139–41) preceding the sing, though it is equally possible to presume that Silko's embedding storyteller[9] provides this portion of text. Formally, the identity of the storyteller in this case remains ambiguous, as is so often the case in the novel wherever embedded story occurs, an ambiguity which invites a reader to understand that all possible tellers (and all possible auditors) are in homological identity with one another by virtue of knowing (or hearing) the story.

The story of Coyote and the hunter appears frequently in Navajo chantways. In the section of his book subtitled "The Mythology of Red Antway," Wyman notes that "the motif is also found in the myths of Waterway, Excessway, and Beadway" (74). Wyman's list is not exhaustive: another accessible print version of the Coyote transformation story, including some of the accompanying songs, can be found in Berard Haile's *Legend of the Ghostway Ritual in the Male Branch of Shootingway* (54–77, 253–56). However, the wording in this version is dissimilar throughout to Silko's.

Recovery Chant and Unraveling

Formally, this second story of transformation itself transforms, as Betonie moves from recounting the hunter's departure from home and human identity, delivered in oral narrative form, to re-enacting the recovery part of the story, the text of which is delivered in the chanted ritual poetry that accompanies the elaborate hoop ritual (already treated at some length in chapter 5 of this study). The ritual poetry portion of this story appears as four portions of embedded text; the first three (142–44) are clearly integrated with the acted-out ritual alignment of Tayo's identity as Pollen Boy with his identity as the hunter-coyote, and they can easily be read as a single embedded text interrupted briefly by two passages of prose narrative description of the accompanying ritual. The fourth portion (260–61) is located so as to bundle this Navajo hunter-coyote thread with the Laguna nine-part backbone story discussed in chapter 3 above. Like the Coyote transformation story, these chant texts bear strong formal and thematic resemblances to passages in Wyman, most of which are pointed out by Bell.

[1]

The first of these passages (142) is composed of four stanzas. The first stanza is composed of the vocable phrase "en-e-e-ya-a-a-a-a!" repeated four times; in the songs reproduced in Wyman on pages 176–205, the most frequent vocable (which seems to be the signature of Monster Slayer) is "en-e-ya-a-a-a," sounding very similar to, albeit two syllables shorter than, Silko's. The second stanza ("In dangerous places you traveled/in danger you traveled/to a dangerous place you traveled/in danger e-hey-ya-ah-na!"), all save the verb tense and the vocable, looks much like the opening line ("En-e-ya-a-a-a, in a dangerous place you are traveling, in danger you travel, in a dangerous spot you are traveling," 189) to the first "cutting song" (Wyman 189) that normally accompanies one of the several ceremonies comprising the Red Antway.[10] The third and fourth stanzas ("To the place/where whirling darkness started its journey ...") replicate a portion of the last of six "Thunder Prayers" given in Wyman (143–44).

[2]

The second passage (143), located immediately after Betonie suddenly (and for Tayo, unexpectedly) uses a "dark flint"[11] to "cut Tayo across the head" and immediately before a prose narrative description of Tayo stooping through the series of hoops while the blood "ooze[s] along his scalp,"[12] consists of the vocable phrase "eh-hey-yah-ah-na!" repeated five times. This vocable, which also appears once in the first passage (in the last line of the second stanza), may be related to one of the vocables in a "series of vocables, 'en-e-he-ya eye-ne-ah e-ya ya-ena-a' or the like," which closes each line of one set of songs of Red Antway (184).

[3]

The third passage (143–44) contains seven stanzas, the first and fourth of which consist of the vocable of the previous passage repeated four times. The second and third stanzas ("At the Dark Mountain ... Following my footprints ..."), along with the fifth and sixth ("At the Dark Mountain ... I have the dew ..."), replicate the texture and text of the chant in Wyman entitled "Bear's Prayer" (134–35). The final stanza of this passage, though remaining center-justified on the page, shifts from ritual poetry to narrative mode to describe, as does Wyman, what occurs after the completion of the Great Hoop portion of the Coyote transformation rite: in both cases, the patient is spun sunwise and returns home via the crossed rainbows of the ritual sandpainting, though "all kinds of evil were still on him" (Silko 144, Wyman 136).

[4]

The fourth portion of chant text (260) is found nearly 100 pages away from the first three, where it works to seal the homological identity of the disease Coyote inflicts upon the Navajo hunter with the disease Pacayanyi conveys to the Laguna brothers. Like the third portion, it is composed of seven stanzas, and it picks up where the first portion left off, providing a version of the final movement of the sixth "Thunder Prayer" (Wyman 144). However, the texture of Silko's version appears much more chiseled and carefully phrased —"ritualized"— than the version in Wyman, and although both versions conclude with a phrase repeated four times, the triumphant finality of the closing phrase of the Wyman version, "now it is dead for good," stands in stark contrast to Silko's chillingly open-ended "it is dead for now."

[5, 6]

Additionally, Silko includes two closely related narrative (rather than ritually poetic) portions of embedded text, center-justified like the others, describing stages of the "unraveling," that is, ritual undoing of the evil that, first in the form of coyote skin and subsequently in the form of raveled hoops, envelops the recovering hunter. Edith Swan, in "Healing Via the Sunwise Cycle," argues that these "unraveling" passages derive from Fr. Berard Haile's *Legend of the Ghostway Ritual in the Male Branch of Shootingway*; however, I cannot find evidence for her claim in either the narrative translation or in the ritual poetry ("songs") provided in Haile's text. The passages in Silko's novel do, though, bear resemblance to passages in the Wyman text (see Appendix G).

The first of these ("The dry skin/was still stuck/to his body./But the effects/of the witchery/of the evil thing/began to leave/his body ...," 153) functions formally as a bridge connecting Tayo's time with Betonie in the Chuska Mountains (139–52) to the event of his return from the Chuskas to Laguna (153–70). The second ("They unraveled/the dead skin/Coyote threw/on him ...," 258) appears among the crescendo of five embedded texts at the end of the novel (255–62), the coming together of four strands of motif informing the novel; interestingly, Silko locates this penultimate Navajo fragment immediately following an episode set in the Laguna kiva, so that syntactically the "they" who complete Betonie's recovery ceremony can be understood to be the old men (including, of course, Ku'oosh) of the preceding paragraph: "When the sun was dropping near the center of the west window, they stood up. They were going home to rest and eat supper; they would be back later, after dark, old man Ku'oosh told him" (258). Up to this point in the novel, it might appear that there are two backbones to the prose narrative, a Laguna one and a Navajo one; here, it becomes more apparent that these two backbones are but two functionally homologous strands of a single bundle of backbone story, either strand and both strands working to hold the prose narrative and its protagonist Tayo upright.

THE BIG HOOP CEREMONY

The Coyote unraveling songs are the verbal component of the so-called Big Hoop ceremony[13] that (in Wyman as in Silko) is designed to undo the damage caused by Coyote. In this ceremony, which involves sandpaintings and upright hoops and physical motion, Betonie conducts what many first-time readers assume is the "real" ceremony of the novel. In rather minute detail, Silko describes how Betonie and Shush create a sandpainting and how they then lead Tayo through a series of upright hoops from one side of the hogan to the other and out into the northwest New Mexico night.

This episode is central to the novel in many ways. The most obvious index of centrality is a page count: these events occur in and about the dead center of the novel. Another index is that with respect to the prose narrative's plotline this episode functions as the turning point of the novel: prior to this episode, the novel is the story of how Tayo had become separated from his spiritual identity with the Laguna community, that is, how Tayo has moved away from his natal Indianness and become "lost" in the context of the dominant culture; after this episode, it's clear to even casual readers that Tayo is in the process of recovering his Laguna identity, of seeing himself as Indian and moving back into identity with a community who come to own him as one of their own. Departure and recovery: this episode stands at the pivot point of that process.

One more way this episode matters is that here Silko provides Tayo, and the reader, with a color-coded teleological map for the remainder of the novel, a map overtly modeled on an "authentic" Navajo ceremonial text.

In the sandpainting that accompanies both Betonie's and Wyman's Big Hoop ritual, each of the four sacred mountains is painted a certain color and set in a certain order. In Wyman's version, the colors of the mountains, from closest to the patient to closest to the outside of the *hogan* in which this sandpainting is placed, are black (or "dark"), blue, yellow, and white. Accompanying these colored mountains are a series of bearprints, color-coded in the same sequence, and beyond the footprints are five hoops placed upright in the ground:

Betonie's Medicine

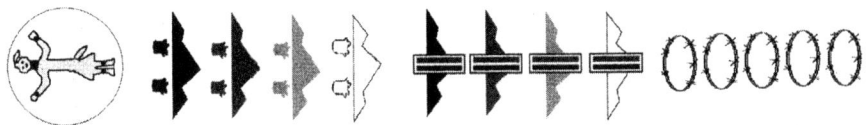

(after Wyman Figure 26A [251])

In the Big Hoop ritual, the patient rehappens the story of how the Navajo hunter is recovered, step by step, back from Coyote identity into full human identity; the patient in this ritual is walked through the sequence of painted mountains, then over the footprints, then through the hoops, in time to a series of chants promising return to home, happiness, and a state of *hozho*.

There is, of course, no mention of "white culture" or "white people" in the Navajo ceremony or in the story (or "myth," in Berard's terminology) it derives from. A human who has been tricked into wandering unprepared into a dangerous place, the "dark mountains," is restored by degrees to full human identity, and the locus of this *state* of recovery is just past the white mountain. Clearly, in this ceremony darkness is associated with separation from community and human identity, while whiteness is the color most closely associated with recovery and restoration of Navajo identity.

The version of this ritual given in the novel, and in particular the color-coded sequence of recovery that is provided by the sandpainted mountains and bearprints, becomes the template for Tayo's recovery of his Laguna identity in the second half of the novel. Silko's text—both the embedded text and the prose narrative—follows Wyman's very closely at his point, sometimes even verbatim; interestingly, Silko's description of the ritual shares some of the deep ambiguity of Wyman's text with respect to where elements of the sandpaintings lie in relation to one another, as well as in relation to the patient and the cardinal directions. In the case of Wyman's text, it would be highly improbable that anyone not already familiar with the pattern would be able to reproduce it from the prose description (hence, perhaps, his decision to include the drawing reproduced above). Silko's description, though still somewhat ambiguous, is a little clearer. Here, according to Silko, is how Betonie and Shush lay out the hoops and sandpaintings of this ritual in Silko's text:

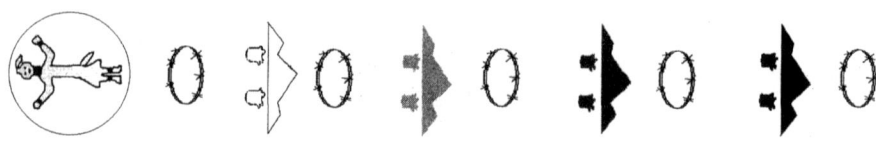

Comparing the two patterns shows that Silko has telescoped the Navajo pretext, so that the hoops now occupy the liminal, transformative zones between six ceremonial stages of identity: the state the patient is in at the beginning and the four color-coded transitions that connect him to the other side of the hogan and to the final phase, identity with the world that awaits on the other side of this ritual recovery walk. Unlike the traditional version also, Silko clearly specifies the east-west order of the hoops, placing the softest one, the "wild rose" one, nearest the door—which would be east; the doorway to a traditional Navajo dwelling (hogan) always faces sunrise—and the hardest one, the "hard oak" one, closest to Tayo and the Pollen Boy painting, at the "back" or west side of the hogan. Recall that when the trackers finally locate the hunter-turned-Coyote in the embedded narrative, he is lying under a wild rose bush (140).

However, perhaps the most intriguing change Silko makes to the Wyman version is to reverse the sequence of colors for both the footprints and the mountains: instead of moving the patient from darkest to lightest, as in the diagram reproduced in Wyman's book, the ritual for Tayo obliges him to move from the white mountain painted "in front of him" past the yellow, then the blue, and finally past the "dark mountain range beside the farthest hoop" (141–42).

Why this reversal? Several possible explanations occur to me, but I think the most likely is that Silko has purposely reversed the order of the colors of the mountains and the footprints in this episode of the novel. Betonie's ceremony is designed to show Tayo how he became lost and came to be wandering, disoriented, in the "dark mountains" where Coyote and Bear, rather than humans, are most at home. In passing, the ritual literally leads Tayo from the realm of sacred story—from being seated as a part of the sandpainting of the holy person called Pollen Boy made at the back of the hogan—out into his personal history as part of the cold night air of the literally dark Chuska Mountains. From there, theoretically, Tayo need only follow this route in reverse to find himself back home and back in identity with his source community. Tayo, that is, is set to act out in historical time/space what the patient in traditional Navajo ceremony acts out in the hoop transformation ceremony: to move from the dark mountains through the blue and the yellow ones to the white one, the one closest to the locus of sunrise both inside and outside the ritual setting. In fact, this is just what he does: subsequent to this orientation ritual in the volcanic dark mountains of the Chuska range, and cued by the star pattern that Betonie draws for him in the sand there (152), Tayo proceeds next to the episode set on Mount Taylor, called Tse-pi'na at Laguna but conventionally called the Turquoise Mountain by the Navajo, the appearance of which, both inside and outside the novel, is always distinctly blue. Tayo then spends the following summer with Ts'eh in the vicinity of Pa'toch Butte, a traditional Laguna holy place that is composed of mainly yellow sandstone, after which he is ready to return, by way of the Jackpile Mine, to the white gypsum mesa upon which the village of Old Laguna is built, to personal and cultural restoration.

I still think it is interesting that Silko elected to use a Navajo pretext as a template for a story about recovery of Laguna identity. Historically, Navajos and Pueblo peoples did not begin getting along with one another until about the mid-1800s, and the oral traditions of both groups would suggest that, from earliest contact, hostility rather than cooperation characterized the rules of engagement between the two. Even so, they have one interesting thing in common: in the origin and early migration stories of both the Navajos and the Keresan-speaking peoples, including the Laguna stories that Silko takes as the pretexts for most of the rest of the traditional-sounding embedded texts in the novel, white is one of the four cardinal colors. I have already argued that white signifies home and return to fully human identity in the Navajo story underpinning the Big Hoop ritual; I want to end this chapter by saying something about the traditional status of the color white in the Keresan traditional worldview—by which I also mean the Keresan pre-Contact worldview.

RE-APPROPRIATING WHITENESS

Prior to contact with the colorful European notion of blood quantum as an index of racial or cultural purity, the Laguna People had already assigned a cardinal spiritual importance to whiteness. When this novel is read in the light of traditional Keresan color conventions, the fact that Tayo is part "white" could easily signify that he is more, not less, essentially Laguna. It works like this: According to traditional Laguna reckoning, we are all now living in the Fifth World. Prior to this world, and also *within* this world, positioned "below" with respect to the "earth-surface world" but also within, as in the relationship of womb to belly, are the previous worlds from which life has emerged. In several renditions of the Laguna origin story recorded by Franz Boas in *Keresan Texts*, the First World (the room in which Spider Grandmother wills the world into motion) is white, the Second World red, the Third blue, and the Fourth yellow.[14] These four colors are the traditional Keresan "cardinal colors," the colors of the spiritual "elements" of Keresan life, the colors of the degrees of spirit which, woven correctly together, produce the forms of life that we know in the Fifth World. In the Laguna origin and migration stories, the first place in the Earth Surface World that the People call their home is "Kush-Kutret," a phrase that translates into English as "White House."[15] Like this place that the People first called "home," the color white was always, is always a part of—indeed, the *source* of—Laguna individual and collective identity.

With this traditional Keresan paradigm in mind, then, the novel can be read as Silko's attempt to imagine a successful re-appropriation of whiteness to Indian identity. To do so, she fashions a protagonist whose personal story represents the effects of nearly 500 years of history driven by those who would like nothing better than to separate the People from their own life source. By making Tayo a "half-breed," she overtly invites us, along with Tayo, to "read" his identity as hopelessly separated from some hypothetical pure Indian status, but then through a series of inversions and reclamations, leads Tayo (and us) to a less diseased, and diseasing, understanding of how life works, when it is working for regeneration rather than for separations.

At the end of Silko's novel, when Tayo is sequestered in the kiva while he delivers the story of Our Mother Nautsityi's postwar recovery, we are told that the kiva walls are in the process of being whitewashed in anticipation of the winter ceremonies (256). On one axis of significance, this whiteness aligns the interior of the kiva, the spiritual center of nowaday Laguna life, with the time/space of Kush Kutret and the White House stories, the restorative origin stories of the People. On an even more fundamental axis, the whitewashed kiva symbolically re-connects the lives and stories of all its occupants to the Place of Origin for all of Laguna life and story, the First World, the White World, that is Ts'its'tsi'nako's, Spider Grandmother's, most immediate home.

CHAPTER 12
The Witchery

At the heart of the novel, formally bracketed by the two Navajo transformation stories, lies the long, central embedded story about the origins of a virulent new strain of witchery created, as Betonie tells it, at a witches' convention held in the dark "lava rock hills/north of Cañoncito" (133). This portion of text is marked formally for special attention both by its central location and by its length, for it is the longest of any of the embedded texts in the novel.

It is an especially important piece of text on several other counts as well. For one, it is an origin story, a story about an event that precedes and puts into motion subsequent Fifth World history. As an origin story, it points to the "dark side" of the power of words to make worlds, and thus it stands in stark formal and thematic contrast to the Keresan origin story that Silko contrives to precede, and set in motion, the prose narrative of her novel. If Ts'its'tsi'nako, the grandmother of all generative storytellers, is the ultimate protagonist in *Ceremony*, then the anonymous witch, the genderless archetype of all destructive storytellers ("the destroyers," 247), is surely the novel's prime antagonist. For another, the immediate prose narrative context for this portion of text is the only place in the novel where anyone who seems to know what he or she is talking about directly addresses the relationship between Native American identity and the dominant ideological force in North America, color-coded here and elsewhere in the novel as "the white people." Last but not least, it is one of the few embedded texts in the novel for which I have been unable to locate a written pretext, and very probably one doesn't exist: and in a 1976 interview Silko herself refers to it as "this awful story I made up" (Evers and Carr 20). This set of anomalies leads me to speculate that Silko may have had to create this story in order to get the rest of her novel to move in a way not anticipated in either Keresan or Navajo oral or ethnographic tradition.

Like the first three portions of text on the first three pages of the novel, this portion of text also features a story within a story, an embedding voice (in this case, Betonie's) and an embedded voice (the anonymous witch's). Although no print pretext seems to exist for this story, Native oral traditions are rich in stories, cast variously as histories and as prophesies, of contact with pale-skinned outsiders, and many of these oral narratives have been recast in print by both Indian and non-Indian writers. The most familiar example of the former is Wovoka's prophecy recounted in Mooney's 1892 account of the Lakota Ghost Dance, eventually published by the BAE four years later; perhaps the most notorious of the latter is the "Hopi Prophecy" published in Frank Waters' *Book of the Hopi*. More recently, James Ruppert has analyzed a Tlingit version of this motif in "The Russians Are Coming, the Russians Are Dead" (1990), while Cherokee poet and novelist Robert Conley's wonderful historical/prophetic poem "We Wait" concludes with a stanza subtitled "The Old Prophecy":

> it came in various forms
> from the Creek
> & the Navajo
> but the message is always clear
> *white men will come*
> (they did)
> *they will take the land*
> (they did)
> *they will nearly destroy the People*
> (they tried)
> *they will waste the land*
> (they have)
> *then they will go away*
> (we wait).

Silko's own deep ongoing interest in this motif also informs her second novel, *Almanac of the Dead*: in the final "Book" of the novel, titled "Prophecy," a character known as "the Barefoot Hopi" embodies the spirit of prophecy embodied by Conley's anonymous narrator in "We Wait" and by Wovoka almost exactly a century earlier. The important difference between these prophesies and the one launched by the anonymous witch in Betonie's story is that these prophecies foresee Native recovery from the disease carried by the infected and infecting Other, while the witch in Betonie's version foresees the end of Native identity—

indeed, the universal end of mankind—and the triumph of the spirit of annihilation.

ORIGIN OF THE GUNNADEYAH

In what some might take to be a postmodernist gesture, within the story the main action is the telling of a story; this doubly embedded story tells of how a powerful belief—terribly shortsighted, but nonetheless powerful—will come to underpin, and then generate, contact and postcontact history. The belief is that, to quote Betonie who in turn is quoting the storytelling witch, "*The world is a dead thing/ the trees and rivers are not alive the mountains and stones are not alive*" (135).[1] This belief will be a disease that originates in "*caves across the ocean in caves of dark hills*" and that will be brought to Indian country by "*white skin people like the belly of a fish/ covered with hair*" (135). The disease will be carried across the ocean, and it will infect the descendants of all the people who were already in the world prior to the advent of the disease. This disease will manifest not only as a failure of vision but also as a series of physiological catastrophes, including the historical epidemics of smallpox and influenza that decimated Native populations on both American continents:

> *They will bring terrible diseases*
> *the people have never known.*
> *Entire tribes will die out*
> *covered with festered sores*
> *shitting blood*
> *vomiting blood.*

By the time Tayo hears about this story in the postwar twentieth century, we are to understand, the world all over has indeed become acutely ill—so ill that Tayo, for instance, cannot see beyond the effects of the witchery and is ready to believe that "Indians have nothing compared to white people" and that "the sickness [which he sees all around him] comes from their wars, their bombs, their lies" (132).

One corollary of this witchery-induced belief, of course, is the conviction that white is "*their*" color and the color of *their* characteristic medicine—a color designed to make Indians sick. However, by embedding the idea of "white people" in the larger context of a pre-European, pre-Contact event, Silko through Betonie reappropriates the power that Tayo, like Emo and the other members of the Indian veteran generation, has come to assign to non-Indian identity. "White people are only tools that the witchery manipulates," Betonie tells Tayo, "and I tell you, we can deal with white people, with their machines and beliefs. We can because we invented white people; it was Indian witchery that made white people in the first place" (132). This statement, like the story in the embedded text that follows it,[2] turns the usual colonialist paradigm inside-out: diseased Native American identity is presented not as a creature of the European imagination but rather as a creature of a (tribally nonspecific) Native American medicine-story.

"THE LAVA ROCK HILLS"

As I have already argued in chapter 11, Silko's choice to make Laguna *cheani* Ku'oosh's medicine ineffective against twentieth-century witchery, and to make Tayo the patient of Navajo *hataali* Betonie instead, suggests her desire to broaden Tayo's quest so as to recover not only specifically Laguna identity but also, in the process, map a template for the recovery of (pan-)Indian identity in the postwar years. Within the embedded text she attributes to Betonie, this linking of Laguna concerns to Navajo ones is made plain in the composition of the audience to the story-within-the-story, those originally infected by the disease set in motion by the words of the anonymous, genderless storyteller to end all storytellers. Silko specifically makes this first generation of Gunnadeyah witches not only multiracial —"Some had slanty eyes/others had black skin"—but also pan-tribal: "witches from all the Pueblos/and all the tribes./They had Navajo witches there,/some from Hopi, and a few from Zuni" (133).

For those who agree with Silko that the life of the people as well as the life of the stories derives from the land,[3] this connection is sealed from the outset of the embedding narrative, in which we are told that the witches' convention was held "Way up in the lava rock hills/north of Cañoncito" (133), a location that figures as a contact zone where Laguna and Navajo stories overlap both inside and outside the novel. From a Navajo perspective, Cañoncito is the area that gives its name to the Cañoncito Indian Reservation, one of several small Navajo reservations scattered through northcentral New Mexico, which is virtually embedded within the northeast quadrant of the Laguna Reservation.[4] Within the novel, this is the vicinity Tayo remembers when old Ku'oosh, working to call Tayo back into identity with Laguna, "describe[s] a cave, a deep lava cave northeast of Laguna" (34) inhabited by bats and rattlesnakes: "He nodded to the old man because he knew this place. People said back in the old days they took the scalps and threw them down there. Tayo knew what the old man had come for" (35).[5] Later in the novel, Tayo also recalls how Josiah's Mexican cattle pause awhile at the "Cañoncito windmill," on Laguna land, during their flight southwards from the Sedillo Grant (just south of the lava hills and caves) toward the home encoded in their hearts and bones (79). This area shows up for the fourth and final time near the end of the novel when Tayo awakens from his final drunken truck ride with Harley and Leroy to find himself in country "that was dry, and the hills were covered with dark lava rock.... These were the hills northwest of Cañoncito" (241), from which Tayo then moves southwest (toward Laguna village) in time to encounter the old witchery of Betonie's story in its latest manifestation, Emo's ceremony at the Jackpile Mine. The structure here locates the anonymous witch of Betonie's story, whose medicine is the story set into motion by its oral performance, as the homological template for all other manifestations of witchery that appear in the novel, including Laguna tradition's Old Woman Ck'o'yo and her spawn Pa'caya'nyi and Kaup'a'ta, Navajo tradition's Coyote in his dark aspect, and, in the novel's prose narrative, Emo and his minions—all those who, like Harley, Leroy, and Pinkie, have wittingly or unwittingly become Gunnadeyah destroyers, agents of Ck'o'yo medicine.

In sum, then, this portion of embedded text functions in two major ways with respect to the prose narrative. Most immediately, as an origin story the embedding narrative presents the protagonist Tayo (and the reader) with a midcourse correction of vision regarding the origin of the disease from which Tayo must recover if he is to become the figure of twentieth-century Indian survivance. At the same time, the prophecy embedded in that narrative—the story set in motion by the anonymous witch—foreshadows the Native significance of the final showdown in the novel between Tayo and Emo and, by extension, between the generative (and regenerative) medicine set in motion by Spider Grandmother Ts'its'tsi'nako and the Gunnedeyah medicine set in motion by Silko's anonymous hama-ha witch.

CHAPTER 13
Arrowboy

>Arrowboy got up after she left.
>He followed her into the hills
>up where the caves were.
>The others were waiting.
>They held the hoop
>and danced around the fire
>four times.
>The witchman stepped through the hoop
>he called out that he would be a wolf.
>His head and upper body became hairy like a wolf
>But his lower body was still human.
>"Something is wrong," he said.
>"Ck'o'yo magic won't work
>if someone is watching us."

When read without reference to the body of Laguna story, this portion of embedded text seems fugitive and fragmentary, maybe even less germane to the prose narrative than the Reed Woman fragment (which, interestingly, is located about the same narrative distance from the beginning of the prose narrative as this fragment is from the end of it). Even when read with some awareness of the way that oral tradition informs the prose narrative in *Ceremony*, unless the reader has seen (or heard) the longer story of which this episode is a part, this portion of text may look like a fragment from some longer traditional narrative, but its relevance to the prose narrative is likely to seem at best strained—limited, perhaps, to the coincidence of a pair of shared motifs, animal transformation and Ck'o'yo medicine.

PRETEXTS

As much as this passage looks like an excerpt from some longer print narrative, it is not. The passage is, however, in homological identity with an episode that is part of a much longer traditional Laguna narrative, one usually set at neighboring Acoma Pueblo.[1] At least four[2] versions of this story appear in print: Charles F. Lummis's

1910 publication of "The Sobbing Pine" in *Pueblo Indian Folk Stories* (194–99); a version in John Gunn's 1917 *Schat-chen* titled "Yo-A-Schi-Moot and the Kun-Ni-Te-Ya" (195–203); a version recorded in 1920 and published in Boas's *Keresan Texts* under the title "The Witches and Arrow-Youth" (130–40); and Silko's own "Estoy-eh-muut and the Kunnedeyahs," published in *Storyteller* (140–54).³ In the broader story informing all four of these versions, the protagonist, Arrowboy,⁴ is married to Kochinninako, Yellow Woman, who in this story is also one of the Kunnedeyah, a secret society of witches also known (throughout Silko's writing) as the Destroyers.⁵ Arrowboy secretly follows Kochinninako one night and discovers that his wife is a witch, but he is then captured by the witches and, after he refuses or fails to pass the initiation ceremony, he is spirited to a high ledge and left there to die of thirst and starvation; small animals, however, contrive to keep him alive (in some versions, for years) long enough for him to escape, after which he returns and, with the aid of Spider Grandmother, effects the destruction of his witch-wife.⁶ The embedded text in *Ceremony* rehearses the discovery phase of this story.

As can be seen from a quick glance at the comparable passages contained in Appendix F, the closest print homolog of the novel's Arrowboy fragment is contained in the story given by Ko·´Tʸe in 1920 titled "The Witches and Arrow-Youth" (*Keresan Texts* 130–40; Ko·´Tʸe, it may be recalled, was also the informant whose Pacayanyi story is remarkably similar to the one Silko gives in *Ceremony*). As in the novel's version, the witches begin their ceremony, but, as long as Arrow-Boy is watching them undetected, the animal transformation (from human to wolf, as in Silko's *Ceremony* version) is only partially effected—in both cases, the witches' upper half transforms to wolf while the lower half remains human, and in both cases the chief of the witches immediately deduces that someone must be spying on them.

HOOP/TRANSFORMATION MOTIF AND VISION

Arguably, one of the major functions of this embedded text is to signal congruence between what Tayo is about to witness at the Jackpile Mine and the idea, seeded in the Navajo coyote transformation story and ritual given to Tayo by Betonie in the Chuska Mountains episode (see chapter 11), that the process of physical and spiritual recovery, at least from Ck'o'yo witchery, goes hand in hand with a process of literal and metaphorical *dis*-covery—that is, the removal of some kind of layer that hinders or prevents clear vision. This is, we may recall, also one of the major motifs of the Kaupata-Sun Man showdown, in which Sun Man must be able to "see through" Kaupata's trickery and identify what is covered by "the bag on the east wall" and the "sack hanging from the south wall" of Kaupata's mountain abode "up North/around Reedleaf town" (175, 170). However, the homology between the Arrowboy fragment and the Betonie series is much more apparent, mainly because much more detailed: in both cases, transformation is effected by passing through hoops[7]; in both cases, transformation is between human form and animal form; and in both cases, the transformation from human form to animal form is, according to the storyteller, prime evidence that Ck'o'yo witchery is at work. By reactivating these motifs through the agency of an embedded fragment having no context except the events of the novel itself, the Arrowboy fragment here serves to telegraph homological identity between whatever is happening here on the northeast edge of the Laguna landscape and whatever was happening in the Chuska Mountains.

This identity also aligns, not only *what* Tayo sees in the Jackpile episode with what he "sees" in the story of witchery narrated earlier by Betonie and what Arrowboy sees, but also *how* Tayo sees in those two episodes and the quality of Arrowboy's vision in the embedded fragment. What's there to be seen in all three cases is clear enough: witchery, in the form of those who practice it. In the story Betonie gives Tayo, "they got together/to fool around in caves/with their animal skins. Fox, badger, bobcat, and wolf/they circled the fire/and on the fourth time/they jumped into that animal's skin" (133–34); in the Arrowboy fragment, "[t]hey held the hoop/and danced around the fire/four times./The witchman stepped through the hoop/he called out that he would be a wolf"; at the Jackpile Mine, Emo and the other members of the Laguna Ck'o'yo brotherhood, disguised as drunken vets, "circling the fire" (248), are "[t]he destroyers. They would be there all night, he knew it ... The witchery would be at work all night" (249). *How* Tayo sees, or rather comes to see, the witchery—and, probably more importantly, his relationship to that witchery—is a subtler matter.

In the available Keresan Arrowboy pretexts, as in Silko's own "Estoy-eh-muut and the Kunideeyahs," to witness the goings-on in the cave is to become part of the goings-on. In one case (Gunn), once Arrowboy is discovered by the witches he has to eat with them; in most cases (DeHuff, Gunn, Lummis, Silko), he is required to fetch a sacrificial heart (or two) to bring to their ceremony; but in every case, Arrowboy is captured by the witches and stranded on a ledge, so that he survives this encounter only thanks to the assistance of [ground] squirrels. My point is that, "traditionally," the witchery (which is specifically C'ko'yo witchery only in the novel) is irresistible. Tayo, that is, is the only "Arrowboy" homolog whose medicine is equal to that of the Destroyers.

Perhaps this is because we are to understand that Emo is only a watered-down agent of the Ck'o'yo way. But I doubt it. I think we need to look, rather, to what Tayo has acquired (by this point in his story) that his homologs have *not* acquired in theirs. One thing Tayo has acquired, of course, is a series of stories that encode a variety of witchery's strategies of deception and appropriation as well as a variety of strategies for coming to terms with such medicine. As the story of Kaupata and Sun Man demonstrates and highlights in the lengthy point-for-point reiteration of Spider Grandmother's prophetic advice, simply knowing that the story *can* end on a note of survival or triumph rather than destruction or defeat is empowering. My own sense, though, is that Tayo has acquired more than the spirit backbone of all these stories: he has also acquired, whether he seems conscious of it or not, a special quality of vision that enables him to see the Living Land[8]—a quality of vision adumbrated at the end of Betonie's ritual (145), reinforced during the Mt. Taylor episode (201), and anchored in the figure of Ts'eh's relationship to Patoch Butte during the Dripping Springs episode (222, 230), at which time it also becomes anchored in Tayo's sense of his relationship to Ts'eh. That is, even as he then proceeds to the showdown with witchery at the Jackpile Mine, as long as he continues to "see" the land as alive he also remains in immediate contact with Ts'eh, even if she is not "visible" as a form differentiated from other non-human forms that Life takes hereabouts. This is the special quality of vision that enables Tayo to see again that one of the important life forms enlivened by the life of the land is the story, that *au fond* stone, story, and human history are homologous forms of a single, ongoing event:

> He walked to the mine shaft slowly, and the feeling became overwhelming: the pattern of the ceremony was completed there. He knelt and found an ore rock. The gray stone was streaked with powdery yellow uranium, bright and alive as pollen; veins of sooty black formed lines with the yellow, making mountain ranges and rivers across the stone.... He cried the relief he felt at finally seeing the pattern, the way all the stories fit together—the old stories, the war stories, their stories—to become the story that was still being told. He was not crazy; he had never been crazy. He had only seen and heard the world as it always was: no boundaries, only transitions through all distances and time. (246)

A paragraph later in the text, the Arrowboy fragment appears; in the fragment as in the prose narrative, part of the story is "Ck'o'yo magic," the witchery that works to take life out of circulation, metaphorically to pen it up in chainlink fencing, as Floyd Lee does on Mt. Taylor, or to lock it up in four separate rooms or enclose it in sacks hanging on the walls, as Kaupata does, or to cut it from Harley's living body and drop it in a bloody paper sack, as Emo does in the ritual that Tayo is about to witness—an element of Emo's ceremony which aligns him with those prototypical witches in Betonie's story who work with "skin bundles of disgusting objects ... Whorls of skin/cut from fingertips/sliced from the penis end and clitoris tip" (134). My sense is that what differentiates Tayo from his Arrowboy precursors and enables him to resist being drawn into the circle of witchery here is the one additional element of insight that Tayo brings to his encounter with his antagonist in his version of the "old story/the long story of the people." He recognizes that he is a part of the story of witchery, just as he recognizes that witchery is a part of his story and both of those stories are homologous versions of the story and the life of the land and its people; but he *further* has come to recognize that, in the story/life/ceremony which all individual performances are but versions, there are no endings but only the *choices*, among possible versions waiting to be enacted, that people make to keep the story in motion.⁹ In some important way, the traditional story of Arrowboy and Silko's story of Tayo diverge during the moment between the time the witches realize that someone is metaphorically *seeing through* the secrecy surrounding their ceremony and the moment when, in Silko's prose narrative, Tayo outlasts his powerful desire to enter the circle of witchery and exercise his own capacity for violence and destruction. In this crucial differentiating moment, Arrowboy is brought into the circle of witchery—becomes not only a part of it, but becomes located *in* it, the story proceeding accordingly—while Tayo remains a part of it but also a part of the landscape outside it and surrounding it. Continuing to move with and like Ts'eh and her harbinger the water snake,[10] at nightfall Tayo "squeezed himself into a hollow space between" some huge boulders ("It was warm there, the sandrock still held the sun's heat," 248) when headlights suddenly appear "from the northeast," and he retains his newfound position with respect to the witchery even when Emo sends him a compelling invitation to transform into his mountain lion self and finish the story set in motion in an earlier bar fight. In that episode, in response to Emo's taunt ("You drink like an Indian, and you're crazy like one too—but you aren't shit, white trash. You love Japs the way your mother loved to screw white men"), "[h]e moved suddenly with speed that was effortless and floating like a mountain lion" (63); here, in response to a similar taunt ("Look at this, you half-breed! White son of a bitch! You can't hide from this! Look! Your buddy, Harley"), and armed with a screw driver instead of the earlier broken beer bottle, Tayo visualizes but resists the impulse to close the distance between himself and the agent of Ck'o'yo witchery:

> He knew he could get to Emo before Pinkie or Leroy could stop him.... He visualized the contours of Emo's skull; the GI haircut exposed thin bone at the temples, bone that would flex slightly before it gave way under the thrust of the steel edge.... This was the time. (252–53)

In order to complete the integrative ceremony that will restore his own life to the People, Tayo must see—acquire an accurate vision of—the witchery in motion at the Jackpile Mine, but he must not attempt to kill Emo or the others, because Ck'o'yo energy, like any other kind of energy, can neither be created nor destroyed but only transformed. This is the insight Sun Man exercises, an insight which goes one step further than the preview given to him by Grandmother Spider and a step too beyond Arrowboy's understanding of witches and witchery, when he refuses to cut out Kaup'a'ta's heart, even when invited to by Kaup'a'ta. In the story as told by Silko, it is enough for the protagonist to witness the Ck'o'yo/Kunideeyah work with a good heart, and then to publicize that vision, to disable it.

FROM ACOMA TO LAGUNA

In Gunn, as in Boas and Lummis, "they say" this story happened around Acoma, and certainly Silko provided herself ample opportunity to bond Arrowboy to this story's traditional provenance as well as to her protagonist. The night after Ts'eh leaves Tayo at the end of the Dripping Springs episode, we are told, Tayo "climbed up the big boulders, feeling his way slowly, remembering ledges and cracks in the cliff wide enough for a person to climb to the top of the mesa," and then "He ran north until he hit the wood-hauling road, and he followed it east to the Acoma boundary fence. He trotted along the fence" (235). In the actual landscape to which the novel refers, the trail being described in the novel moves along the Acoma side of the Acoma-Laguna border, roughly paralleling the dirt road that runs from the (paved) Acoma road through the mesas on Laguna land south and east past Dripping Springs and Patoch to the Marmon ranch—the same road that, we are reminded, "a year ago he and Harley had ridden down ... on the burro and mule" (234); Tayo ends this night sleeping in a culvert near Engine Rock, alongside the Acoma road. The next morning at sunrise Tayo begins to think simultaneously about two kinds of cave: "He realized that all long the valley the cliffs were full of shallow caves and overhangs with springs. But there were other caves too, deeper and darker. He turned away" (237). A sentence later, contemplating the beauty of Enchanted Mesa, whose "cloudy yellow sandstone was still smoky blue before dawn," Tayo realizes that part of this landscape is "the other [which] was distinct and strong like the violet-flowered weed that killed the mule, and the black markings on the cliffs, deep caves along the valley the Spaniards followed to their attack on Acoma" (237). The immediate allusion here is to the bloody Oñate campaigns of 1598-99, but "the other" in these descriptions surely includes those "other caves too, deeper and darker" where, according to both Laguna and Acoma tradition, Arrowboy witnessed the witchery working in the shadows for destruction.

However, even given this opportunity, Silko chooses to resituate the story, and in fact she resituates it about as far from Dripping Springs—where it would also attach to Ts'eh, perhaps unfortunately suggesting that she is about to betray Tayo —as she could possibly place Tayo and still have him witnessing the witchery on the body of Laguna land. To be more precise, this fragment occurs in the text when Tayo himself has returned to the reservation and the Jackpile Mine (locus of the coming Ck'o'yo performance by Emo et al.) from that place where Tayo wakes up after a drunken truck ride with Leroy and Harley. A place of dark lava rock, dry weeds, cholla cactus, and salt bush, "[t]hese were the hills northwest of Cañoncito" (241), the very same "lava rock hills/north of Cañoncito" where "they got together/to fool around in caves/with their animal skins" in the origin story given to Tayo by Betonie in those other dark mountains earlier in the novel (137). Like Arrowboy, Tayo knows he is in the presence of witchery here—"this was their place, and he was vulnerable"—(243) and the conference of witches still occurs here in the form of the "voices, low and steady tones coming from the top of the hill" (242) where Tayo surmises Harley and Leroy have gone.[11] The betrayal of Arrowboy by Kochinninako is here recapitulated in the betrayal of Tayo by Harley, an event Tayo had already begun to suspect (240); it remains only for Tayo to see, literally, the ongoing ceremony of witchery at the Jackpile Mine to complete the transformation from possibility to certainty. The Arrowboy fragment, then, functions to bridge the short distance (both literal and figurative) between the site of original Ck'o'yo witchery and the site of the latest, and to date most monstrous, manifestation of that witchery and its practitioners.

As Silko positions it, then, this story fragment works to connect the shadowy world of Acoma witchery to the dark side of Laguna ceremonialism, rather than to differentiate between them. By extension, the fragment functions to liminalize the separations we tend to make between "traditional"/Acu and "progressive"/Laguna,[12] "West" of Laguna and "North" of Laguna, and even—and most uncomfortably, I suspect, for many readers—Tayo's Ts'eh and Arrowboy's Kochinninako. From a formal perspective, after all, they are not so different: both know how the Ck'o'yo witchery works. Both have seen it practiced. Both are a part of its story, as it is part of theirs.

"ESTOY-EH-MUUT AND THE KUNIDEEYAHS"

As we might have come to expect, Silko gives a detailed version of this longer story in *Storyteller* under the title "Estoy-eh-muut and the Kunideeyahs" (140–54).

Contrary to these same expectations, however, the wording of the relevant episode in the *Storyteller* version (145–46) is quite different from the text given in the novel. In the *Storyteller* version, Silko gives the English translation of the name, Arrowboy, only once, in the first line of a 14-page performance; elsewhere only the Keresan name, Estoy-eh-muut, appears. Nowhere in the *Storyteller* version does the term "Ck'o'yo" appear—throughout the *Storyteller* version, the witchery is associated with the Kunideeyah clan. In the novel's version, the witches want to turn into wolves, but in the *Storyteller* version the desired forms are bear and crow. In Boas's and Lummis's versions, as in the novel, the shapeshifters undergo a partial but incomplete transformation while Arrowboy spies on them, whereas in the *Storyteller* version (as in Gunn's) "nothing happened" when the witches pass through the transformative hoop.[13]

The difference in the telling of these two versions serves as a reminder of a very important element of successful storytelling in the oral mode: the role of context. This episode occurs very early in the story of Arrowboy's discovery of how intimate his own life has become with the Kunideeyah witchery, but in the novel this episode occurs very late in the story of Tayo's quest to learn how to come to terms with Ck'o'yo medicine. By this point in the novel, Tayo's story is working its way into homological identity with the entire body of Laguna story, and Silko is in effect "footnoting" the point that the backbone of Tayo's story is now aligned also with the backbone of a powerful story that usually stresses the element of Yellow Woman's betrayal of the culture hero; by including a reference to "Ck'o'yo magic" but making no mention here of the Kunideeyah, and by downplaying the element of betrayal (the storyteller of this fragment never mentions Kochinninako by name, and in fact alludes to "her" only once in the passage) and foregrounding instead the element of covert witness, Silko as literary Skeleton-fixer once again works here to reassemble "the whole story/the long story of the people" (*Storyteller* 7).

"ESTOYMUUT AND THE GUNNADEYAH"

It should probably be noted that Silko has a special attachment to this storyline. It is the subject of her videotape "Arrowboy and the Witches," now titled "Estoymuut and the Gunnadeyah," a 60-minute video version of *Storyteller*'s "Estoy-eh-muut and the Kunideeyahs." Silko's project was originally for a trilogy of films, to be collectively entitled *Stolen Rain*, but "Arrowboy and the Witches" is the only one of the three to be completed (though it never underwent final editing).[14] To film it, she returned to the mesa country south and west of Old Laguna, a landscape of cottonwoods and sandstone caves in an area locally known as Dripping Springs, which has been in the care of the Marmon family for several generations and where, in *Ceremony*, Tayo and Ts'eh spend their summer together near the end of the novel. As part of the setting for this film but also partly, perhaps, fulfilling the words she attributes to her father in *Storyteller*—"You could even live/up here in these hills if you wanted" (161)—Silko erected a stone cottage near the base of the Dripping Springs mesa. It burned down shortly thereafter, but its ruins are still there, along with the shell of the dwelling occupied by Spider Grandmother in that film, parts of yet another story attaching to this place.[15]

This film version of the story of Arrowboy underscores another link between the Arrowboy fragment that appears in *Ceremony* and the larger body of Laguna story, including other episodes in the novel's prose narrative: the site where the event takes place. The Dripping Springs where Silko sites the convention of the witches or Kunideeyah in her film version of the Arrowboy story is also the place where Tayo and Ts'eh spend their summer together,[16] as well as the place Tayo sees in the dream he has immediately following the hoop ritual Betonie performs for him about a year earlier in the chronology of the prose narrative:

> He dreamed about the speckled cattle. They had seen him and they were scattering between juniper trees, through tall yellow grass, below the mesas near the dripping spring.... They were gone, running southwest again, toward the high, lone-standing mesa the people called Pa'to'ch. (145)

By juxtaposing the Arrowboy fragment with the prose narrative as she does near the end of the novel, Silko contrives to juxtapose the theme of recovery and regeneration (associated with Tayo and Ts'eh's work together at Dripping Springs) with its antithesis, the Ck'o'yo medicine and its practitioners: the caves at Dripping

Springs can be home to either and to both, just as the body of Laguna story contains both.[17]

APPENDIX A

Mapping the Embedded Texts

Embedded text vs. prose narrative

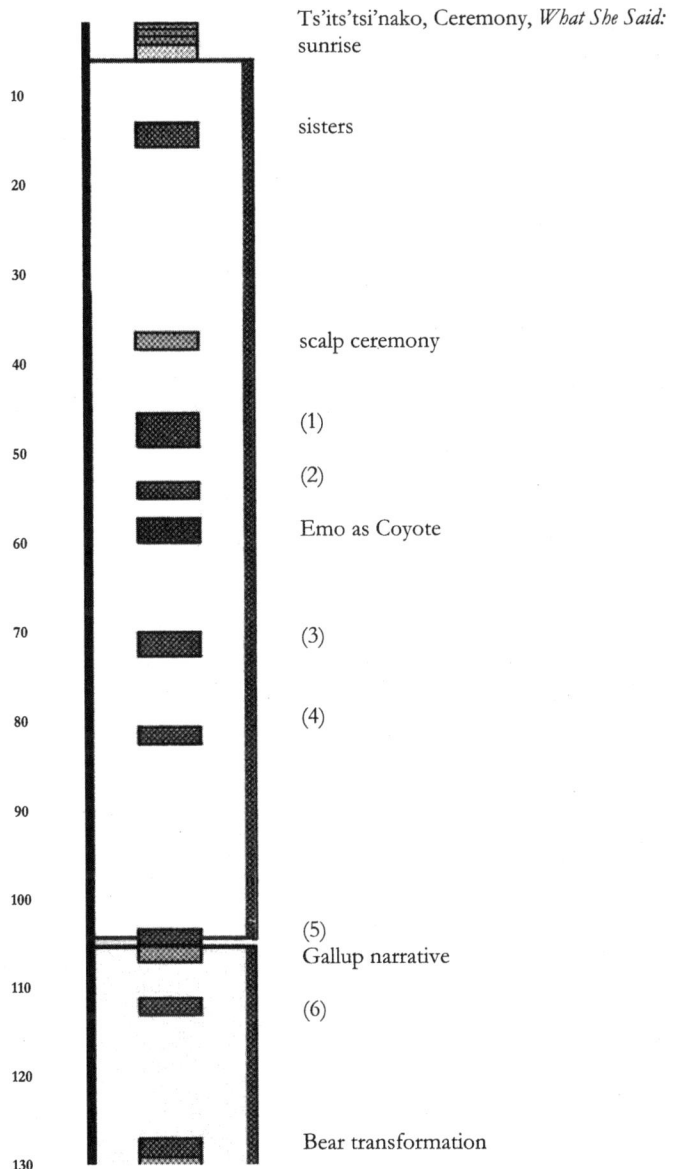

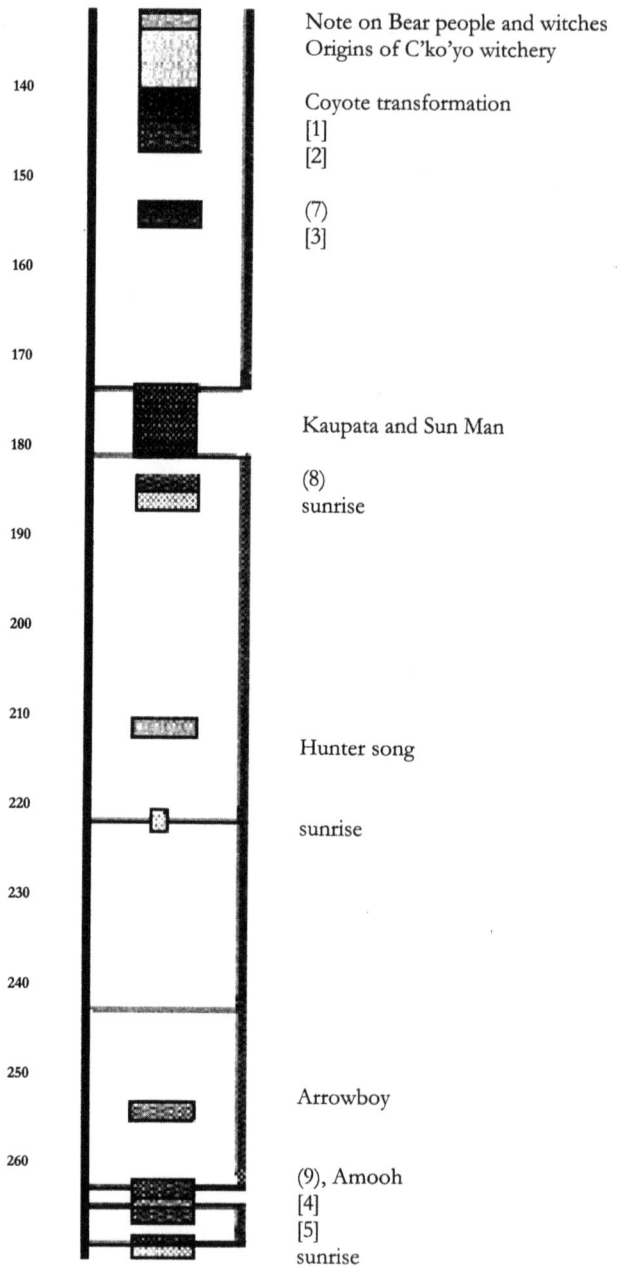

Note on Bear people and witches
Origins of C'ko'yo witchery

Coyote transformation
[1]
[2]

(7)
[3]

Kaupata and Sun Man

(8)
sunrise

Hunter song

sunrise

Arrowboy

(9), Amooh
[4]
[5]
sunrise

Appendix A 141

Acoma, Laguna, and Cañoncito Reservations

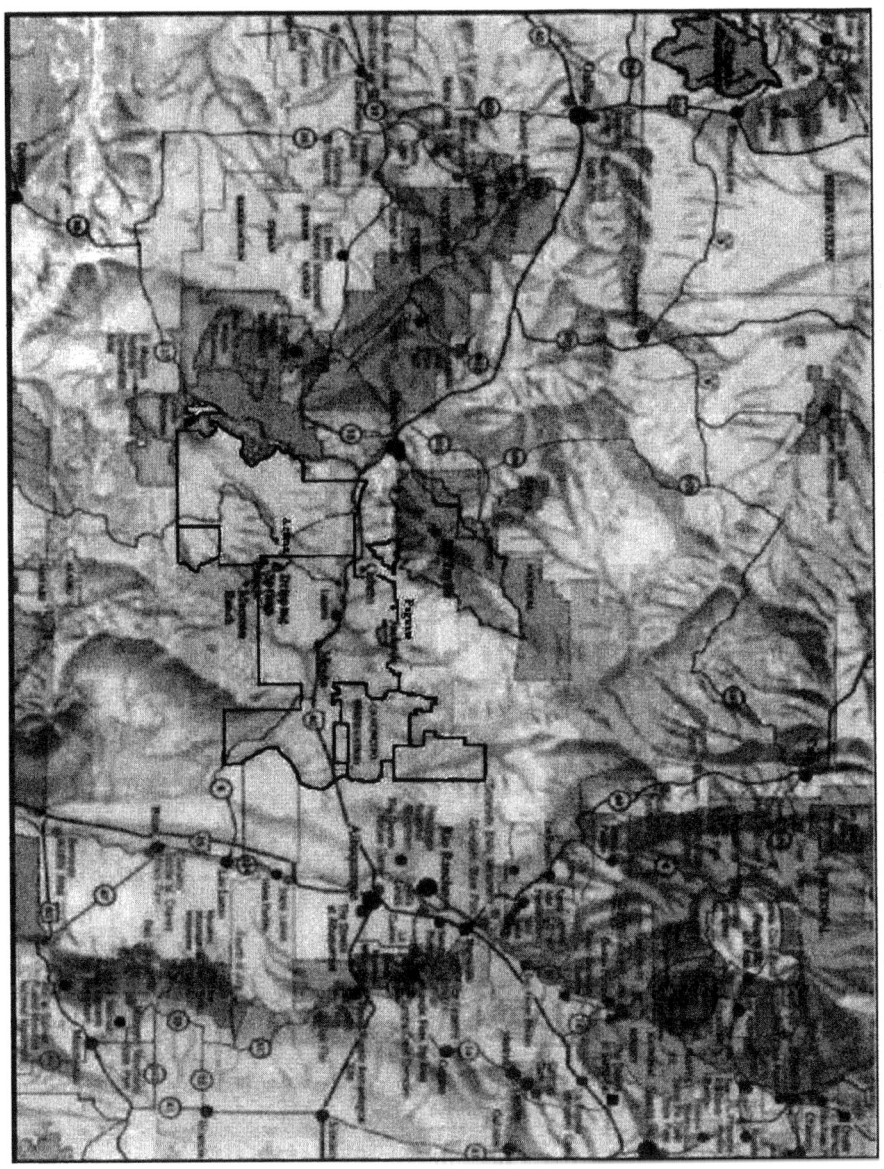

Laguna Sites Referred to in the Novel

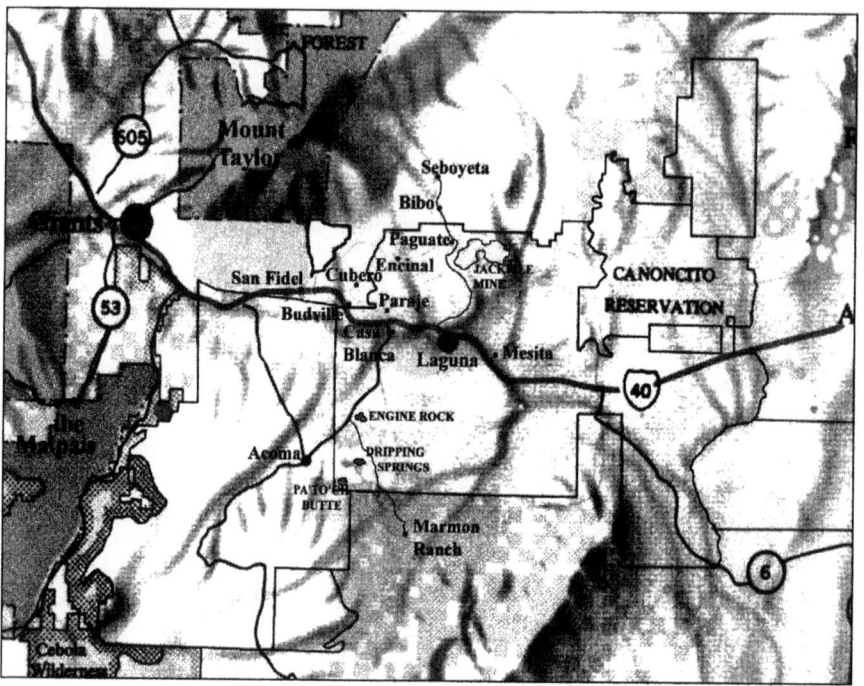

APPENDIX B

Laguna Sisters: Parallel Passages from Silko's *Ceremony* and Gunn's *Schat-chen*

(Silko, *Ceremony* 13–14 [also *Storyteller* 158–59])

It was summertime
and Iktoa'ak'o'ya-Reed Woman
was always taking a bath.
She spent all day long
sitting in the river
splashing down
the summer rain.

But her sister
Corn Woman
worked hard all day
sweating in the sun
getting sore hands
in the corn field.
Corn Woman got tired of that
she got angry
she scolded
her sister
for bathing all day long.

Iktoa'ak'o'ya-Reed Woman
went away then
she went back
to the original place
down below.

And there was no more rain then.
Everything dried up
all the plants
the corn
the beans
they all dried up
and started blowing away
in the wind.

The people and the animals
were thirsty.
They were starving.

[Gunn, "Ko-pot Ka-nat" in *Schat-chen* 115]

I-ye-ti-ko and her sister, I-sto-a-ko-ya, lived in the Kush Kut-ret of the southwest. I-sto-a-ko-ya was in the habit of bathing in the big water. This she did almost continually, and it sorely tried the patience of her sister, so that one day I-ye-ti-ko scolded her because of it. This angered I-sto-a-ko-ya and she went back to Ship-op.

Now it was because of the fact that I-sto-a-ko-a was almost constantly in the water that the rain fell at Kush Kut-ret. When she had gone the rains stopped, everything became parched and dry and Kush Kut-ret was threatened with famine. I-ye-ti-ko, who divined the cause of the drouth, repenting of her harshness to her sister and fearful I-sto-a-ko-ya had been overcome by hunger and had died, sent a blue-bottle fly to find her.

APPENDIX C

Kaupata: A Sample of Parallel Passages from Silko's *Ceremony* and Boas's *Keresan Texts*

(Silko 170–76)

Up North
around Reedleaf Town
there was this Ck'o'yo magician
they called Kaup'a'ta or the Gambler.
...
But the people didn't know.
They ate the blue cornmeal
he offered them.
They didn't know
he mixed human blood with it.
...
And one time
he even captured the stormclouds.
He won everything from them
but since they can't be killed,
all he could do
was lock them up
in four rooms of his house
...
The Sun is their father.
Every morning he wakes them up.
But one morning he went
first to the north top of the west mountain
then to the west top of the south mountain
and then to the south top of the east mountain;
and finally, it was on the east top of the north mountain
he realized they were gone.
For three years the stormclouds disappeared
while the Gambler held them prisoners.
The land was drying up
the people and animals were starving.
...
Go ahead
gamble with him.
Let him think he has you too.
Then he will make you his offer—
your life for a chance to win everything:
even his life.
He will say
"What do I have hanging in that leather bag
on my east wall?"
You say "Maybe some shiny pebbles,"
then you pause a while and say "Let me think."
Then guess again,
say "Maybe some mosquitoes."

(Boas, "Ka͡up'a·tɑ'" 76–82)

Long ago. — Eh. — long ago there in the northwest region at Reed-Leaf-Town, there lived a man. Thus was his name, Ka͡up'at·ɑ'. And so always every day he gambled.

...and also there in a room in the east there dead bodies were hanging down. Always blood was dripping down. Therefore red cornmeal piled on a dish all mixed with blood he gave them to eat.

Then at that time from Ca'k'ak' and Cu'isi and all the (other) storm clouds, from everyone he won clothing and their storm clouds and also Ma'yɛt'cinɑ's and Cui'Tɾɑⁱ's storm clouds and their clothing, all were lost. Then for this reason in four rooms he locked them up, because not in any way could he kill them, for they were storm clouds.

Then for three years never clouds came up and also it never rained. Then, therefore, the earth and the whole ground cracked. Then there in the east at KOaikʻᵃtc', the Sun-Youth spoke thus, "I wonder why it is never raining," said the Sun-Youth. "In general every morning I awaken the storm clouds. From here I go to the north top of the west mountain and also to the west top of the south mountain and also to the south top of the east mountain and from here to the east top of the north mountain. There I always wake up the storm clouds," said the Sun-Youth.

"Then also this I will tell you," said she, "If you bet everything then Ka͡up'a·tɑ'-Man will say to you, 'What have I above on the east wall?' thus Ka͡up'a·tɑ'-Man will say. Then you will say, 'I wonder what,' thus you will say. Then again a little while you will think. Then you will say, 'Maybe beads,' you will say. Again you will say, 'I wonder I what,' you will say. 'I guess pebbles,' you will say. Then again he says thus, 'What have I up there?'" thus she said. "Then again you will say, 'I wonder what, — maybe honey-bees.' Then again he will speak for the last time. Then you will say, 'Oh, I think the Pleiades.' Then Ka͡up'at·ɑ" will say, 'Heheya',"

He'll begin to rub his flint blade and say
"This is your last chance."
But this time you will guess
"The Pleiades!"
He'll jump up and say "Heheya'! You are the first
to guess."
Next he will point to a woven cotton bag
hanging on the south wall.
He will say
"What is it I have in there?"
You'll say
"Could it be some bumblebees?"
He'll laugh and say "No!"
"Maybe some butterflies, the small yellow kind."
"Maybe some tiny black ants," you'll say.
"No!" Kaup'a'ta will be smiling then.
"This is it," he'll say.
But this is the last time, Grandson,
you say "Maybe you have Orion in there."
And then
everything—
his clothing, his beads, his heart
and the rainclouds
will be yours."
...
"Heheya'! You guessed right!
Take this black flint knife, Sun Man,
go ahead, cut out my heart, kill me."
Kaup'a'ta lay down on the floor
with his head toward the east.
But Sun Man knew Kaup'a'ta was magical
and he couldn't be killed anyway.
Kaup'a'ta was going to lie there
and pretend to be dead.
So Sun Man knew what to do:
He took the flint blade
and he cut out the Gambler's eyes
He threw them into the south sky
and they became the horizon stars of autumn.

thus he will say. 'Never anybody told me like this,' Kaupʻa·taʼ will say. Again he will ask you. There above in the south is something that is inside. Kaupʻa·taʼ will say, 'What is up there on the east wall that I have?' thus he will say. Then you on your part will say, 'I wonder what it may be that he keeps up there?' thus you will say. For a little while you will think. Then you will say, 'Maybe bumble-bees,' you will say. 'No, it isn't that,' Kaupʻa·taʼ will say. Then again you will say, 'Maybe butterflies,' you will say. Then again for the last time Kaupʻa·taʼ will say. 'No, not that;' and again you will say, 'Maybe these are ants,' you will say. 'No, not that,' Kaupʻa·taʼ will say, and so for the last time he will speak. Then you will say 'Maybe, the Orion,' you will say," said Old-Woman-Spider-Woman. "And then everything, his clothing, the storm clouds and his heart you will win," thus said Old-Woman-Spider-Woman.

"Heheya'! heheya'!" said Kaupʻa·taʼ.... "Now go ahead, kill me," said he. "You will take the yellow knife." Then Sun-Youth took it. Then Kaupʻa·taʼ there to the east lay down on his back. Then Sun-Youth sat down there. For a while he thought what he would do to him. Then Sun-Youth spoke thus, "I wonder, am I going to kill him?" said he. Then he was looking at his face and his body. After a while spoke Sun-Youth, "It comes to this. Let me take out his eyes," said he. "Presently then up to the north let me throw them," said he. "because he has supernatural power," said Sun-Youth. Then he took the flint knife. Then one eye he took out and again the other eye he took out. Then (up) went out Sun-Youth. Then Kaupʻa·taʼ's eyes southward he threw up. Then Kaupʻa·taʼ's eyes became stars.

APPENDIX D

Pacayanyi: A Sample of Parallel Passages from Silko's *Ceremony* and Boas's *Keresan Texts*

(Silko 46–49)

One time
Old Woman K'yo's
son came in
from Reedleaf town
up north.
His name was Pa'caya'nyi
and he didn't know who his father was.

He asked the people
"You people want to learn some magic?"
and the people said
"Yes, we can always use some."

Ma'see'wi and Ou'yu'ye'wi
the twin brothers
were caring for the
mother corn altar,
but they got interested
in this magic too.

"What kind of medicine man
are you,
anyway?" they asked him.
"A Ck'o'yo medicine man,"
he said.
"Tonight we'll see
if you really have magical power," they told him.

So that night
Pa'caya'nyi
came with his mountain lion.
He undressed
he painted his body
the whorls of flesh
the soles of his feet
the palms of his hands
the top of his head.
He wore feathers
on each side of his head

He made an altar
with cactus spines
and purple locoweed flowers.

(Boas, "*P'acaya·'nʸi.*" 13–14)

... after some time there arrived Old-Woman Ckʻoˑ'yo's child. And from the northwest region he came. Mountain-Lion-Man he brought with him.... "Where do you come from?"[the Chief] said to him. "Yes," he said, "I am P'acaya·'nʸi," thus he said to him. "Who is your mother?" said he to him. Then he said, "Ckʻoˑ'yo, she is my mother," said he. "And who is your father?" said he. "I do not know," said he.... Then, "Let me ask you. Do you want someone of magical power?" thus he said to him. — "Yes," said the Chief, "that is what I want. — Indeed, really one of supernatural power I want," thus said the Chief. "Indeed?" said P'acaya·'nʸi.

Long ago Ma·'sɛɛ·wi and Uyu·'yɛ·wi his brother from the place of emergence upward came out. Then the sacred ear of corn and the altar they watched, because they were very brave, therefore it belonged to them, to Ma·'sɛɛ·wi and his brother Uyu·'yɛ·wi.... Ma·'sɛɛ·wi and his brother Uyu·'yɛ·wi verily always took care of their mother Altar and the sacred ear of corn.

Then spoke Ma·'sɛɛ·wi, "Who are you, man? Where do you come from?" said he. "From the northwest," said P'acaya·'nʸi, and in the northwest region from Reed-Leaf-House, there I come from," said P'acaya·'nʸi. "Who is your father?" said he to him. "I don't know," said he. "But who is your mother?" said he to him. "Old-Woman-Ckʻoˑ'yo, she is my mother," said he. "Is that so?" said Ma·'sɛɛ·wi. Then spoke again P'a'cayanʸi, "I came here," said P'acaya·'nʸi, "maybe, indeed, you want some man of magical power," thus said P'acaya·'nʸi. "Yes," said Ma·'sɛɛ·wi, "what kind of a shaman are you?" Thus he said, "I am Ckʻo'yo shaman," thus said P'acaya·'nʸi. "Indeed?" said Ma·'sɛɛ·wi. "Then tonight we shall see you," thus he said to him, "(to see) if you have really magical power," thus he said to him.

Then some time (P'acaya·'nʸi) went there with his Mountain-Lion.... Then P'acaya·'nʸi undressed. He took off his shirt and took off his trousers. Then next he put feathers on each side of his head and also he painted himself.[2] [Boas's note: "He put on the paint of the shaman on the front and back of his body, on the soles of his feet, on the palms of his hands and on the crown of his head."] Then he painted his head.

He lighted four cactus torches
at each corner.
He made the mountain lion lie
down in front and
then he was ready for his magic.

He struck the middle of the north wall
He took a piece of flint and
he struck the middle of the north wall.
Water poured out of the wall
and flowed down
toward the south.

He said "What does that look like?
Is that magic power?"
He struck the middle of the west wall
and from the east wall
a bear came out.
"What do you call this?"
he said again.
"Yes, it looks like magic all right,"
Ma'see'wi said.
So it was finished
and Ma'see'wi and Ou'yu'ye'wi
and all the people were fooled by
that Ck'o'yo medicine man,
Pa'caya'nyi.

...

Our mother
Nau'ts'ity'i
was very angry
over this
over the way
all of them
even Ma'see'wi and Ou'yu'ye'wi
fooled around with this
magic.

"I've had enough of that,"
she said,
"If they like that magic so much
let them live off it."

So she took
the plants and grass from them.
No baby animals were born.
She took the
rainclouds with her.

Then he lighted in four places cactus (torches). Then again he put down the altars, candelabra cactus spines and tuna spines and Jameson weed. "Enough," said P'acaya·´nʸi. Then there in front he made lie down his Mountain-Lion. Then he was ready for his magic work.

Flint he took up. Next there he struck the north wall of the house, the middle of the wall. There south downward came out water. "Have I magical power?" said he to him. Again to the west he came and next there in the west he struck it. Then there eastward a bear came out. "Have I no supernatural power?" said he to him. "Indeed, it is true," said Ma·´sɛɛ·wi. "Enough," said Ma·´sɛɛ·wi. "That is all," said he. Thus Ma·´sɛɛ·wi and his brother Uyu·´yɛ·wi were deceived by P'acaya·´nʸi, the Ck'o·´yo shaman. Then it was finished. From that time (forward) on Holding-Prayer-Stick's, the Chief's people, those who were shamans, were entirely deceived by the Ck'o·´yo shaman, P'acaya·´nʸi. Thus it was that Ma·´sɛɛ·wi and his brother Uyu·´yɛ·wi made trouble long ago. From that time on they were very bad, both of them.

(Boas 223)
Then the cïts'Ma·´sɛɛ·wi and the War Captains entered, followed by P'acaya·´nʸi. He took his flint knife and stabbed the north side of the house. Immediately water rushed out of it. Then he stabbed the west wall and a bear came out.

(Boas, "*P'acaya·´nʸi.*" 13–15)
Then there below our mother was very angry. She spoke thus, "Enough," said she. "My children make all trouble for themselves. I will punish them. For four years I shall hide all cultivated plants," thus she said. Then she hid everything and from that time on the next year the people tried to plant something, but for a long time there was no rain, and on account of this the people starved.

(Boas 223)
Then the War Captain called all the shamans to assemble. He said, "Mothers and fathers, what is going to happen? What are you going to choose? Are you going to follow Our Mother Nau´ts'ïtʸ'i's shamans or are you going to follow the ways of P'acaya·´nʸi?" Then all the shamans said they would accept P'acaya·´nʸi's teachings. This was the cause of great trouble because Our Mother became angry; for they had not obeyed her commands. For a long time there was a drought and they had nothing to eat.

APPENDIX E

Hummingbird: A Sample of Parallel Passages from Silko's *Ceremony* and Boas's *Keresan Texts*

(Silko 53–54)

The wind stirred the dust.
The people were starving.

"She's angry with us,"
    the people said.
"Maybe because of that
    Ck'o'yo magic
    we were fooling with.
We better send someone
    to ask our forgiveness."

They noticed hummingbird
    was fat and shiny
    he had plenty to eat.
They asked how come he
    looked so good.

He said
Down below
Three worlds below this one
    everything is
        green
all the plants are growing
the flowers are blooming.
    I go down there
        and eat.

"So that's where our mother went.
How can we get down there?"

Hummingbird looked at all the
    skinny people.
He felt sorry for them.
He said, "You need a messenger.
    Listen, I'll tell you
    what to do":

Bring a beautiful pottery jar
painted with parrots and big flowers.
Mix black mountain dirt
some sweet corn flour
    and a little water.

Cover the jar with a
new buckskin
and say this over the jar

(Boas, "The Hummingbird" 11)

Long ago. — Eh. — Long ago at White-House they lived. Then the shamans took each their means of working their art, and on top of their house in the east they danced. Then our mother Nau´ts'it'ⁱi hid from them entirely the food for seven years. Then it happened so that they called a meeting. They here discussed where they might find again our mother.

Then in the middle of the south wall above, Hummingbird-Boy stayed at night. Then they asked him, "Where from, behold, do you eat? Always you have enough to eat." — "Do you wish for it?" — "Yes," said all the shamans and chiefs and war chiefs, and all [the others].

Then spoke thus Hummingbird, "There in the fourth place in the earth there is our mother." — "Then how will she look to us again, — and her food and her body?"

(Boas 226)
In the south wall there was a hole and every evening the humming bird came in through this hole. He always looked well but they did not know how he obtained food. Finally they asked him where he was obtaining food. He replied, "It is too difficult for you; I go to Nau´ts'it'ⁱi." They asked him, "Where is she?" He replied, "She is in the fourth world, below." And they asked, "How can we go there?" He said, "You will have to create a large fly (iwa·pa·´ctⁱ). Tell Yellow-Woman to rub cuticle off from her knee and give it to you." Then they sent the War Captain to ask Yellow-Woman to rub cuticle off from her knee. She complied with his request and she gave a small ball to the War Chief. They put it into a new jar which was covered with buckskin. Soon something began to move inside. A buzzing sound was heard and when the jar was opened they found the fly....

(Boas, "The Hummingbird" 11–13)
— "Find a chief's daughter. From her knee take dirt. Then you will bring it here to me; then also a jar and a

and sing this softly
above the jar:
After four days
you will be alive
After four days
you will be alive
After four days
you will be alive
After four days
you will be alive

(Silko 82)

    On the fourth day
something buzzed around
      inside the jar.

They lifted the buckskin
   and a big green fly
with yellow feelers on his head
    flew out of the jar.

"Fly will go with me," Hummingbird said.
      "We'll go see
    what she wants."

They flew to the fourth world
       below.
      Down there
was another kind of daylight
  everything was blooming
     and growing
everything was so beautiful.

(Silko 105–06)

    Fly started sucking on
      sweet things so
Hummingbird had to tell him
       to wait:
"Wait until we see our mother."
     They found her.
They gave her blue pollen and yellow pollen
  they gave her turquoise beads
   they gave her prayer sticks.

"I suppose you want something," she said.
"Yes, we want food and storm clouds."
  "You get old Buzzard to purify
     your town first
and then, maybe, I will send you people
    food and rain again."

    Fly and Hummingbird
      flew back up.

new buckskin. Then down you will put it into it." Then (down) they put it into it."

After some time Fly [Boas's note: "A large greenish fly with yellow antennae, on cantaloupe vines"] became alive. It arrived in one place after another. "For what am I needed here?" — "Hummingbird and you will go to the fourth earth below. Then take these beads and prayer sticks and pollen, " — "Give these to us," they said. Then all blew on them (on the beads, prayer sticks and pollen). "Now let us go," said the two.

Then the two went, that way down there to the fourth world below. When they arrived, there was another daylight. There eastward they went. How beautiful everything, — corn stalks and wheat and water melons, — everything they saw.

The Fly was going to eat. He was stopping in places and honey he was sucking. Then spoke Hummingbird, "Don't, — let us first meet our mother." — "All right," said he. Then they met our mother. Then they conserved [sic] with her. "Here are pollen and beads and prayer sticks. We brought them here."

— "I suppose you want something." — "Yes, we want food and your body and storm clouds." — "Well," she said, "first up above on the cast wall Old-Turkey-Buzzard you will meet. First he will purify above towards the south down and above towards the east down and above towards the north down and above towards the west down, he will purify." — "All right," they said, " let us go ahead." Then the two went. Then, when they arrived there they said, "How are things"? — "It is good. Did you come here?" — "Yes," they

Appendix E 151

    They told the town people
that old Buzzard had to purify
        the town

(Silko 113)
    They took more pollen,
more beads, and more prayer sticks,
and they went to see old Buzzard.

They arrived at his place in the east.
      "Who's out there?
Nobody ever came here before."
  "It's us, Hummingbird and Fly."
    "Oh. What do you want?"
"We need you to purify our town."
"Well, look here. Your offering isn't
  complete. Where's the tobacco?"

  (You see, it wasn't easy.)
    Fly and Hummingbird
had to fly back to town again.

(Silko 151–52)
     The people asked,
    "Did you find him?"
"Yes, but we forgot something,
      Tobacco."
  But there was no tobacco
so Fly and Hummingbird had to fly
    all the way back down
   to the fourth world below
  to ask our mother where
  they could get some tobacco.

   "We came back again,"
   they told our mother.
"Maybe you need something?"
      "Tobacco."
   "Go ask caterpillar."

(Silko 180)
     So they flew
  all the way up again.
They went to a place in the West

(See, these things were complicated....)
  They called outside his house
"You downstairs, how are things?"
  "Okay," he said, "come down."
    They went down inside.
  "Maybe you want something?"
   "Yes. We need tobacco."

said. — "What did you find out?" — "Oh, first above on the east wall meet Old-Turkey-Buzzard that he may purify [the town]." — "Indeed?" they said, "go ahead."

Then they took pollen and beads and prayersticks and there up they went. There they arrived and there inside he was. Then the two said, "You, inside, how are things?" — "It is well. Who is this? Nobody has ever been walking here." — "We are Hummingbird and Fly." — "Indeed, what do you want?"

— "We want you to purify the people and the earth and the thunder clouds." — "Indeed? Wait a while. Your offering is not complete. There is no tobacco." — "Is that so? Let us go." They went down. "Let us go," they said. "Go along," they were told. Then down they went.

When they arrived there they were asked, "Did you meet Old-Turkey-Buzzard? —" "Yes," they said, "it was not complete what we took there." — "And what more was needed?" — "Tobacco." — "That is it. Then where shall we find it?" — "To our mother go again." — "Let us go." Then they went. Down there they arrived in the fourth world. There was another daylight.

They met our mother. "We have come back here." — "Maybe you want something." — "Yes," they said, for tobacco asked us Turkey-Buzzard. Where are we going to find it?" — "There in the southwest above, there on a hill, there right in the middle is a doorway. There Caterpillar lives. Him you will ask for tobacco." — "Permit us to go. Let us go" — "Go ahead," she said to them.

Then there west they went. There in the west they arrived.

When they came to the edge they said, "You downstairs, how are things?" — "It is well. Come down." — "Indeed, we will go (down)." — "Indeed, now sit down. Maybe you want something?" — "Yes," they said, it is tobacco we want." — "Then I will give it to you." Then down he spread corn husks. There on them he wiped off [his hands]. Then tobacco came off

Caterpillar spread out dry corn husks on the floor. He rubbed his hands together and tobacco fell into the corn husks. Then he folded up the husks and gave the tobacco to them.	from them. Then he gave it to them.
(Silko 255–56) Hummingbird and Fly thanked him. They took the tobacco to old Buzzard. "Here it is. We finally got it but it sure wasn't very easy." "Okay," Buzzard said "Go back and tell them I'll purify the town."	After they had taken it they said, "Let us go." — "Go ahead," said he to them. Then up they went. They came out above and they entered the kiva. "Did you find it?" — "Yes," they said. "Indeed, it is well." Then they divided it and one half they took to Old-Turkey-Buzzard. There above they arrived. "We have come again." — "Indeed?" — "We have found tobacco." — "Indeed, it is well. Now I shall purify [the town].
And he did— first to the east then to the south then to the west and finally to the north. Everything was set straight again after all that ck'o'yo' magic.	… Then he purified first from the south down; afterwards from the east down; afterwards from the north down; and afterwards from the west down.
The storm clouds returned the grass and plants started growing again. There was food and the people were happy again.	Then everything could become clear all around; storm clouds, crops and happiness there around was spread. Then was renewed the food. They saw it again.
So she told them "Stay out of trouble from now on.	Then our mother said, "Do not from now on in the future make trouble." Thus our mother gave instructions in olden times long ago.
It isn't very easy to fix up things again. Remember that next time some ck'o'yo magician comes to town"	

APPENDIX F

Arrowboy/Estoy-eh-muut: Parallel Passages from Silko, Lummis, Gunn, and Boas

(Silko, *Ceremony* 247)

Arrowboy got up after she left.
He followed her into the hills
up where the caves were.
The others were waiting.
They held the hoop
and danced around the fire
four times.
The witchman stepped through the hoop
he called out that he would be a wolf.
His head and upper body became hairy like a wolf
But his lower body was still human.
"Something is wrong," he said.
"Ck'o'yo magic won't work
if someone is watching us."

(Silko, "Estoy-eh-moot and the Kunideeyahs" 247)

Estoy-eh-muut followed her
wondering where Kochinninako was going
in the middle of the night.
He followed her north
far from the village
to a place in the hills
where there are many caves
in the sandstone cliffs.
...
Let's go ahead with our meeting,"
the leader of the Kunideeyah said.
"Each one of you will go under
this cottonwood bow and say
which animal form you want to take."

"I want to be a bear,"
the first one said
going under the cottonwood bow.
"I want to be a crow,"
said the second one.

Nothing happened.
"something is wrong,"
the leader said.
"Kochinninako, go and see
if an outsider is spying on us."

(Lummis, "The Sobbing Pine" 196)

Ees-tée-ah Muts crept softly up and peered in [to their cave]. He saw a great firelit room full of witches in the shapes of ravens and vultures, wolves and other animals of ill omen. They were gathered about their feast and were enjoying themselves greatly, eating and dancing and singing and planning evil to mankind.

For a long time Ees-tée-ah Muts watched them, but at last one caught sight of his face peering in at the hole.

"Bring him in!" shouted the chief witch, and many of them rushed out and surrounded him and dragged him into the cave.

(Gunn, "Yo-A-Schi-Moot and the Kun-Ni-Te-Ya" 197)

[the Ho-chin – chief – announces] "We will now proceed with our ceremonies. I will cause the rainbow to appear." In lieu of the rainbow a large hoop is started rolling and members wishing to change their shape must jump through the revolving ring at the same time making a wish. "You will each and all walk under it and, by merely willing it, assume whatever shape of animal you may choose."

The rainbow appeared at his command, and, one by one, the Kun-ni-te-ya passed under it. The transformation hoped for did not take place. Those who expected to assume the forms of animals still remained men and women. They all marveled greatly at the failure of the magic that had ever before been so potent.

"Hold," cried the Ho-Chin. "There is a spy, an unbeliever in our midst. We must find him. Search the cave."

(Boas, "The Witches and Arrow-Youth" 132)

...After a while the chief said, "Now let us be ready to work," thus said he. "Go ahead," said they [witches]. Then they made ready. "What are you going to become?" (said he). After a while a bow was put up between them. Then the chief said, "Four at a time and two at a time shall go together," thus said he. "Then first two wolves shall go out under there," thus said the chief. Then the two arose and went under (the bow) but they did not entirely put on the wolf shirt. The

Kochinninako went out
as she was ordered and
there she found Estoy-eh-muut,
her husband,
creeping around the cave.
This was why the magic
had not worked.

lower halves of their bodies remained human. Then the chief of the witches said, "Yellow-Woman," said he. "Hey," said she. "Maybe your husband, Arrow-Youth, is looking on," thus said he. "I don't know," said Yellow-Woman. "He was already asleep," thus she said. "Indeed?" said the chief. "Go ahead again and try." Then the two tried again, and again they did not put on the wolf shirt. Then said the chief, "Probably Arrow-Youth came here," thus said he.

APPENDIX G

Navajo Pretexts: Parallel Passages from Silko and Wyman

(Silko 139–41)

His mother-in-law suspected something.
She smelled coyote piss one morning.
She told her daughter.
She figured Coyote was doing this.
She knew her son-in-law was missing.

There was no telling what Coyote had done to him.
Four of them went to track the man.
They tracked him to the place he found deer tracks.
They found the place the deer was arrow-wounded
where the man started chasing it.
Then they found the place where Coyote got him.

Sure enough those coyote tracks went right along there
Right around the marks in the sand where the man lay.

The human tracks went off
toward the mountain
where the man must have crawled.
They followed the tracks to a hard oak tree
where he had spent a night.
From there he had crawled some distance farther
and slept under a scrub oak tree.
Then his tracks went to a piñon tree
and then under the juniper where he slept another night.

The tracks went on and on
but finally they caught up with him
sleeping under the wild rose bush.
"What happened? Are you the one
who left four days ago, my grandchild?"
A coyote whine was the only sound he made.
"Four days ago you left,
are you that one, my grandchild?"
The man tried to speak
but only a coyote sound was heard,
and the tail moved back and forth
sweeping ridges in the sand.
He was suffering from thirst and hunger
he was almost too weak to raise his head.
But he nodded his head "yes."

"This is him all right,
but what can we do to save him?"

(Wyman 131–33)

On the morning of the fourth night he left again. So she entered her mother's home. But when she warmed up, she clearly smelled of coyote urine. "So it is Coyote doing this, I see! Where is the place in which he has not yet schemed! From that time on it did not seem right to me!" the old woman said. "Suppose now, that you begin to track the young man from the place he left four days ago! There is no telling what he has done to him! He certainly did not leave him unharmed!" they said. At once four of them set out to track him. And they tracked him to the spot where he had found the deer tracks, then where it had been arrowwounded, then where he had given it chase. Then they followed him up to the point where Coyote had waylaid him and, sure enough, coyote tracks led along there. The signs were unmistakable that the man had lain there.

And from there on a human track led off, while the other way, towards the mountain, the person must have crawled. So they followed this track some distance and found that he had crawled below a hard oak, where evidently he had spent the night. From here he had crawled farther on below an oak tree, where again he had spent the night. From here he had crawled some distance farther under a pinyon tree, where he had spent the night. Again they found that he had crawled on until he had reached a juniper, below which he had spent another night. Then he had crawled on until he had crawled below a wild rose bush. There they overtook and found him lying below the wild rose bush. Here Talking God came and stood before him. "What has happened? Are you the person who left four days ago, my grandchild?" he asked him. Perhaps he would have replied, but a coyote sound alone was heard, the person's tail only twirled, digging a hole in the ground. He certainly was a sight, he was found suffering with thirst and hunger, and apparently in a very critical condition. He then repeated the same question, "Are you the one, my grandchild, that left here four days ago?" A coyote whine only was the answer. Again he repeated the same question, "Four days ago you left here, are you that one, my grandchild?" he repeated. Again a coyote only answered him. "Four days ago you left us, are you the one, my grandchild? We have missed you!" he said to him. Again a coyote whine alone was heard, he only shook his head in consent, they say.

"Truly it is he!" they said. "How now? What shall be done? Go ahead, you who are fleet of foot, quickly

They ran to the holy places
they asked what might be done.
"At the summit of Dark Mountain
ask the four old Bear People.
They are the only possible hope

they have the power to restore the mind.
Time and again
it has been done."

Big Fly went to tell them.
The old Bear People said they would come
They said
Prepare hard oak
scrub oak
piñon
juniper and wild rose twigs
Make hoops
tie bundles of weeds into hoops.
Make four bundles
tie them with yucca
spruce mixed with charcoal from burned weeds
snakeweed and gramma grass and rock sage.
Make four bundles.

The rainbows were crossed.
They had been his former means of travel.
Their purpose was
to restore this to him.

They made Pollen Boy right in the center of
the white corn painting.
His eyes were blue pollen
his mouth was blue pollen
his neck was too
There were pinches of blue pollen
at his joints.

(Silko 141–42]
He sat in the center of the white corn sand painting. The rainbows crossed were in the painting behind him. Betonie's helper scraped the sand away and buried the bottoms of the hoops in little trenches so that they were standing up and spaced apart, with the hard oak closest to him and the wild rose hop in front of the door. The old man painted a dark mountain range beside the farthest hoop, the next, closer, he painted blue, and moving toward him, he knelt and made the yellow mountains; and in front of him, Betonie painted the white mountain range.

The helper worked in the shadows beyond the dark mountain range; he worked with the black sand, making bear prints side by side. Along the right side

spread the news in the holy places!" was said. This they did, and from these places they met here. "What in your opinion shall be done? Here your young man is lying!" they said. "Yonder, beyond Hesperus Peak, at the summit of a place called Dark Mountain, is the home of four elders who belong to the Bear People. These, possibly, offer the only hope. They have hoops called once-they-are-to-be-seen, they have footprint figures, they have sitting place figures, they have hand place prints with power to restore the mind time and again; notify them!" was suggested.

Immediately Big Fly sped away. The elders arrived here in full number. "It is only this, that this happened herein some manner. That accounts for the news being sent to you." And the story of how it had happened was related to them. "All right, we shall do as you wish! Bring some hard oak, also some ordinary oak, pinyon, juniper, and wild rose twigs!" Immediately they went to work on their preparation, and robes were spread for the hoops as they were being made. And the first one in the set was provided with a forehead, the next one was made with its forehead cut at an angle, another was provided with a forehead, another with its forehead cut at an angle, while the wild rose twig was left untrimmed. Bundles of weeds were placed in four places and tied to them with yucca, namely, spruce and burned-mixture-weeds (mixed charcoal), that is, snakeweed, grama grass and rock sage (for the four bundles). That completed the preparations.

Then a sandpainting was made inside the hogan. Rainbows lying in cross form only were made, because these had been his former traveling means and their purpose was to restore his travel means to him. At a point beyond where the hoops were to be placed the white corn sandpainting also was made, similar to a sun figure, inside of which Pollen Boy was drawn with pollen. Blue pollen was used for his eyes and mouth and the same for his neck. At the various joints too, pinches of it were strewn.

(Wyman 133–34)
After that, on this side of it, (small trenches) were dug in which the hoops were to stand, with spaces left between them. The hoops were then lined up at a distance from the hogan and at the end farthest from the hoops, a dark mountain range was placed. The next range this side of it was blue, the next range this way was yellow, and the next range white. Beyond the dark mountain range, coming from its rear, bear tracks were set in black, resting their feet side by side because he was to stand on these. On this side of them their paws were placed in blue. Next their footprints again were placed in yellow, and next to these their paws again in white. And, stringing over the mountain ranges just mentioned, a rainbow was strewn, which represented

Appendix G

of the bear footprints, the old man painted paw prints in blue, and then yellow, and finally white. They finished it together, with a big rainbow arching wide above all the mountain ranges. Betonie gave him a basket with prayer sticks to hold.

...

The helper stepped out from the shadows; he was grunting like a bear. He raised his head as if it were heavy for him, and he sniffed the air. He stood up and walked to Tayo; he reached down for the prayer sticks and spoke the words distinctly, pressing the sticks close to his heart. The old man came forward then and cut Tayo across the top of the head; it happened suddenly. He hadn't expected it, but the dark flint was sharp and the cut was short. They both reached for him then; lifting him up by the shoulders, they guided his feet into the bear footprints, and Betonie prayed him through each of the five hoops.

his former travelling means.... Then he (the patient) was placed upon the drawing in white corn mentioned before. There the talking prayersticks were laid upon him, while here inside, the turquoise arrow and white bead arrow were laid in a basket, and placed on the sandpainting here.

As soon as all was about ready a song was intoned inside to fetch him and, at mention of the proper words, he (Bear, the singer) started walking towards him, and continued so until he reached the patient. After applying the talking prayersticks to him he pressed them against his heart. "He certainly cannot be left in this condition! How can it be removed from him! Here, any of you that have knives, you that possess flint hand it here!" they said to each in turn. "I do not know, I have none, I know nothing of this particular way of doing things," they were saying. Whatever may be meant by it, the bird is called big wood snapper (?), in whose possession a dark flint was found. With this a diagonal crosscut was made at the top of the person's head. From there they supported him in walking to the said foot place prints, on top of which they placed his right foot, then his left one. Then a prayer was recited for him, the Bear's own prayer, although sometime in the past it used to be the Red Ant's prayer, but was exchanged with the Bear's prayer. This prayer proceeded on through the hoops, he was talked through the five hoops with it.

(Silko 142)
    In dangerous places you traveled
        in danger you traveled
    to a dangerous place you traveled
        in danger e-hey-ya-ah-na!

    To the place
where whirling darkness started its journey
    along the edges of the rocks
    along the places of the gentle wind
    along the edges of blue clouds
    along the edges of clear water.

Whirling darkness came up from the North
Whirling darkness moved along to the East
    It came along the South
    It arrived in the West
Whirling darkness spiraled downward
    and it came up in the Middle.

(Wyman 189)
En-e-ya-a-a-a, in a dangerous place you are traveling, in danger you travel, in a dangerous spot you are traveling.

(Wyman 144)
[from the sixth Thunder Prayer]
And beyond that, along places of gentle breezes,
    whirling darkness started out with its witchery.
And beyond that, along the edges of rocks,
    whirling darkness started out with its witchery.
And beyond that, along the ends of mountains,
    whirling darkness started out with its witchery.
And beyond that, along the ends of clouds,
    whirling darkness started out with its witchery.
And beyond that, along the ends of waters,
    whirling darkness started out with its witchery.

(Silko 143–44)

At the Dark Mountain
born from the mountain
walked along the mountain
I will bring you through my hoop,
I will bring you back.

Following my footprints
walk home
following my footprints
Come home, happily
return belonging to your home
return to long life and happiness again
return to long life and happiness.

At the Dark Mountain
born from the mountain
moves his hand along the mountain
I have left the zigzag lightning behind
I have left the straight lightning behind

I have the dew,
a sunray falls from me,
I was born from the mountain
I leave a path of wildflowers
A raindrop falls from me
I'm walking home
I'm walking back to belonging
I'm walking home to happiness
I'm walking back to long life.

When he passed through the last hoop
it wasn't finished
They spun him around sunwise
and he recovered
he stood up
The rainbows returned him to his
home, but it wasn't over.
All kinds of evil were still on him.

Silko 153)

The dry skin
was still stuck
to his body.
But the effects
of the witchery
of the evil thing
began to leave
his body.
The effects of the witchery
of the evil thing
in his surroundings
began to turn away.
It had gone a great distance
It had gone below the North.

(Wyman 134–36)
Bear's Prayer

At the Dark Mountain, who was reared in the mountain, who walks along the mountain, I have started through your red hoop! I have started through your dark hoop, I have started through your blue hoop, I have started through your yellow hoop, I have started through your white hoop, I have started through your sparkling (pink) hoop.

I have left on the foot place prints of white corn, I left on the trail of white corn.

In the rear recess of the white corn home zigzag lightning has dropped with me.

Happily I have returned to my home, happily I have returned belonging to my home, happily my home has become mine again.

...

At Dark Mountain, reared in the mountain, who moves his hand along the mountain, I have started out through your dark hoop. ("Red hoop" is omitted in this part which otherwise repeats the first part until): In the rear recess of the white corn home straight lightning has dropped with me (etc., until the end).

At Dark Mountain, reared within the mountain, who shoves the dew (etc., as in the first part, but "dark hoop" is omitted, and "sunray dropped with me" is substituted for "zigzag lightning" of the first part).

At Dark Mountain, reared within the mountain, who leaves a path walking over nice flowers (etc., as in the second part, but "rainray dropped with me" is pronounced here).

...

Of the Winds some spin sunwise, others spin sunward, but this later is not a good one," they said. So one of those that spin in the proper sun-wise direction went into him, and by means of this the person began to breathe again. ... When this had occurred the person stood up, but all kinds of evils were still on him. They then set out to return, and they arrived with him at the hogan. The rainbows which, as said, had been crossed diagonally, went below him; these dropped him at his home.

(Wyman 148)
[from the Hoop Prayer]

...the effects of the witchery of the wicked thing that used to exist in my surroundings have turned away from me, it has gone a great distance, therefore I say this, it has gone below the north therefore I say this.

(Silko 258)

> They unraveled
> the dead skin
> Coyote threw
> on him.
>
> They cut it up
> bundle by bundle.
>
> Every evil
> which entangled him
> was cut
> to pieces.

(Silko 260-61)

> Whirling darkness
> started its journey
> with its witchery
> and
> its witchery
> has returned upon it.
>
> Its witchery
> has returned
> into its belly.
>
> Its own witchery
> has returned
> all around it.
>
> Whirling darkness
> has come back on itself.
> It keeps all its witchery
> to itself.
>
> It doesn't open its eyes
> with its witchery.
>
> It has stiffened
> with the effects of its own witchery.
>
> It is dead for now.
> It is dead for now.
> It is dead for now.
> It is dead for now.

(Wyman 145–46)

Then five unravelings were made, which purposed to have the moving power straightened out again. These, of course, were made with snakeweed, grama grass, rock sage, red grass, with one feather of the bundle (brush) placed upon them. In accord with this, at a chant, (the patient) is pressed with them, one is unraveled at his soles, another at his knees, at his heart, at his mouth and at the top of his head ... and thus a one night ceremonial had been completed.

(Wyman 144)

[from the sixth Thunder Prayer]

And beyond that, on through the ends of the sky, whirling darkness entered here with its witchery.

And beyond that, at the trail on white earth, whirling darkness started out with its witchery.

And beyond that, where its brothers live, whirling darkness entered there with its witchery.

And beyond that, where its neighbors live, whirling darkness entered there with its witchery.

Then things, by which it wickedly bothered me in the past, by which it wickedly thought of me in the past, by which it wickedly spoke of me in the past, all of which it caused previously, when it has taken these out of me this day, its witchery has returned upon it, its witchery has killed it, its witchery has returned into its interior, its witchery has returned all around it, and now it keeps all of its witchery to itself, now it does not open its eyes with its witchery, now it does not say a word with its witchery, now it is stiffened with the effects of its witchery.

Now it is dead for good, now it is dead for good, now it is dead for good, now it is dead for good!

NOTES

CHAPTER 1: INTRODUCTION

1. For a good analysis of the history of the novel's reception, see Kenneth Roemer's "Silko's Arroyos as Mainstream."
2. The term Keres (sometimes spelled Queres) refers to the people of the two Western pueblos, Laguna and Acoma, as well as to the people of several of the Rio Grande pueblos (Santa Ana, San Felipe, Santo Domingo, Zia, and some of the inhabitants of Isleta); "Keresan" is the indigenous language of these pueblos.
3. "Oracy," a term coined by Andrew Wilkinson in 1965 to denote "general ability in the oral skills" (O.E.D.), is now frequently used by literary critics who deal with oral traditional materials to draw attention to the idea that cultural literacy (in E. D. Hirsch's sense of that term) may be measured in terms of not only how much of one's written traditions but also how much of one's oral traditions one is familiar with.
4. This apparent paradox is one of the most interesting formal features of Silko's formally intriguing text, and I try to address it throughout this study but especially in chapters 2 and 5.
5. This essay was first published in the 1976 issue of Ishmael Reed's radical *Yardbird Reader* (volume 5).
6. I take this phrase from the title of Silko's videotape made for PBS: see below.
7. The term is Mary Louise Pratt's: see "Arts of the Contact Zone"; see also Gloria Anzaldúa's *Borderlands/La Frontera*.
8. See, for instance, "Yellow Woman" (62), "Storytelling" (94–95), and "The Man to Send Rain Clouds" (182).
9. *Ceremony* 182; see also Auntie's story about Tayo's mother Laura, which positions her at this place at sunrise, returning to Laguna (70). This is also the place that Tayo positions himself at sunrise at the first sunrise following the autumnal equinox (and the Jackpile mine episode) at the end of the novel (255). A videotaped image of this site, marked by a large cottonwood tree, appears in "Running on the Edge of the Rainbow."
10. For a discussion of these sources see Linda Danielson, "The Storytellers in Storyteller." For photographs of the family storytellers Silko credits in *Storyteller* see Lee Marmon, "A Laguna Portfolio."
11. See, for instance, "Landscape, History, and the Pueblo Imagination," *Antaeus* 51 (1986): 83–94. Silko reiterates her formative connection to the landscape of Laguna Pueblo in one of her most recent essays, "Interior and Exterior Landscapes."
12. This was her second, and last, marriage; her first, also short-lived, was to Richard Chapman while she was still a student at the University of New Mexico. She bore two sons (one from each marriage), Robert and Cazimir.
13. "Running on the Edge of the Rainbow: Laguna Stories and Poems" is one of the series of videotapes of oral literary performance entitled *Words and Place*, produced by Larry Evers at the University of Arizona; available from Norman Ross Publishing Co., 330 W. 58th St., New York NY 10019.
14. For more on this film project of hers see chapter 13, "Arrowboy."
15. For more on the Kochinninako/Yellow Woman motif in *Ceremony* and *Almanac of the Dead*, see Elizabeth Hoffman Nelson and Malcolm Nelson's "Shifting Patterns, Changing Stories," in

Barnett and Thorson's *Leslie Marmon Silko*.
16 For two notable exceptions to this otherwise positive consensus, see Paula Gunn Allen's "Special Problems in Teaching Leslie Marmon Silko's Ceremony" and Shamoon Zamir, "Literature in a 'National Sacrifice Area'."

CHAPTER 2: MAPPING THE EMBEDDED TEXTS

1 For more on the idea of hama-ha stories, see chapter 3; briefly but more precisely, the stories that Silko chooses to embed in her novel come mostly from the conventional Keresan category of oral narrative called "maaíma uúbeétaányi," those "true" stories that get re-happened in the ceremonies (as distinguished from secular coyote stories and stories about talking frogs and wrens that are also included in the term "hama-ha").
2 One might also discern some visual analogy between the structure of Silko's novel thus seen and the structure of storykeeping wampum belts used under traditional circumstances in some other American Indian cultural traditions, and until the mid-1990s many readers might have been put in mind of the legendary Walam Olum, the encoded story of the Lenape (Delaware) people, which David Oestreicher exposed as a hoax in his essay "Unraveling the Walam Olum" (*Natural History*, October 1996, 14–21).
3 Silko's own affinity for snakes, which is congruent with Laguna story tradition (see her essay "The Fourth World" on the Great Serpent of Keresan myth in *Artforum*, rpt. as "Fifth World: The Return of Ma ah shra true ee, the Giant Serpent" in *Yellow Woman* 124–34) probably has something to do with the appearance of the "light yellow snake, covered with bright copper spots" who is "the first to emerge, carrying this message on his back to the people" just prior to Ts'eh's re-emergence at Dripping Springs (221). This interest shows up much more dramatically near the end of *Almanac of the Dead*, where she also incorporates the image of Maahastryu (= Ma ah shra true ee), as well in the spectacular mural she painted in Tucson in 1986–87 while writing *Almanac*: see "Stone Avenue Mural" in *Yellow Woman* 149–51.
4 See, for instance, the title of Melody Graulich's 1993 edited collection of critical essays on Silko's work, *"Yellow Woman," Leslie Marmon Silko*, and also the title of Silko's own 1996 collected essays, *Yellow Woman and a Beauty of the Spirit: Essays on Native American Life Today*, as well as the Nelson and Nelson essay cited earlier in chapter 1.
5 Readers interested in an extended analysis of the relationship of Silko's prose narrative to the landscape of Laguna might start with Nelson, "The Function of Landscape in *Ceremony*."

CHAPTER 3: RE-FLESHING THE BACKBONE

1 Susan Reyes Marmon, her paternal great-aunt; Marie Anaya Marmon, her paternal great-grandmother. On these and other family sources, see Linda Danielson, "The Storytellers in *Storyteller*" and Lee Marmon, "A Laguna Portfolio."
2 Louis Owens offers a more intriguing reading of the presence of these embedded texts within the context of the surrounding prose narrative:

> Haunting the total ceremony of the novel, like figures in a sandpainting, are the dimly perceived physical presences of Holy Persons dispersed throughout the text in the physical dimensions of the poems/stories that bridge the distance between oral and written narrative. (95)

3 More particularly, the Keresan embedded texts derive mainly from Franz Boas's 1928

publication *Keresan Texts*, while the Navajo ones derive mainly from Leland Wyman's translations of his and others' transcriptions of the oral component of Navajo ceremonial texts. For some discussion of the former, see Nelson, "He Said/ She Said"; on the latter, see Robert Bell, "Circular Design in *Ceremony*."

4   See, for example, Helen Sekaquaptewa's opening comments on the Hopi frame elements "aliksai" and "poyuqpölö" in the videotape "Iisaw: Hopi Coyote Stories," as well as Andrew Wiget's comments on these elements in "Telling the Tale" and Larry Evers's program notes to the Sekaquaptewa video transcript. Analogously, Scott Momaday uses the traditional Towan frame elements *dypaloh* and *qtsedaba* as the first and last words of his novel *House Made of Dawn* to invoke the spirit of traditional Jemez oral performance (Nelson, *Place and Vision* 43).

5   I'm aware that attempts to subvert this convention in postwar fiction are legion. I also think most readers do not fall for it, though: what goes on before and after the first and last words of the written performance, after all, isn't copyrighted.

6   More precisely, *Keresan Texts* is Boas's edition of Elsie Clews Parsons's transcriptions of tales she collected at Laguna. As volume 8 of the Publications of the American Ethnological Society, *Keresan Texts* was published in two parts: 8.2, comprised of holographs of handwritten phonetic transcriptions of performances in Keresan of 47 stories plus miscellaneous materials (biographical tidbits about one of the informants, lyrics to several songs and chants, texts of several prayers) was published in 1925; 8.1, the English-language text, was published three years later in 1928, and contains translations of the pieces in Part 2 (in roughly the same order) but also several additional fragments and a section in which Boas collates these materials with other extant ethnographic materials.

7   Boas attributes each of the stories collected in *Keresan Texts* to one of six informants, all of whom initiate at least one of their performances with the phrase "hamaha" or "hamaha-eh!" Of the 47 story texts, 36 are initiated with this phrase, while another nine include the term "hama" or "ha'ma" in their first sentence. In *Storyteller*, Silko's Aunt Susie tells her that *"The Laguna people/ always begin their stories/ with 'humma-hah': that means long ago"* (38). This phrase is still conspicuously in use at Laguna today: in 1991, for instance, a showing of 16 photographs of Laguna and Acoma old-timers mounted at the Wheelright Museum in Santa Fe by Silko's father, Lee Marmon, was titled "Humma-Ha."

8   This is exactly how Paula Gunn Allen translates the term in *Sacred Hoop* (147).

9   Roughly three-fourths (35 out of 47) of the stories and story fragments given to Parsons and Boas end with some version of this phrasing, and all six of their informants use it at least once.

10 In *Notes on Ceremonialism at Laguna*, Parsons gives the term as "*Heme tsich* (thus long)" (98 n. 5); in *Laguna Genealogies* she spells the longer version "*tometsish s'ak'oya-k'ayodzesh-povits*" and referes to it as "the regular conclusion of Laguna folktales" (196).

11 For more on the significance of this male storyteller figure see the "Ceremony" section of chapter 5 of this book.

12 See, for instance, Silko's "Skeleton Fixer" (*Storyteller* 242–45) and Simon Ortiz's *A Good Journey* (42–43).

13 I am not the first to recognize this trope in Silko's work or its application to the nine-part departure-recovery story embedded in the novel. Edith Swan comments on it in her 1977 article "Healing Via the Sunwise Cycle":

> Like vertebrae composing the backbone, sequential segments of this myth occur throughout the text of *Ceremony*, showing how difficult it is to correct the insidious and lingering effects of witchcraft as well as how carefully this must be done. Furthermore, this metaphor on the structural analogy of form is in keeping with the art of telling Laguna stories; the storyteller often closes with a phrase like "That long is my aunt's backbone" (Boas 1928). (316)

14 For a more detailed accounting of this story thread in terms of its ethnographic antecedents, see chapter 8 of this study.

15 "P'acaya·´nʸi" (the orthography varies, both within Boas and between Boas and Silko) appears in both Parts 1 (13–16) and 2 (19–23), as does "The Hummingbird" (1.11–13, 2.16–18). The section titled "Origin Legend" is only in Part 1; the relevant passages are on pp. 223 ("At one time the son of the Giantess (ck`o´yo) who was called "P'acaya·´nʸi" arrived from the north-west. He was accompanied by the Mountain-Lion-Man.... He took his flint knife and stabbed the north side of the house. Immediately water rushed out of it. Then he stabbed the west wall and a bear came out") and 226 (in which well-fed Hummingbird reveals Nautsityi's whereabouts, "in the fourth world, below," and oversees the creation of "a large fly" inside "a new jar that was covered in buckskin"). For closer inspection of the relevant Boas pretexts, see Appendices D and E.

16 Here and throughout the rest of this chapter, except where required by the context, I have simplified and regularized the orthography of Keresan words.

17 A more complete analysis of this motif is given in chapter 11 of this study.

18 A more complete analysis of this motif is given in chapter 4 of this study.

19 Perhaps this is why even living informants become archaicized in Boas's presentation: for instance, the name of one informant gets consistently spelled out phonetically as *Gʸi´mi* ("Jimmy").

CHAPTER 4: ANALOGY vs. HOMOLOGY

1 See Ruth Benedict, n. 1 to "Eight Stories"; see also pp. 114 and 117 of John Gunn's *Schat-chen*, featuring hand drawings of the Laguna version(s) of this figure, the katsina brothers Kopot and Ko-kah-ki-eh. A facsimile of Gunn's story "Ko-pot Ka-nat," including these drawings, appears in *SAIL* 5.1 (Spring 1993): 25–30.

2 Linda Danielson identifies six such sources acknowledged by name in *Storyteller* alone in "The Storytellers in *Storyteller*" (22).

3 On Silko's use of Wyman's account of the Red Antway, see Robert Bell, "Circular Design in *Ceremony*"; on her use of Boas's Pacayanyi and Hummingbird Man stories, see Nelson, "Rewriting Ethnography."

4 There is little doubt that Gunn's "Kopot," Boas's "Kaup`a·t´a," Benedict's "Kaupat´a," and Silko's "Kaup'a'ta," are variant spellings of the same word, the spelling of which I have regularized in this study as "Kaupata." Gunn's text includes two page-sized drawings, both reproduced in *SAIL* 5.1 (Spring 1993: 25, 30): one (verso to the first page of Gunn's text of "Ko-pot Ka-nat") labeled "Kopot" and the other (Gunn 117) labeled "Ko-kah-ki-eh—Brother of Kopot"; both of these drawings are reproduced also in Parsons's *Notes on Ceremonialism at Laguna*, identified (with others) as drawings of katsinas who visit Laguna annually. Boas (253–54) discusses Gunn's Kopot as a variant of "The Gambler" Kaup`a·t´a depicted in a story told by Ko·´Tʸe. In a note to her story "Kaupat´a" gathered at Acoma, Benedict says that "Kaupat´a appears as a masked dancer at the Winter Solstice ceremony. He is blind and is led by his old grandmother" (62 n. 5).

Additionally, in her 1920 *Notes on Ceremonialism at Laguna*, Parsons includes, in her list of about a dozen Laguna "gods" included in the generic term *kupishtaiya* (a category that includes, incidentally, "Shiwanna": see below), the figure Kopot'ε, one of "two brothers who became two stars close together and of which one is very red.... Both brothers are very wicked" (95). Parsons's account tallies closely with Gunn's account of the brothers Kopot in *Schat-chen*.

Another interesting cognate story is "How KauBat Lost His Eyes," published by Leslie White in *The Acoma Indians*, 47th annual report of the BAE pp. 165–68. In this version, Grandmother Badger acts the part of Spider Grandmother while the role of Sun Man is filled by twin boys who are sons of an Acoma woman who was seduced and impregnated by the gambler KauBat´; they visit KauBat´ and his mother at his place, a few days to the west of Ako (Acoma), and (as in other versions) finally end up gambling with him, the stakes of the ultimate wager being the gambler's heart against everything the boys have won from him; also as in other versions, the boys win by knowing (thanks to Grandmother Badger's preview story) that the contents of a bag are stars, and as in other versions the boys choose to take the gambler's eyes rather than his heart, which eyes become stars too. The blind KauBat´ then sets fire to vats of pitch, which then boil over and set fire to the countryside until the fires are put out by the shiwanna and "the pitch became cold and hard. You can see it near Grants to-day (the lava beds)" (168). Note the difference between other versions and this one as regards motive: in others, the protagonist seeks the return of the stormclouds; here, the (twinned) protagonist is visiting an absent father (as in several Laguna stories in which the twins Maseewi and Ouyuyewe seek, and are tested by, their father the Sun).

5   See Nelson, "He Said/She Said."
6   For some examples of this correspondence see appendix C.
7   See, for instance, Kroeber, "An Introduction" 3 and Wiget, *Native American Literature* 2–3.
8   Kenneth Roemer provides a methodical study of these and other grounds of the novel's canonization in "Silko's Arroyos as Mainstream."
9   On the crucial implications of the backbone metaphor, see Nelson, "Rewriting Ethnography"; Swan also touches on the traditional Keresan significance of this trope in "Healing Via the Sunwise Cycle" (16).
10 I find it a little puzzling that the novel's embedded text locates Kaupata's place "high/in the peaks of the Zuni mountains" (170), which would put him to the west and south of Laguna, whereas Tayo's proper destination is Mt. Taylor, to the north and west of Laguna. On this detail Silko's version differs from Boas's, in which it is located "in the northwest region at Reed-Leaf-Town," placing it (with respect to Laguna) in the vicinity of Mt. Taylor. In Leslie White's Acoma version, KauBat´ and his mother live a few days west of Acoma; in Ruth Benedict's version (also from Acoma), Sun Man's homolog Tsutea arrives at "Kaci ka´tcutʸa, White House of the North" (63 n. 4)—the place Gunn spells "Kush kut-ret," Mt. Taylor—to teach "the katcinas, the gamblers" there not to play for the lives of the people, but then travels "many days" to find Kaupat´a and the rainclouds, so that conceivably this Kaupata also lives in the Zuni Mountains.
11 The important presumption that vision is a form of control over, as well as defense against, evil suffuses Silko's novel. In the prose narrative see, for instance, Betonie's strategic placement of his hogan with respect to Gallup (117); in the embedded text see, for instance, the Arrowboy fragment (chapter 13 of this book); and finally, see Tayo's own strategic response to Emo's equinoctial ritual in the climactic Jackpile Mine episode.
12 Boas 76, 283–84; Swan, "Laguna Symbolic Geography" 231–32. Boas spells the word "shiwana," Parsons "shiwanna," and Kurath "ší·wana" (Keresan) and "shiwana" (English).
13 This is, incidentally, also the "diaphanous morning cloud" that is the locus of the narrative perspective in Simon Ortiz's beautiful early poem "Heyaashi Guutah." This book adopts Ortiz's orthography; Boas gives the word as "Hi· ´Tcats'ɛ" (284), Kurath as "héaši̧."
14 In the account given in Boas, four days after Sun-Youth leaves, blind Kaup`a·ta', vowing to "destroy the people," gathers pitch at the south end of his mountain and spreads it to "the west mountain at the south end," then sets fire to it and, stirring the pitch in front of the fire as he goes, moves back northward. When he eventually veers eastward, the storm clouds take note of his coming and vow to "extinguish" the fires and "kill" the Gambler. As the storm clouds run "alongside eastward" the fires, putting out the fires there, Kaup`a·ta' "was surrounded by flames and was ablaze" and dies.

In Benedict's account, the people whose lives the Gambler has previously won are revived and directed by Tsutea (Sun Youth) to strip Kaupat´a's house of everything of value; all they leave is "a powerful torch which was hidden in the ceiling between two rafters," which the blind Gambler later finds and sets ablaze. Then, setting fire to "pitch from the piñon trees," he sets his house afire and stirs it so that "the lava flowed in both directions to the north and east." Several species of white birds then attempt to "beat out the fire with [their] wings," only to turn brown or black forever; but "hummingbird flew around to the great waters to the north, west, south and east, to rouse the tides to put out the fire"; the clouds then converge from all directions and, after hail fails to extinguish "the burning lava rock," rain succeeds.

Notable in both these versions is that Kaupata's revenge takes the form of volcanic eruption and burning rock—lava—rather than the form of a flood, as it does in Gunn's "Kopot Kanat"; however, and again interestingly, burning rock and water are cast as one another's neutralizers in all three of these texts (including Gunn's). If Boas's Kaupata were located on Mt. Taylor but Benedict's in the vicinity of Acoma, the pattern of the burning pitch/lava's movement in these two versions would be consistent with an eruption of Mount Taylor and with the resulting configuration of the so-called Malpais in relation to the current locations of Acoma and Laguna.

CHAPTER 5: THE HOOP SERIES

1   This is the case in the original 1977 Viking edition, as well as in at least the first several Penguin paperback editions of 1986: the Arabic numeral 1 is set at the bottom center of the page (the number is printed top center on all subsequent pages save for the recto page [179, in the Penguin edition] depicting "Old Betonie's stars").

2   See, for instance, the publication in 1979 of G. M. Mullett's *Spider Woman Stories*; more recently, see Paula Gunn Allen's 1989 *Spider Woman's Granddaughters*.

3   As Boas notes, Stevenson goes on to refer to this figure as "he" even though the -nako suffix in Keresan clearly denotes female gender. Boas attributes this male [re-]gendering to recent Catholic influence; however, such gender ambivalence appears to be a characteristic of Keresan treatment of particularly powerful figures. For instance, a Keresan community's cacique or *tiamunyi*, who is invariably a man, is always to be referred to as "she" during his time in office. Jay Miller offers this explanation:

> Throughout their culture the nexus for all mediators was and is the Keres paramount deity, often called Thought Woman, although Consciousness Deity is a better translation, the source and summary of Keres culture.... The embodiment of this deity living in each town is the Inside or Town Priest (tiamunyi), invested wearing bridal robes and thereafter officially called "mother," although he is a husband and father in private life. Each has a separate official office, regarded even more than similar kivas as a tysic of and for the pan-Keresan primordial abode named Shipop^u. (500)

4   Six, to be precise: "The Emergence," (Ko´t'e [1919] 1–5 and Gɣi´mi [1919] 5–7), "Ts'its'ts'i·´na·´k'o" (Ko´t'e [1921] 7–8), "Nau´ts'it'i" (Ko´t'e [1919] 8–9) "White-House" (Ko´t'e [1919] 9), and "The Emergence" (Gɣi´mi [1919] 9–11).

5   Walter's full middle name was Gunn, a Marmon family name and the surname of several cousins of the Marmon brothers, one of whom also migrated to Laguna; both John Gunn, author of *Schat-chen*, and Paula Gunn Allen, perhaps best known as the author of *The Sacred Hoop*, are his descendants and thus related to Silko as well.

6   Specifically, the *shikani cheani*, one of whose duties it was to recite the all-night winter rites.

Notes

7   See Parsons, *Notes* 87.
8   Parsons' "ma'sewi" is the same as Silko's "Maseewi," the elder of the usually paired Laguna hero twins Masewi and Ouyuyewi: see chapter 8.
9   Because Keresan is the language of both Laguna and Acoma, and these two pueblos are virtual next-door neighbors (Acoma shares its eastern border with Laguna), the following thumbnails of relevant Acoma ethnography may be of interest to some.

In Matthew Stirling's BAE edition of a version told to him by an Acoma informant during a visit to Washington, DC in 1928,

> In the beginning two female human beings were born. These two children were born underground at a place called Shipapu.... After they had grown considerably, a Spirit whom they afterward called Tsichtinako spoke to them, and they found that it would give them nourishment. After they had grown large enough to think for themselves, they spoke to the Spirit when it had come to them one day and asked it to make itself known to them and to say whether it was male or female, but it replied only that it was not allowed to meet with them. (1)

Later in this story, when they emerge from below and while they are experiencing their first sunrise, the sisters are given their names, Nautsityi and Iatiku, by Tsichtinako, who then tells them that they were created "by your father, Ūch'tsiti ... and it is he who made the world" (3).

In a somewhat similar version from Acoma published by Leslie A. White in 1932, which he titled "Origin and Emergence," we are told that "The first supernatural being was Utc´tsiti (male). Then there were two sisters, Nau´tsiti and Ia´tik^u" (147); curiously, there's no mention of a Tsitstsinako cognate anywhere in this version or elsewhere in the 48 pages of White's "Myths and Tales." In a footnote to this version, White says

> This version, I suspect, is one that was told at Laguna, or Zia, perhaps. I do not believe it is common at Acoma, for other informants did not know about it. (147)

It would seem that White and Stirling moved in different Acoma circles.

10 It's also possible that the gendering in Silko's version is designed to reproduce an important feature of Laguna (as opposed to English) grammar: according to Lee Francis, a native speaker,

> Laguna (Keres) is a language which is "genderized" depending on the speaker. That is, there is "men's talk" (when a Laguna male speaks the language) and "women's talk" (when a Laguna woman speaks the language). (Personal communication, 26 August 2002)

This would not, however, account for a storyteller of either gender referring to one sibling in the story as "our mother" and the other as "our father"; it would imply only that the storyteller of the version in *Ceremony* is to be understood as a female.

11 Conventional genealogical parlance would relate them as great-grandaunt to great-grandniece, but in the Laguna way of thinking, context dictates degree of relationship, so that my granddaughter may also be my daughter or even my sister, or my cousin may also be my brother (or even my cousin-brother), depending on the degree of sharedness the speaker wishes to establish.

12 In some of the stories collected by Boas the four worlds are also, somewhat like the floors of the Pentagon, color-coded: according to Boas (228), the four worlds below are colored, from first (earliest/farthest) to fourth (latest/closest), white, red, blue, and yellow.

13 See Tedlock, "The Spoken Word and the Word of Interpretation" in Kroeber's *Traditional Literatures of the American Indian*.

14 See, for instance, "Aunt Susie had certain phrases" (7–15) and "The Two Sisters" (100–03).
15 Though this line of analysis may sound a little sophistic, I offer it in evidence of my thesis in this chapter that Silko is going all out in these first fragments of embedded text to inculcate a Laguna way of reading the coming prose narrative. Here, the four narrative presences are formally congruent with Laguna cosmology, in which there are always four worlds before/within the one we all live in, always four dimensions, four "places" or phased sources of life moving in some kind of relationship to one another. The function of ceremony is to align, or re-align, those relationships. This is also the function of storytelling, whenever it is being used to heal rather than to dis-ease.
16 Louis Owens speculates that the "She" on page 3 is "possibly a clan mother or Thought-Woman reentering the text" (94). Curiously, Owens also reads page 3 as the final lines of a "poem," a "male-female dialog," that begins with the word "Ceremony" on page 2.
17 As old man Ku'oosh puts it: "There are some things that we can't cure like we used to, not since the white man came" (38).
18 First published in 1932, the text enjoyed a resurgence of interest after the popular University of Nebraska Press Bison edition was published in 1961.
19 So she says in her "Introduction": "When I was small, my mother often told me that animals, insects, and plants are to be treated with the kind of respect one customarily accords to high status adults. 'Life is a circle, and everything has its place in it,' she would say. That's how I met the sacred hoop, which has been an integral part of my life, though I didn't know to call it that until the early 1970s when I read John G. Neihardt's rendering of the life story of Oglala Holy Man Black Elk in *Black Elk Speaks*" (1).
20 The reference is to a memorable passage in James Welch's 1979 *The Death of Jim Loney* describing "three framed paintings by an Indian artist [Kate] had met in South Dakota':

> Two of the paintings were of Indian dancers, "fancy dancers," and their movements were kinetic and exaggerated. The third was of a dancer walking home along a highway, still in full regalia but lonely and tired.... But then a feeling of dread came over her and she knew things were not right and she felt, as she watched the fancy dancer walk home, that she would not see her brother again. (164–65)

21 As Silko renders it, Gallup, a Fifth-World, twentieth-century site located on the edge of Navajo ceremonial influence, is clearly enough in homological relationship with the Fourth World, myth-time domain of Laguna's own Kaupata the Gambler in that both sites are spirit traps for those who wander into them—in the Kaupata story, Laguna hunters; in the Gallup of *Ceremony*, "Navajos, but he had seen Zunis and Lagunas and Hopis there too" (115). In this respect also both places can be understood to have the power of places like the transformational zone so brilliantly depicted in Silko's poem "Story From Bear Country."
22 It's customarily *de rigeur* for the patient or his/her family to pay for the services of a Navajo singer, or *hataali*; no doubt Silko knew this, and she acknowledges this exigency by having Tayo reach for his billfold at the end of this episode and say "I want to pay you for the ceremony you did tonight." Very uncustomarily, though, Betonie "shook his head"—perhaps to underscore that the debt Tayo has incurred is the responsibility to finish the recovery Betonie has set in motion with his "ceremony": "It's up to you," he tells Tayo; "Don't let them stop you. Don't let them finish off this world" (152).
23 Robert Bell and I have both argued elsewhere that the description of the ritual that Silko gives in the novel is based on Leland Wyman's published account of the Navajo Red Antway ceremony. See also chapter 11. However, ceremonial hoopwork occurs in any number of Navajo chantways: see, for instance, Wheelwright and McAllester's *The Myth and Prayers of the Great Star Chant and The Myth of the Coyote Chant* (1956), in which a baby, a grandson of Kleesto (Great Snake) wanders away from his people and becomes transformed into the Great Snake; when the

Great Snake is passed through a series of five hoops, the skin of Kleesto peels back gradually to reveal "a grown person who had been their baby four days before" (11). According to McAllester's footnote on these ceremonial hoops, or *tse-panse*:

> *Tse-panse* are ceremonial hoops made of various kinds of branches and variously decorated. They are large enough for a person to pass through and the passage is a symbolic transformation rite. Such concepts as star symbolism, concentration of sacred power in an enclosed space and purification are also associated with ceremonial hoops. (10)

24 Indeed, judging from listening to many years of student responses to the novel, I think most readers seeking a referent for the title of the novel assume that the "ceremony" to which the title refers is the ritual involving hoops, painted mountains, and chanting that Betonie conducts for Tayo out in the Chuska Mountains.

25 I have in mind, for instance, Kenneth Lincoln's early essay "Blue Medicine" and Carol Mitchell's "*Ceremony* as Ritual"; more recently, see Brewster Fitz in his book *Silko: Writing Storyteller and Medicine Woman*.

26 Since writing this chapter, I have noticed I am not alone in this conclusion; Brewster Fitz, for one, makes much of this kind of "silence" in the early chapters of *Silko: Writing Storyteller and Medicine Woman* and goes on to use its presence to invite a poststructuralist reading of her work.

CHAPTER 6: THE SUNRISE SERIES

1 See chapter 3, n. 3, in this study.
2 See my discussion of Gunn's desire to legitimize Keresan story by claiming Phoenecian and Cushite roots for Laguna culture in "He Said/She Said."
3 Allen footnotes a chapter title, "The Ceremonial Motion of Indian Time: Long Ago, So Far" with the statement that "Lagunas start their stories by saying 'humma haa,' which means 'long ago, so far,' among other things" (147); in her 1983 novel, *The Woman Who Owned the Shadows*, she spells the term "hame haa" (175). For more on this term, see chapter 3, esp. n. 6.
4 The term is Silko's. See "Notes on *Almanac of the Dead*" in *Yellow Woman and a Beauty of the Spirit*:

> For the old-time people, time was not a series of ticks of a clock, one following the other. For the old-time people, time was round—like a tortilla, time has specific moments and specific locations, so that the beloved ancestors who had passed on were not annihilated by death, but only relocated to the place called Cliff House. At Cliff House, people continued as they had always been, although only spirits and not living humans can travel freely over this tortilla of time. All times go on existing side by side for all eternity. No moment is lost or destroyed. There are no future times or past times; there are *always all* the times, which differ slightly, as the locations on the tortilla differ slightly. (136–37)

5 Given Silko's sensitivity to the issue of cultural appropriation, Tayo's uncertainty here is ironic, since the text we are given is in English not Keresan: of course these words are not the "right ones" (182), the authoritative text.
6 According to Paula Gunn Allen in her influential early essay "Kochinninako in Academe," "summer" and "winter" in the sense used here align, more or less, with the two seasons composing the ceremonial year personified, respectively, by Miochin and Shakok, two of the *shiwanna* or Cloud People.

7   Boas also describes the ritual hand sign for "sunrise": "Thumb touches points of fingers. Then fingers and thumb stretched and hand thus opened" (299).
8   One is reminded here of the way that Momaday in *House Made of Dawn* similarly frames the whole of his novel within a double bracket composed not only of initiating and concluding bracket phrases (*dypolah* and *qtsedaba*) but also, within these bookend cues, identical portraits of Abel, running, at sunrise, both in myth time (1–2) and on 28 February 1952 (211–12).

CHAPTER 7: THE LAGUNA SISTERS

1   But not until he crosses paths with the Kopot brothers in the vicinity of Ship-op and promises to run a race with them after he has recovered Reed Woman. At this point in Gunn's version, the story of Our Mother's recovery transforms into a Kopot/Kaupata story, two filaments of Laguna story that Silko separates out from each other in her handling of these motifs.
2   In a novel that works hard to privilege the oral tradition (as well as to reclaim space within the circle of the People for twentieth-century homologs of Yellow Woman), I suspect the homophony between the English "Sis[ter]" and the Laguna "Ts'its['tsi'nako]" is not an accident: as easy as it is (even for the Laguna Older Sister) to forget, both daughters of Our Mother bear exactly the same relationship to Our Mother, however different they might appear to one another.
3   On the sunrise motif, see chapter 6 in this book. On Kochinninako/Yellow Woman, see Paula Gunn Allen's now-classic "Kochininako in Academe" in *The Sacred Hoop* and, especially, the title essay of Silko's own *Yellow Woman and a Beauty of the Spirit*. On the idea of liminal zones, see for instance Larry Ellis, "Trickster: Shaman of the Liminal."

The image of the emptied purse recurs when the story of Helen Jean, another of Silko's Yellow Women in the novel, intersects with Tayo's as he is returning to Laguna from his encounter with Betonie in the Chuska Mountains. A truck containing Leroy, Harley, and Helen Jean (says Harley, "We found her in Gallup last night," 156) intercepts Tayo near Cerritos, near the western edge of the Laguna reservation, and the four of them then drive past Mesita (on the eastern edge of the reservation) to the Y Bar. There, as Helen stumbles out of the truck, "her tooled leather purse with the rose designs" (159) spills out its contents, a total of four items (billfold, lipstick, mirror, powder puff); a few beers later, after some Mexicans signal their interest in her, "Helen Jean reached down by her feet for her purse" (160) as prelude to departing from the three Lagunas, one of whom (Tayo) sees it coming, the other two of whom "never even saw her go." There follows immediately in the text (161–66) the story of Helen Jean's past year, beginning with her departure from her own family at Towac on the Ute reservation in order to find a job and her subsequent inability to return home again. The story ends with Helen Jean once more "reach[ing] into her purse for the little pink compact" (166) and telling herself that "this time she really was going to send some money to Emma" back at Towac.

Purse and story both align the image of Helen Jean with Laura. As though to complicate any potentially reductive analogy, though, Silko's description of this particular purse—covered "with the rose designs"—links the figure of Helen Jean to the story of departure and recovery that is the backbone of the ceremony conducted by Betonie. In that ceremony, as in the Navajo pretext about the hunter transformed by Coyote trickery and his recovery, the fifth (easternmost) hoop through which Tayo must pass is constructed of "wild rose."
4   As Tayo recalls during his first morning on Mt. Taylor, this is also precisely the spot where the katsina materialize during their transition from the Fourth World to the Fifth World in late November:

> Before dawn, southeast of the village, the bells would announce their approach ...
> And at the moment the sun came over the horizon, they suddenly appeared on the riverbank, the Ka't'sina approaching the river crossing. (182)

For more on this connection between sunrise, the Katsina, and the motif of recovery, see chapter 6 in this book.

5   In the prose narrative, as Tayo positions himself for reentry,

> In the west and in the south too, the clouds with round heavy bellies had gathered for the dawn. It was not necessary, but it was right, and even if the sky had been cloudless the end was the same. The ear for the story and eye for the patterns were theirs: we came out of this land and we are hers. (255)

6   This association of Tayo with the warrior twins of the backbone story is another point of homological integration between the two departure stories under discussion. When we recall that the Corn Woman-Reed Woman fragment is formally bracketed by Tayo's memory of praying against the rain during World War II, we can better appreciate the fact that the account of the falling-out between Thelma and Laura (including the story the older sister gives to Tayo about the younger sister, who is also the missing mother) is formally bracketed by the appearance of the Army recruiter (64–65, 72). The first time the recruiter appears in the text, his presence occasions Rocky's reference to Tayo as his "brother":

> "And my brother," Rocky said, nodding at Tayo. "If we both sign up, can we stay together?"
> It was the first time in all the years that Tayo had lived with him that Rocky ever called him "brother." Auntie had always been careful that Rocky didn't call Tayo "brother," and when other people mistakenly called them brothers, she was quick to correct the error. (65)

The second time he appears, Tayo's and Rocky's status as brothers is once again the foregrounded issue:

> The Army recruiter looked closely at Tayo's light brown skin and his hazel eyes.
> "You guys are brothers?"
> Rocky nodded coolly.
> "If you say so," the recruiter said. (72)

CHAPTER 8: THE BACKBONE SERIES I

1   Perhaps a better way to speak of this process is to say that Silko has, to use Susan Scarberry-García's very useful term (from *Landmarks of Healing*, her study of Momaday's use of traditional materials in *House Made of Dawn*), assembled some traditional "storysherds" to suit her own esthetic purposes.

2   The 1977 Viking (first, hardback) edition and the popular 1986 Penguin paperback edition appear to be printed from identical plates and contain identical pagination, with the exception that later Penguin editions delete the Arabic numeral on page 1. Below are the 17 variora between the *Ceremony* and *Storyteller* versions of the backbone story.

	Ceremony	*Storyteller*
46.2	Old Woman K'yo's	Old Woman Ck'o'yo's
46.15	mother corn altar,	Mother Corn altar,
47.13–14	[no line break]	[line break]
47.29–30	[line break]	[no line break]

47.32	Is that magical power?"	Is that magical powers?"
48.13	...the mother corn altar	... the Mother Corn altar
49.3	rainclouds with her.	rain clouds with her.
71.9– 72.10	[left justified, left margin centered]	[center justified]
72.2–3	[no line break]	[line break]
113.12	(You see, it wasn't easy.)	*You see, it wasn't easy.*
151.9	to ask our mother where	to ask our Mother where
151.12	they told our mother.	they told our Mother.
180.3	They went to a place in the West	They went to a place in the West.
180.4	[unitalicized line]	[italicized line]
255.9–11	[left justified, double indent]	[center justified]
256.3	after all that ck'o'yo magic.	after all that Ck'o'yo magic.
256.17	some ck'o'yo magician	some Ck'o'yo magician

3. The story given by Stevenson is set prior to the flight to Jemez of the handful of Pecos survivors in the seventeenth century. Scott Momaday refers to coming of the Pecos people (or "Bahkyush" as Momaday spells the term orthographically) to Jemez (or "Walatowa" as its name is given in the novel) several times in *House Made of Dawn*, the first and fourth movements of which are set at Jemez pueblo.

4. One of Boas's informants, José (1919), also seems to have translated ck'o'yo as "giant," referring to Pacayanyi as "the son of the Giantess (ck'o'yo)" (223).

5. Here as elsewhere in Gunn's book *Schat-chen*, orthography is inconsistent. Gunn names this character three times in his account; the first time (72) it is spelled "Po-chai-an-ny," the other two times (73) it is spelled "Po-chi-an-ny."

6. In a footnote in *Notes on Ceremonialism*, Parsons mentions that the brothers Walter and Robert Marmon settled at Laguna in 1862 and both married Laguna women (109 n. 4); Robert in fact married two Laguna women, first the older sister Agnes Anaya and, when she died, the younger sister, Marie Anaya, the "Grandmother A'mooh" whom Silko mentions several times in *Storyteller*. Robert and Marie had four children, including Silko's paternal grandfather Henry C. Marmon ("Grampa Hank" in *Storyteller*). Photographs of these and other family storytellers appear not only in *Storyteller* but also in a photoessay co-authored by Silko's father, Lee Marmon, entitled "A Laguna Portfolio" (*Studies in American Indian Literatures* 5.1 [Spring 1993]): 62–74, available online at <http://oncampus.richmond.edu/faculty/asail/sail2/51.html#62>).

Parsons describes her informant, Silko's great-grandmother's sister-in-law, this way: "Mrs. Marmon remained unsophisticated and uncontaminated by American shoddiness. She was a strong, gentle, and very lovable person. She died in 1918" (*Notes* 87).

7. As Parsons points out, at Laguna as at Keresan-speaking Cochiti and Zia the term *ma'sewi* (Silko's "Ma'see'wi") was commonly used to refer to either the younger of the two brothers (the older being Oyoyewi [Parsons] or Ou'yu'ye'wi [Silko]) or to them both, or perhaps as a term for the warrior-ness they both share. Some of Boas's informants use the term this way too, speaking of "cïts' Ma·´sɛɛ·wi" to refer to both brothers (223).

8. As one final probable version of this story, see Matthew W. Stirling's 1942 *Origin Myth of Acoma and Other Records* (BAE Bulletin 135). Shortly after the emergence, in this version, the corn mother Iatiku and her children, still living in the vicinity of Shipapu (26), have made peace with the katsina to the east and the Kopishtaiya to the west;

> Some time after this the evil spirit (Pishuni) came to the people of Iatiku in the form of disease. It had by this time grown of itself into a big power, and the people were stricken with a plague. It is not known what form of disease it was for the people had never known sickness before. They were panic stricken.... So Iatiku thought of

choosing a man to be chaianyi (medicine man). (28)

An elder of the Oak clan, who is selected by a council of the people, then journeys to the North Mountain where under Iatiku's direction he gathers materials for what will become the altar "which is commonly called Iatiku" (29), after which (inter alia) the Oak man acquires Bear medicine, learns how to orient himself at night by the stars, and participates in the creation of the Koshare before "it was finished" (31).

Given that this version is a redaction of a performance delivered 14 years earlier in Keresan by "a group of Pueblo Indians from Acoma and Santa Ana visiting Washington," that during the original performance "in many places the younger interpreters were unable to translate and the elderly informant would have to explain in modern Acoma phraseology," and that "other paraphrases may have been made for the benefit of the White man or as interpretation of Acoma religion by one who is an exceptionally good Catholic and no longer a participant in the ceremonial life of Acoma" (vii)—not to mention that the printed version is a product of editorial "collaboration" among Stirling, Leslie White, and Elsie Parsons (viii)—it's hard to say how much was lost or distorted via multiple translation and redaction. Nevertheless, I'm guessing "Pishuni" is Stirling's spelling of the word behind Gunn's "Po-chi-an-ny," Parsons's "*bacheani*," Boas's "P'acaya·´nʸi," and Silko's "Pa'caya'nyi; that "Iatiku" and the Nautsityi of the other versions are homologically identical figures of the mother of the people; and that the spirit that is spoken of as a man who comes to the people from the north is simultaneously, in all the versions, to be understood (as he is foregrounded to be, in this version) as a *disease* that infects the *body* of the people.

9 See Appendix D, "Pacayanyi," for some sample comparison of Silko's and Boas's versions.

10

Then next she said, "Enough," said she. "Let Ma·´sɛɛ·wi and Uyu·´yɛ·wi run around the ends of the world four times." Thus she told the storm clouds and the wind. Then after one year she made go out Ma·´sɛɛ·wi and Uyu·´yɛ·wi. There below in the Chief's house arrived Feather Man (the wind). He spoke thus. "Come now, stand up Ma·´sɛɛ·wi and Uyu·´yɛ·wi," said he. Then stood up Ma·´sɛɛ·wi and Uyu·´yɛ·wi. Then the window opened the Wind-Man. He picked them up. There west he took them. To the middle west he carried them. There he put them down. From there west they ran. From the west southward, from south to east, from east to north and from north to west; from west to south; from south to east he took them. From east to south he took them again. In the middle of the south there he made them arrive. Then east he took them. They were almost dead tired; then there in the northwest region in Reed-Leaf-House, when there they arrived in the west out came their sister K'oo·´ko. In the east they arrived. Then she said to them, "Enough that far," she said to them. "Poor brothers! From here (forward) on you will be good," said she to them. There they sat down. (16)

11 Part of their punishment, it seems, is having to witness the transformation of K'oo·´ko's appearance:

Then she said to them again, "She told me, 'I will punish you.' Behold, look at me well," said she. Then she went a little to the west. Then there westward they looked. Very ugly she was, that wide was her mouth and her teeth showed and her eyes were big and her head was big. Then next to the east she turned. Then very beautiful of white complexion she was and also she had an embroidered woman's dress and also very long earrings of turquois. (16)

      Although K'oo·ˊko doesn't appear in Silko's version of the Pacayanyi story, her name (and by extension the body of Laguna story containing that name) does show up, spelled "K'oo'ko," in an embedded text located ten pages earlier in the novel, as a figure who haunts the dreams of warriors who haven't been ceremonially cleansed after contact with "dead enemies": see chapter 10 of this study.

12   The home of Ck'o'yo medicine is always to the north or northwest of the people's home; recall that Silko's Kaup'a'ta episode (see chapter 4) begins

> Up North
> around Reedleaf Town
> there was this Ck'o'yo magician
> they called Kaup'a'ta or the Gambler.

13   In Silko: "He struck the middle of the west wall/ and from the east wall/ a bear came out"; in Boas: "Again to the west he came and next there in the west he struck it. Then there eastward a bear came out."

14   For more on this motif as it informs the Kaup'a'ta story, see chapter 4; for more on the Arrowboy fragment, see chapter 13. David Moore discusses this motif in "Silko's Blood Sacrifice": see especially pp. 162–63 and notes 13 and 15.

15   Here as elsewhere in this episode, Silko works to establish the recruiter as both a con man (note his "rehearsed" sincerity) and a racist (note his use of "we" to distinguish himself and his presumed kind from these Indian "boys"), and in any case as alien to this place and the people who live life there.

16   Where Silko uses the verb "strike," the verb is "strike" in one of Boas's two versions and "stab" in the other (*Keresan Texts* 15, 223 or see Appendix D).

17   Even prior to his acquisition of identity with Mountain Lion during the Mt. Taylor episode, Tayo is associated in the novel with mountain lion energy: when Tayo is remembering the history of his encounters with Emo, and in particular a drunken episode (55–63) in which Emo finally alludes crudely to Tayo's mother as a modern-day Yellow Woman and to Tayo as a halfbreed ("You drink like an Indian, and you're crazy like one too—but you aren't shit, white trash. You love Japs the way your mother loved to screw white men," 63), we are told that Tayo "moved suddenly, with speed which was effortless and floating like a mountain lion" (63). Here as throughout most of the novel, Tayo has all the pieces of the puzzle but not the template for assembling it correctly: like Pa'caya'nyi, he moves with (here, he even moves as) Mountain Lion, but here (as with Pa'caya'nyi in the backbone story) he misdirects that energy to primarily destructive rather than primarily regenerative ends. In the backbone story, Pa'caya'nyi uses a flint knife (recall that his cousin the Gambler Kaup'ata also urges the protagonist Sun Man to unwittingly betray his mission by using the Gambler's own flint knife); here, Tayo uses a broken bottle; in either case the natural capacity for violence (which is also, as we shall see again more clearly in the Mt. Taylor episode, the capacity for graceful action) is being harnessed by Pa'caya'nyi and also by Tayo to work for destruction rather than for regeneration.

CHAPTER 9: THE BACKBONE SERIES II

1   On Betonie's ritual, see chapters 5 and 11; on the episode structure of the novel, see chapter 2 and Appendix A.

2   A very remote homolog is "Ko-pot Ka-nat," one of the stories redacted by Gunn in *Schat-chen* which also bridges the sisters motif (see chapter 7) and the Kaupata motif: once I-ye-ti-ko realizes the necessity of recovering her sister I-sto-a-ko-ya, we are told, she "sent a blue-bottle fly to find her" (115). However, Gunn's fly finds only her footprints, and it is up to Stchi-mu-ne-moot

(who en route encounters the Ko-pot [Kaupata] brothers) to recover the missing mother. Hummingbird Man figures in none of Gunn's stories; Gunn's fly is bluebottle, not greenbottle, and unlike Green Fly in Boas and Silko Gunn's fly is not a custom-made element of the ceremony of recovery.

3   Emo's role in the novel is discussed more fully in chapter 12.
4   See, for instance, Tyler: "... [hummingbirds] have both great speed and endurance, which fits them to be messengers to the spirits who send rain" (92).
5   For more on parrot (macaw) and its relationship to flowers and to the south, see Tyler, whose generalizations about Pueblo tradition happen to hold true for Laguna tradition in this case:

> The multicolored plumage of macaws is also directly related to the many colors found on ears of Indian corn, represented by the Corn Maidens, who are brought back to the Pueblo world each summer. Then the sun reigns supreme from germination time until harvest, but with the approach of winter he returns to his home in the far southland. Macaws, parrots, and parakeets are birds which belong to the distant south but have been brought to the northland and are thus fellow travelers with the sun. (13)

Silko's abiding fascination with the blue-south-flower-female-regeneration-return complex (in *Ceremony* most strongly embodied in the figure of the Night Swan) appears very prominently in her later novels *Almanac of the Dead* (in which *wacah* or macaw spirits direct the revolution brewing in Central America and Mexico) and *Gardens in the Dunes* (in which young Indigo's animal companions are the parrot named Rainbow and the monkey Linnaeus).

6   This line of argument is developed more fully in Nelson, *Place and Vision* 16–17.
7   For the significance of the color white with respect to place and particularly to the First World, where the creatrix Ts'its'tsi'nako is always and ever spinning the story of life for the people and where Hummingbird and Fly go to visit Our Mother Nautsityi in the backbone story, see chapter 11, esp. the section "Re-appropriating Whiteness."
8   For more on Betonie's own associations with tobacco in the prose narrative, see Weso 56–57.
9   Actually, more northwesterly: see the map Laguna sites referred to in the novel in Appendix A.
10 Readers who rightly expect the novel's signifiers to come in batches of four rather than three will recognize that, as far as Tayo's introduction to plant medicine is concerned, "it's not over yet": not until the following summer will Ts'eh introduce Tayo to the fourth flower of this ceremony's pattern, the one that is about the literal and metaphorical light that Tayo will need to "see" what Emo and the others are actually up to at the Jackpile Mine:

> "This one," she said, pointing to a tall dark green plant with round pointed leaves, deep veined like fossil shells. The flat seed pods were sill thick and green, but later, in the fall, the skin would dry thin....
> "What color of sky is in this one?"
> She shook her head. "This isn't for color, she said. "It's for light. The light of the stars, and the moon penetrating the night." (226–27)

Thomas Weso (60–61) identifies this plant with the "moonflower" Tayo finds Ts'eh sitting beside earlier (222) and identifies both as datura, a hallucinogen that also figures importantly in Silko's *Sacred Water* (1993).

CHAPTER 10: SCALP CEREMONY

1   The word means "dear one" or "beloved" and is a term that implies a relationship of grandpar-

ent to grandchild between speaker and auditor. The term appears twice more in the novel: on p. 230, when the Laguna priests address the painting of the she-elk that Tayo and Ts'eh visit during their stay together at Dripping Springs, and on p. 257 when the old men in the kiva finally respond to Tayo's story about his encounters with Ts'eh during the previous year:

>   A'moo'ooh, you say you have seen her
>   Last winter
>   up north
>   with Mountain Lion
>   the hunter
>
>   All summer
>   she was south
>   near Acu
>
>   They started crying
>   the old men started crying
>   "A'moo'ooh! A'moo'ooh!"
>   You have seen her
>   We will be blessed
>   again.

It is interesting that the term functions to identify Tayo with Ts'eh, and old Grandma with the old men of the kiva, in this novel. Silko seals this connection formally by once again relating old Grandma to old Ku'oosh in the sentence following this prayer: "At noon one of old Grandma's grandnieces brought Ku'oosh two lard pails" (257).

2 Quite possibly this informant was Mrs. Walter G. Marmon, Silko's grandmother's sister-in-law: see chapter 7 n. 6.
3 At Laguna, the "enemy" was typically either Navajo or Apache: see Boas 207–10.
4 The question mark indicates a word or phrase that neither Parsons nor Boas could translate.
5 See chapter 8 n. 8 for the relationship between Stirling's "Pishuni" and Boas's (and Silko's) Pa'caya'nyi.
6 That is, the male Laguna representative of that traditionalism—as I argue in chapter 7, old Grandma and her two daughters Thelma and Laura also represent, respectively, the relatively unchanging version of, and two branching historical varieties of, the life of the People. A similar argument could be made that brothers-in-law Josiah and Robert represent two branching male varieties of, and old Ku'oosh the relatively unchanging male version of, that same life.
7 See chapter 11.
8 For more on K'oo'ko's relationship to Pa'caya'nyi (as well as to Nau'ts'ity'i and thus to the Warrior Twins Maseewi and Ouyuyewi), see chapter 7 pp. 78–79.
9 Silko's siting of this cave is consistent with Laguna tradition: in her discussion of opi ceremonialism in *Notes on Laguna Ceremonialism*, Elsie Clews Parsons notes that "Scalps were kept in jars in a cave to the north. The *opi* took care of this cave and from this function were called *dyinidit'kaiame* (north cave)" (122).

CHAPTER 11: THE NAVAJO TEXTS

1 Silko's allusions to the Gallup Ceremonial preparations (116-17) locate this episode temporally in late July or early August, or about two months prior to the third (Mt. Taylor) episode.
2 See chapter 3 of this study for a fuller analysis of this function.

3   At least, so it is in the novel. In a gloss on this section of the Red Antway he recounted to Haile, the singer, "Son of the Late Tall Deschini," adds: "Then a prayer was recited for him, the Bear's own prayer, although sometime in the past it used to be the Red Ant's prayer, but was exchanged with the Bear's prayer. This prayer proceeded on through the hoops, he was talked through the five hoops with it" (134). I take this to imply that portions of chants from the Navajo Mountainway (which deals primarily with the acquisition of Bear medicine) found their way into an older version of the Red Antway. As Silko has old Betonie observe earlier, "the ceremonies have always been changing" (126).

4   Readers familiar with Scott Momaday's classic *House Made of Dawn* may recall a portion of embedded text, in a telling attributed to Ben Benally's grandfather, in which the people encounter *ezda shash nadle*, Changing Bear Woman, and in which a child born of the union of Older Sister (who becomes Bear Maiden) with one of two mysterious strangers results in the birth of a bear child; there is, however, no analog to Silko's story in the available text version (Leland Wyman's *Mountainway*) of that myth. The closest analog I have been able to locate is in Mary C. Wheelright's *The Myth and Prayers of the Great Star Chant* (1940, 1956) but the analogy is only very remote. This version of the Great Star chantway (or "Sóntso Hatrál") includes portions of the myths of several other chantways (Wind, Evil-chasing, Water, Hail, and Coyote); in the first of these, a baby, the son of the Son of Kleesto (Great Snake), disappears from camp near a lake and after three days is recovered (with assistance from Black Wind), but he has been possessed by Kleesto rather than Bear, and when (in the form of Kleesto) he is drawn through a series of ceremonial hoops (rather like the ones in Betonie's ceremony) he transforms into "a grown person who had been the baby four days before" (11).

5   For more on Silko and Bear, see chapter 1 of Brewster Fitz's *Silko: Writing Storyteller and Medicine Woman*. Fitz has this to say about the etiology of Silko's Bear-child story:

> It is not clear whether this embedded bear narrative is one of the clan stories whose telling in *Ceremony* has upset Silko's cousin, Paula Gunn Allen, but both the manner in which it is told and its content make it plausible that this could be a story told by Aunt Susie or Aunt Alice to young Leslie and her sisters to warn them about the consequences of straying from the grownups when away from the pueblo. (53-54)

6   See "Circular Design in Ceremony," originally published in *American Indian Quarterly* (1979) and reprinted in Chavkin, *Leslie Marmon Silko's* Ceremony: *A Casebook* (New York: Oxford UP, 2002) 23-39.

7   Readers may recall that, in the story Betonie tells Tayo right after the completion of the hoop ceremony about the origins of the anti-witchery work Tayo has just become part of (145-51), "It all started a long time ago. My Grandfather, Descheeny, was an old man then" (145). It seems we are to understand, then, that Betonie is the son of the "Son of the Late Tall Deschini," which would explain his familiarity with the Red Antway materials he uses in the novel.

8   "Shush" (sometimes spelled "shash") is the Navajo word for "bear."

9   For the distinction between "embedding" and "embedded" storytellers, see chapter 5 of this study.

10 "In the garment ceremony the spruce garment is cut from the patient by the impersonators of Monster Slayer and his brother, therefore Monster Slayer's Songs are used as cutting songs" (Wyman 189). The "garment ceremony" is one of several rites, each enacted on a different day of the overall chantway, in which the hunter's liberation from the coyote skin is commemorated; in the backbone myth of the Coyote transformation ceremony reproduced in Wyman, the first of these "cuttings" involves slicing the patient's head so that the coyote skin can then be peeled off the hunter from head to toe as he passes through the series of five hoops.

11 Compare the "piece of flint" (47) Pa'caya'nyi uses to stab into the earth, causing water to run north to south and Bear to appear in the east, in first movement of the novel's nine-part em-

bedded backbone series; compare also the "black flint knife" (175) Kaup'a'ta hands to Sun Man in his effort to trick Sun Man into trying to kill him. Of course, these two appearances of flint show how flint is used for destruction in the hands of Ck'o'yo medicine men, whereas Betonie's use of the flint is part of a ceremony designed to undo the effects of witchery.

12 Almost certainly we are to recall in this description Old Ku'oosh's enigmatic allusions to the Laguna "Scalp Ceremony" (37–38) : see chapter 10 of this study.
13 So called, at least, by Wyman: see, for instance, p. 17.
14 See Boas, "The Emergence" 9–10 and a fragment given by José in 1919 (222); see also White 84. This color coding of worlds is not always consistent, however, even within a given telling: in "The Emergence," for instance, the informant (Gʸi·´mi, 1919) also reverses the colors of the Second and Third worlds at one point (9).
15 This identity is reiterated in John Gunn's *Schat-chen*: "When the people came out, the earth or land was soft, not ripe (sah-kun-nut). So they traveled on to the south, and there, finding a place suitable, built their habitations or village and called it Kush-kut-ret (the White Village)" (110). Interestingly, the most venerable of the Navajo chantways, Blessingway or *hozhojii*, is said to grow out of the White House ruins in Cañon de Chelly: see, for instance, Andrew Natonabah's gloss on his performance of one of the songs comprising *hozhojii* in the videotape "By This Song I Walk."

CHAPTER 12: THE WITCHERY

1 Silko uses italic typeface to demarcate narrative voice in only two of the 30 embedded texts, this one and the short "*What She Said:*" piece in the opening hoop series (see chapter 3). However, the opening sentence of witch's discourse is marked conventionally, with quotation marks: "This one just told them to listen:/ 'What I have is a story'" (135). Similarly, all of the discourse attributed to the other witches in this portion of text appears in quotation marks rather than italics. Silko appears to be prodding her reader to distinguish between the voicing of ordinary discourse and the voicing of ritual or ceremonial speech (that is, "ritual poetry").
2 That the story which follows is to be understood as narrated by Betonie is formally underscored by the fact that in the novel the preceding sentence, bounded on the front end by quotation marks, carries no closing quotation marks.
3 For a full-length analysis of this premise and of how it informs the novel, see Nelson, *Place and Vision*, especially the chapter on *Ceremony*.
4 See maps in Appendix A. This chapter of the Navajo Nation recently replaced the (Spanish) name "Cañoncito" with the Navajo word for this place, *To'hajiilee*.
5 For more on the connection between this cave and scalps, see chapter 10.

CHAPTER 13: ARROWBOY

1 See also Helen Jaskoski's "Narrative Art in a Hopi Tale," which focuses on a Hopi version of this "widespread tale" [e-mail, 6 Feb 1996]. In an early interview Silko refers to this Arrowboy story (also called the Black Corn story) as the "classic" witchery story in Laguna oral tradition: "I never heard many of those stories here [at Laguna], except for the classic. I heard that one and that says just about everything you need to know about witches. I heard that one, but that's the only one" (Evers and Carr 18).
2 Boas refers in *Keresan Texts* (228) to an additional version, "The Fate of the Witch Wife," published by Elizabeth de Huff in *Taytay's Tales* in 1922. De Huff's version is written in what she calls a "simple and direct manner" (ix); the style and content of this collection, tellingly sub-

titled *Collected and Retold*, is gentled down to the reading level of children and the mothers whom de Huff presumes will be reading these stories to those children. The provenance of her version is highly uncertain: under the titles of most of the tales in this collection, de Huff gives in parentheses the name of a village or Pueblo, presumably where she heard the prototype of her version, but for "The Fate of the Witch Wife" she gives as her source "Seama Pueblo, San Juan Pueblo, Sia Pueblo and Hopi, Second Mesa" (172). She gives the protagonist's name as Redflower and his wife's as White Corn.

In addition to the Hopi correlatives noted by Jaskoski (see note 1 above), Toby C. S. Langen references three print versions of this story collected at Tewa-speaking pueblos (two from San Juan and one from Santa Clara), as well as one from Cochiti, in her essay "Estoy-eh-muut and the Morphologists."

3   For complete transcripts of the homologous passages from Lummis, Gunn, and Boas, see Appendix F.
4   "Arrowboy" is an approximate translation of the word "Estoy-eh-muut," and in the first line of "Estoy-eh-moot and the Kunideeyahs" (*Storyteller* 140–54)—but only there—Silko gives the appellation "Estoy-eh-muut, Arrowboy"(140); elsewhere in this 14-page text the protagonist's name is given as simply "Estoy-eh-muut." Lummis's spelling and translation are almost identical to Silko's: "Among the folk-lore heroes of whom every Quères lad has heard is Ees-tée-ah Muts, the Arrow Boy" (*Pueblo Indian Folk Stories* 194). Though his spelling varies, Gunn agrees with Lummis's translation: In *Schat-chen* Gunn includes two stories featuring the protagonist "Is-to-a-moot," a name he translates "the arrow boy, [...] one of the most celebrated characters in Qe-res history" (184), making it all the more curious that the protagonist of his most analogous witchery story is "Yo-a-schi-moot." Boas gives the spelling of the name in Keresan orthography as *icto·ˈa miḍʳᵉ* and translates the word as "Arrow-Youth."

Elsewhere in *Storyteller*, Estoy-eh-muut appears in a piece titled "The Two Sisters" (100–03), a performance in which the storyteller's glosses on her own story are presented as italicized interpellation; early in this story, we are told that once two sisters "were interested in a young man/by the name of Estoy-eh-muut./ *'Muut' means 'youth.'*/ *'Estoyeh' means that he was a great hunter*" (100). See also Boas's discussion of the near-homonyms "ιcτο·ˈa kʼo·ˈya, arrow-woman, or ιcτοa·ˈa kʼo·ˈya, reed woman"and the probable pun on "ιcτο·ˈa ikʊˈyɑnyi," "tobacco" (Boas 238); see also chapter 7, especially pp. 68–69, of this book).

5   The spelling varies, even within Silko's work. Though curiously she does not use this term in her novel (the agents of witchery are referred to only as "the destroyers," 229), she gives the spelling "Kunideeyah" in *Storyteller* (140–54) but "Gunnadeyah" in her video title. Gunn spells it "Kun-ni-te-ya"; Boas (who invariably translates the term as "witch") variously as "kʼanaτvɛʼya" (Pt. 2 208) or "tcʼaˊnaτ·εʼya" (Pt. 2 205); and Parsons in *Notes on Ceremonialism at Laguna* as *kanadyeya*, defining the term as "witch, evil spirit" (97, 118).
6   A good precis of the print versions available in the mid-1920s is given in Boas, "The Witches and the Youth" 263–65).
7   For an extended discussion of hoop imagery in Betonie's ritual and elsewhere in the novel, see chapter 5, esp. Part 2, "Jumping Through Hoops." As an aside, it may be worth noting that at the end of the *Storyteller* version (and also at the end of Boas's version), Spider Grandmother teaches Arrowboy to use a different kind of hoop—one constructed of yucca, which when thrown frisbee-style transforms into a snake—to destroy Kochinninako. In this case as in Navajo and Laguna story more generally, practically any form of energy can be deployed against, as well as for, the Destroyers: what matters is not the form of energy *per se* but rather who is deploying it, or in what spirit it is being deployed.
8   See *Place and Vision* for a more thorough explication of this idea.
9   In the section subtitled "Ritual of the Reader" in his essay "Silko's Blood Sacrifice: The Circulating Witness in *Almanac of the Dead*," David Moore also highlights a relationship between

vision and the need to keep story in motion. In his argument Arrowboy serves as a role model for the reader in both *Almanac of the Dead* and *Ceremony*:

> Through vision, the ritual circulation of [the] passive powers of time, land, and dreamed stories gradually interpellates the reader of *Almanac* as witness.... In Arrowboy's context, this watching becomes a strategy of undoing. The dynamic functions ritualistically, 'a good ceremony' for the reader to test her or his responses against Arrowboy's ethos: am I a witness or a voyeur? Am I a protestor or a participant in this violence? The difference bears all the personal-as-political weight of colonial history and psychology. (162)

Moore goes on to argue that Silko works to problematize this dialectic for her reader, just as it becomes problematized for Tayo and for Arrowboy when such binary models work only to entrap, rather than to liberate or keep in circulation, the stories they are part of:

> How does Arrowboy's witnessing stop the witchery from working? By exploding, opening, triangulating the binary of victim and victimizer, the witness creates a circulation of the blood energy among the three poles—and then many in the telling —rather than between an oppositional two. In Bakhtinian terms, the witness makes a dialogic polyglossia out of a dialectic monoglossia. The energy is freed from oppositionality as the witness harnesses her own vulnerability. (163)

10   Just prior to Ts'eh's emergence into the field of Tayo's vision during the Dripping Springs episode, we are told, Tayo notices, and is noticed by,

> a light yellow snake, covered with bright copper spots, like the wild flowers pulled loose and traveling.... He knelt over the arching tracks the snake left in the sand and filled the delicate imprints with yellow pollen. *As far as he could see, in all directions, the world was alive.* He could feel the motion pushing out of the damp earth into the sunshine—the yellow spotted snake the first to emerge, carrying this message on his back for the people. (221; italics added)

Note that Tayo pays snake the same respect earlier paid to mountain lion on Mt. Taylor ("He leaned close to the earth and sprinkled pinches of yellow pollen into the four footprints," 196). Here at the Jackpile Mine, it seems, Tayo himself completes the transition from identity with Mountain Lion, the hunter, to identity with Snake, the waterbearer.

11   On U.S. Geodetic Survey maps there is such a place, north of Jackpile and within walking distance (as described in the text), and it is called "Mesa del Lobo" (in English, "wolf mesa"). Perhaps we are to understand from this that, even though it is getting dark, so that his physiological vision must be somewhat impaired, Tayo is beginning to "see," as it were, "beneath the surface[s]" of things, exercising that special quality of vision that enables him to see, as he learned to see on the Dark Mountain in the Navajo way, that "there were no boundaries" between the life of the stories and the life of the people, that "the world below and the sand paintings inside became the same that night" (145). At any rate, he does come to understand, suddenly and surely, that this place is "theirs"—that whatever enspirits Emo also enspirits this place, and that the spirit they share is conventionally embodied as "lobo" or "wolf" (rather than, say, coyote or bear). Thus, it is probably not just coincidental that the *only* animal mentioned in the fragment, the one the "witchman" half-transforms into, is wolf.

12   Laguna Pueblo was not particularly progressive until a sociopolitical schism developed in the latter part of the nineteenth century, a fallout which resolved when conservatives relocated themselves and their ceremonies in 1881 to neighboring Isleta Pueblo.

Notes

13 See Appendix F for a transcript of the relevant passage from the *Storyteller* version.
14 "Arrowboy and the Witches" is available from The Video Tape Co., 10545 Burbank Blvd., North Hollywood, CA 91601-2280.
15 In a 1978 letter to James Wright, Silko had this to say about her intentions for this project:

> I am pushing to finish the first of the scripts which attempt to tell the Laguna stories on film using the storyteller's voice with the actual locations where these stories are supposed to have taken place. In a strange sort of way, the film project is an experiment in translation—bringing the land—the hills, the arroyos, the boulders, the cottonwoods in October—to people unfamiliar with it, because after all, the stories grow out of this land as much as we see ourselves as having emerged from the land there ... if you do not know the places which the storyteller calls up in the telling, if you have not waded in the San Jose River below the village, if you have not hidden in the river willows and sand with your lover, then even as the teller relates a story, you will miss something which people from the Laguna community would not have missed. (*Delicacy* 24)

16 For a detailed explanation of the location and role of Dripping Springs in the novel, see Nelson, *Place and Vision* 30.
17 Silko makes much the same point within the prose narrative when Robert visits Tayo "at the end of the summer" (227) to remind him of the ongoing life and story of the people that, sooner or later, Tayo's life and story must re-become part of:

> "What should I tell them at Laguna?... They want you to come home. They are worried about you. They think you might need the doctors again.... Old man Ku'oosh and some of the others are wondering too why you haven't come. They thought maybe there might be something you should tell them." The words caught in his throat, and he coughed. "And Emo has been saying things about you. He's been talking about how you went crazy and are alone out here. He talks bullshit about caves and animals." (228)

Robert's reference to "bullshit about caves and animals" is, no doubt, a reference to the kinds of animal transformation stories associated with witchery, i.e., stories easily confused with the recovery stories that also feature the transformation motif: *cf.* Silko's warning about confusing the two ("NOTE ON BEAR PEOPLE AND WITCHES," 131).

 # WORKS CITED

Allen, Paula Gunn. *Grandmothers of the Light: A Medicine Woman's Sourcebook.* Boston: Beacon, 1991.
———. *The Sacred Hoop: Recovering the Feminine in American Indian Traditions.* Boston: Beacon, 1986.
———. "Special Problems in Teaching Leslie Marmon Silko's *Ceremony.*" *American Indian Quarterly* 14 (Fall 1990): 379–86. Rpt. in Chavkin, 83–90.
———. *Spider Woman's Granddaughters.* Boston: Beacon, 1989.
Anzaldúa, Gloria. *Borderlands/La Frontera: The New Mestiza.* San Francisco: Aunt Lute, 1987.
Arnold, Ellen. *Conversations with Leslie Marmon Silko.* Oxford, MS: UP of Mississippi, 2000.
Barnett, Louise, and James Thorson, eds. *Leslie Marmon Silko: A Collection of Critical Essays.* Albuquerque: U of New Mexico P, 1999.
Bell, Robert. "Circular Design in *Ceremony.*" *American Indian Quarterly* 5.1 (February 1979): 47–62. Rpt. in Chavkin, 23–39.
Benedict, Ruth. "Eight Stories from Acoma." *Journal of American Folklore* 43.167 (1930): 59–87.
Boas, Franz. *Keresan Texts.* Publications of the American Ethnological Society, 8. New York: American Ethnological Society, 1928.
Chavkin, Allen, ed. *Leslie Marmon Silko's* Ceremony: *A Casebook.* New York: Oxford UP, 2002.
Conley, Robert. "We Wait." *The Remembered Earth: An Anthology of Contemporary American Indian Literature.* Ed. Geary Hobson. Albuquerque: U of New Mexico P, 1980. 72–73.
Danielson, Linda. "The Storytellers in *Storyteller.*" *Studies in American Indian Literatures* 1.2 (Fall 1989): 21–31.
De Huff, Elizabeth Willis. *Taytay's Tales: Collected and Retold.* New York: Harcourt, Brace and Company, 1922.
Ellis, Larry. "Trickster: Shaman of the Liminal." *Studies in American Indian Literatures* 5.4 (Winter 1992): 55–68.
Evers, Larry, and Denny Carr. "A Conversation with Leslie Marmon Silko." *Sun Tracks* 3.1 (1976): 28–33. Rpt. in Arnold, 10–21.
Fitz, Brewster E. *Silko: Writing Storyteller and Medicine Woman.* Norman: U of Oklahoma P, 2004.
Graulich, Melody, ed. *"Yellow Woman," Leslie Marmon Silko.* New Brunswick, NJ: Rutgers UP, 1993.
Gunn, John M. *Schat-chen: History, Traditions and Narratives* [sic] *of the Queres Indians of Laguna and Acoma.* 1917. New York: AMS, 1980.
Haile, Berard. *Legend of the Ghostway Ritual in the Male Branch of Shootingway.* St. Michaels, AZ: St. Michaels P, 1950.
Jaskoski, Helen. *Leslie Marmon Silko: A Study of the Short Fiction.* New York: Twayne, 1998.
———. "The Witch Lady Story: Narrative Art in a Hopi Tale." *Native American Literatures.* Ed. Laura Coltelli. *Forum* 2–3 / 1990–91. Pisa: SEU. 3–26.
Kroeber, Karl. "An Introduction to the Art of Traditional American Indian Narration." *Traditional Literatures of the American Indian: Texts and Interpretations.* Ed. Karl Kroeber. Lincoln: U of Nebraska P, 1981. 1–24.
Kurath, Gertrude P. "Calling the Rain Gods." *Journal of American Folklore* 73 (1960): 312–15.
Langen, Toby C. S. "Estoy-eh-muut and the Morphologists." *Studies in American Indian Literatures* 1.1 (Summer 1989): 1–12.
Lincoln, Kenneth. "Blue Medicine." *Native American Renaissance.* Berkeley: U California P, 1983. Rpt. in Chavkin, 51–62.
Marmon, Lee. "A Laguna Portfolio." *Studies in American Indian Literatures* 5.1 (Spring 1993): 62–74.

Miller, Jay. "Keres: Engendered Key to the Pueblo Puzzle." *Ethnohistory* 48.3 (2001): 495–514.
Mitchell, Carol. "*Ceremony* as Ritual." *American Indian Quarterly* 5.1 (1979): 27–35.
Momaday, N. Scott. *House Made of Dawn*. New York: Harper, 1968.
Mooney, James. *The Ghost-dance Religion and the Sioux Outbreak of 1890. Fourteenth Annual Report of the Bureau of Ethnology, 1892–93*. Part 2. Washington, DC: G.P.O., 1896.
Moore, David L. "Silko's Blood Sacrifice: The Circulating Witness in *Almanac of the Dead*." *Leslie Marmon Silko: A Collection of Critical Essays*. Eds. Louise K. Barnett and James L. Thorson. Albuquerque: U of New Mexico P, 1999. 149–83.
Mullett, G. M. *Spider Woman Stories*. Tucson: U of Arizona P, 1979.
Nabokov, Peter. "American Indian Literature: A Tradition of Renewal." *Studies in American Indian Literatures* 2.3 (Autumn 1978): 31–40.
Natonabah, Andrew. "By This Song I Walk." *Words and Place: Native American Literature from the American Southwest*. Videocassette series. Prod. Larry Evers. New York: Clearwater, 1982.
Nelson, Elizabeth Hoffman, and Malcolm Nelson. "Shifting Patterns, Changing Stories: Leslie Marmon Silko's Yellow Woman." *Leslie Marmon Silko: A Collection of Critical Essays*. Eds. Louise K. Barnett and James L. Thorson. Albuquerque: U of New Mexico P, 1999. 121–33.
Nelson, Robert M. "He Said / She Said: Writing Oral Tradition in John Gunn's 'Kopot Kanat' and Leslie Silko's *Storyteller*." *Studies in American Indian Literatures* 5.1 (Spring 1993): 31–50.
———. "The Function of Landscape in *Ceremony*." *Place and Vision: The Function of Landscape in Native American Fiction*. New York: Peter Lang, 1994. 11–40. Rpt. in Chavkin, 139–73.
Ortiz, Simon. *A Good Journey*. Sun Tracks 12. Tucson: U of Arizona P, 1984.
———. "Heyaashi Guutah." *The Remembered Earth: An Anthology of Contemporary Native American Literature*. Ed. Geary Hobson. Albuquerque: U of New Mexico P, 1980. 264–65.
Owens, Louis. "'The Very Essence of Our Lives': Leslie Silko's Webs of Identity." *Other Destinies: Understanding The American Indian Novel*. Norman: U of Oklahoma P, 1992. 167-91. Rpt. in Chavkin, 91–116.
Parsons, Elsie Clews. *Laguna Genealogies*. Anthropological Papers of the American Museum of Natural History 19.5. New York: AMNH, 1923.
———. *Notes on Ceremonialism at Laguna*. Anthropological Papers of the American Museum of Natural History 19.4. New York: AMNH, 1920. 85–131.
Pratt, Mary Louise. "Arts of the Contact Zone." *Ways of Reading: An Anthology for Writers*. Donald Bartholomae and Anthony Petrosky, eds. 3rd ed. Boston: St Martin's, 1993.
Roemer, Kenneth M. "Silko's Arroyos as Mainstream: Processes and Implications of Canonical Identity." *Modern Fiction Studies* 45.1 (Spring 1999): 10–37.
Rosen, Kenneth, ed. *The Man to Send Rain Clouds*. New York: Library of America, 1974.
"Running on the Edge of Rainbow: Laguna Stories and Poems. With Leslie Marmon Silko." *Words and Place: Native Literature from the American Southwest*. Videocassette series. Prod. Larry Evers. New York: Clearwater, 1978.
Ruppert, James. "The Russians Are Coming, the Russians Are Dead: Myth and Historical Consciousness in Two Contact Narratives." *Studies in American Indian Literatures* 2.1 (Spring 1990): 1–10.
Salyer, Gregory. *Leslie Marmon Silko*. New York: Twayne, 1997.
Sekaquaptewa, Helen. "Iisaw: Hopi Coyote Stories." *Words and Place: Native American Literature from the American Southwest*. Videocassette series. Prod. Larry Evers. New York: Clearwater, 1982.
Silko, Leslie Marmon. *Almanac of the Dead*. New York: Simon and Schuster, 1991.
———. "An Essay on Rocks." *Aperture 139: Strong Hearts: Native American Visions and Voices* (Summer 1995): 60–63.

---. "An Old-Time Indian Attack Conducted in Two Parts." 1977. Rpt. in *The Remembered Earth: An Anthology of Contemporary Native American Literature*. Geary Hobson, ed. Albuquerque: U of New Mexico P, 1980.
---. *Ceremony*. New York: Viking, 1977.
---. "The Fourth World." *Artforum* 27.10 (Summer 1989): 125–26.
---. "Interior and Exterior Landscapes: The Pueblo Migration Stories." *Landscape in America*. George F. Thompson, ed. Austin: U of Texas P, 1995. 155–70.
---. *Laguna Woman*. Greenfield Center, NY: Greenfield Review P, 1974.
---. "Landscape, History, and the Pueblo Imagination" *Antaeus* 51 (1986): 83–94.
---. *Sacred Water*. Tucson: Flood Plain, 1993.
---. *Storyteller*. New York: Seaver, 1981.
---. *Yellow Woman and a Beauty of the Spirit: Essays on Native American Life Today*. New York: Simon & Schuster, 1996.
Spencer, Katherine. *An Analysis of Navaho Chantway Myths*. Memoirs of the American Folklore Society v. 48. Philadelphia: American Folklore Society, 1957.
Stevenson, Mathilda Coxe. *The Sia*. 11th Annual Report of the Bureau of Ethnology (1889–90). Washington, DC: GPO, 1894. 3–157.
Stirling, Matthew W. *Origin Myth of Acoma and Other Records*. Bureau of American Ethnology Bulletin 135. Washington: GPO, 1942.
Swan, Edith. "Healing Via the Sunwise Cycle in Silko's *Ceremony*." *American Indian Quarterly* 12.4 (Fall 1988): 313–28.
---. "Laguna Symbolic Geography and Silko's *Ceremony*." *American Indian Quarterly* 12.3 (Summer 1988): 229–49.
Tyler, Hamilton A. *Pueblo Birds and Myths*. 1979. Flagstaff, AZ: Northland, 1991.
Waters, Frank. *Book of the Hopi*. New York: Viking Penguin, 1963.
Weso, Thomas F. "From Delirium to Coherence: Shamanism and Medicine Plants in Silko's *Ceremony*." *American Indian Culture and Research Journal* 28.1 (2004): 53–66.
Wheelwright, Mary C. *The Myth and Prayers of the Great Star Chant and The Myth of the Coyote Chant*. Ed. David P. McAllester. Navajo Religion Series v. 4. Santa Fe: Museum of Navajo Ceremonial Art, 1956.
White, Leslie A. *The Acoma Indians*. 47th Annual Report of the Bureau of American Ethnology (1929–30). Washington, DC: GPO, 1932. 17–192.
---. "The World of the Keresan Pueblo Indians." *Primitive Views of the World*. Ed. Stanley Diamond. New York: Columbia UP, 1964.
Wiget, Andrew. *Native American Literature*. Twayne's United States Authors Series 467. Boston: Hall, 1985.
---. "Telling the Tale: A Performance Analysis of a Hopi Coyote Story." *Recovering the Word: Essays on Native American Literature*. Eds. Brian Swann and Arnold Krupat. Berkeley: U of California P, 1987. 297–338.
Wright, Anne, ed. *The Delicacy and Strength of Lace: Letters between Leslie Marmon Silko and James Wright*. Saint Paul, MN: Graywolf, 1986.
Wyman, Leland. *The Red Antway of the Navaho*. Navajo Religion Series 5. Santa Fe: Museum of Navajo Ceremonial Art, 1965.
Zamir, Shamoon. "Literature in a 'National Sacrifice Area'." *New Voices in Native American Literary Criticism*. Arnold Krupat, ed. Washington, DC: Smithsonian Institution, 1993. 396–415.

INDEX

A

Acoma (Pueblo), 34, 62, 109, 161n2
   as locus of Arrowboy story, 127, 133–34
   as locus of Kaupata story, 27, 165–66n4
   in relation to Dripping Springs, 133
   in relation to Pa'toch Butte, 133
   locus of Opi origin story in Stirling, 101–102, 101
   map of, 141–42
   origin story from, 40, 167n8
Allen, Paula Gunn, 17, 19, 23, 26, 50, 162n16, 163n8, 166n2, 170n3
   Fitz on, 177n5
   hama-ha in, 59, 169n3
   related to Silko, 166n5
   shiwanna in, 169n6
a'moo'h (dear one), 48, 95, 175–76n1
   old Grandma's chant, 100
Anzaldúa, Gloria, 161n7
Arnold, Ellen, 1
Arrowboy, 9, 14, 77, 105, 127–37, 179n4
   Hopi version, 178n1
   in Boas, 128
   in DeHuff, 129
   in Gunn, 128, 129, 133
   in Lummis, 127–28, 129, 133
   in Silko and Boas, 153–54, 155
   in Silko and Gunn, 155
   in Silko and Lummis, 155
   in Storyteller, 128
   Tayo as, 127–137 *passim*
   use of hoop to kill Kochinninako, 179n7
   vision and, 165n11n, 180n9
Aunt Susie. *See* Marmon, Susan Reyes
Auntie (Thelma), 16, 81, 85, 107, 171n6
   and Corn Woman, 69–71
   and Laura, 70–71
   and Laura as branching versions of Laguna female, 176n6
   story about Laura, 71–74, 161n9

B

backbone, 58, 63, 108, 130, 135
   and skeletal structure of embedded texts, 15, 24
   as traditional storytelling closing phrase, 22
   in Swan, 163n13
   nine-part backbone story, 14, 19–26, 66, 73, 75–97
      bundled with Coyote transformation story, 111, 113
      old Buzzard in, 18
      Ma'see'wi and Ou'yu'ye'wi in, 74
      tobacco in, 67
      variations in *Ceremony* and *Storyteller*, 171–72n2
Badger, 23, 165n4
Barnett, Louise, 1
Bear, 17, 79, 80, 107–10, 177n3
   and Chuska Mountains, 116
   Bear People, 53
   in "An Essay on Rocks," 109
   in Silko and Boas, 149
   in "Story From Bear Country," 109
   in Red Antway, 177n3
Bear medicine, 79, 107
   in Silko and Wyman, 156–59
   in Stirling, 173n8
   Pacayanyi's abuse of, 79–80
   Pacayanyi's Ck'o'yo version of, 77
      See also Red Antway
bear-child story, 107–09
   in Fitz, 177n5
Bell, Robert, 109, 111, 163n3, 164n3, 168n23
Benedict, Ruth, 27, 36, 164n1, 165–66n10
   "Kaupat´a," 28
Betonie, 24, 95, 103, 168n22
   and Bear medicine, 79–80
   and Gallup, 165n11
   and Nautsityi, 93
   and old Buzzard, 90, 92–94
   and Descheeny/Deschini, 96, 177n7

and old Ku'oosh, 45, 48, 103
and Big Hoop ceremony, 52, 83, 107–17 *passim*, 169n24
and tobacco, 175n8
and the witchery in the Arrowboy story, 128–36
flint knife, use of, 178n11
star pattern, 32, 34, 166n1
witch story, 85, 121–25
Big Hoop ceremony, 110–17
as the turning point of the novel, 114
color coding in, 114–19
departure and darkness in, 115
hoops and transformative zones in, 116
in Wyman, 177n3
in Wyman and Silko, 156–59
recovery and whiteness in, 115
Black Elk, 50, 51, 168n19
Boas, Franz, 21, 27, 60, 66, 100, 118
Keresan Texts, 21, 22, 23, 25, 42, 60, 66, 75, 84, 118, 128, 162–63n3
See also *Keresan Texts*
Budville, 7
Buzzard, 14, 83, 84, 91–95
and Betonie, 90, 92–94
and Nautsityi, 90
in Silko and Boas, 150–52

C

Cañoncito, 105
as locus of both witches' convention and Emo's c'ko'yo cermony, 134
as locus of witches' convention, 121–25 *passim*
cave near, 105
Cañoncito Navajo reservation (*Tohajiilee*), 7, 124
map of, 141–42
Casa Blanca, 6, 16, 90
Caterpillar, 93–94
in Silko and Boas, 151-52
cave
and Scalp Ceremony, 104–05
at Acoma, 133
near Cañoncito, 124
near site of witches' convention, 105
occupied by the Gunnedeyah in the Arrowboy story, 105

where Pacayanyi performs his Ck'o'yo magic, 105
Cerritos, 170n3
Chavkin, Allen, 1
Chuska Mountains, 34, 93, 107, 113
and "dark mountain" of Big Hoop ceremony, 16, 52, 117
as locus of Bear and Coyote medicines, 80, 116
as site of Betonie's ceremony, 128–29, 169n24
in relation to Laguna village, 94
Ck'o'yo, 23, 36, 72
absent in *Storyteller* Arrowboy story, 135
and Coyote, 108
and U. S. government, 79
as disease, 103
as disruption, 96
as infection, 86
as magic, 85
as sister to Nautsityi/Corn Mother, 77
"giantess," 172n4
in Stevenson (Sko´yo), 76
magician, Pacayanyi as, 96
medicine, 95
home in the north, 174n12
in Silko and Boas, 147–48, 149
Tayo's advocacy of, 83
mother of Pacayanyi and Kaupata, 125
witchery, 125, 127–37
Cochiti (Pueblo), 41, 172n7, 179n2
color coding
in Big Hoop ceremony, 114–19
of worlds in Boas, 167n12
of worlds in Boas and White, 178n14
of mountains in Silko and Wyman, 156–57, 159
Conley, Robert, 122
contact zone
Laguna village as, 5
Corn Mother
as sister to K'oo'ko/Ck'o'yo, 77
in Stirling (Iatiku), 172n8
See also Nautsityi
Corn Woman, 13, 16, 65–71, 73, 77, 81, 104, 108, 171n6
and Auntie, 69–71
and Nau'ts'ity'i as homologues, 67
and Tayo, 68–69
in Gunn, 65–67
in Silko and Gunn, 145

Coyote, 14, 17, 24, 40, 53, 107–14, 116, 125, 128
  and Chuska Mountains, 116
  and Ck'o'yo, 108
  and Pacayanyi, 108, 112
  hunter-Coyote transformation in Silko and Wyman, 155–59, 170n3, 177n10
  transformation story, 109–17
Cubero, 7, 16, 34, 77

D

Danielson, Linda, 161n10, 162n1, 164n2
dawn people (kurena moiety), 60, 61
De Huff, Elizabeth, 178–179n2
deer
  and Rocky, 86
  and Ts'eh, 97
DeHuff, Elizabeth, 130
departure
  and darkness in Big Hoop ceremony, 115
  in Big Hoop ceremony, 114
  of Nautsityi in nine-part backbone story, 75–82
  of Nautsityi, Helen Jean, and Laura 170n3
  of Reed Woman, 69
      See also departure-recovery motif
departure-recovery motif, 5, 16–18, 70–71
  in *Almanac of the Dead* and *Gardens in the Dunes*, 10–11
  in Big Hoop ceremony, 52, 107–19 *passim*
  in nine-part backbone story, 14, 23–24, 75–97
  in scalp ceremony, 99–105
Descheeny, 96, 177n7
Dripping Springs, 16, 35, 95, 130, 176n1
  and speckled cattle, 136
  and spotted yellow snake, 180n10
  and Ts'eh, 133, 136
  as site of "Estoymuut and the Gunnadeyah," 136
  cave at, 105
  snake at, 162n3
drought, 19, 108
  and departure of Reed Woman, 65–69
  and departure of Nautsityi, 75–89 *passim*
  caused by Corn Woman's rejection of Reed Woman, 65–69 *passim*
  caused by the introduction of Pacayanyi's ck'o'yo medicine, 104
  caused by peoples' misbehavior, 81
  caused by Tayo's prayer, 104
  caused by violation of Scalp Ceremony, 101–02
  in Silko and Gunn, 145

E

Ellis, Larry, 170n3
emergence, 32, 45, 49, 62, 76, 78, 85, 87
  of Ts'eh at Dripping Springs, 162n3
  of yellow spotted snake at Dripping Springs, 162n3, 180n10
emergence place. *See sipapu*
Emo, 25, 165n11
  ceremony at Jackpile mine, 105, 131–34, 180n11
  and Kaupata, 36
  and Pacayanyi, 86
  and Rocky, 85
  and witchery in Arrowboy fragment, 129
  as advocate of whites, 81, 124
  as ck'o'yo witch, 77, 85, 125
Enchanted Mesa, 133
Encinal, 6
Engine Rock, 133
Estoy-eh-muut
  variant spelling in Silko, Lummis, Gunn, and Boas, 179n4
ethnography
  as pretext for *Ceremony*, 3, 20, 21
  Laguna as ethnographic site, 25

F

Fifth World, 36, 43, 49, 88, 118, 121
  and hoop ceremony, 53,54,56,96
  katsinas' emergence into, 60
  Nautsityi's departure from, 23
  Nautsityi's return to, 73
First World

home of Ts'its'tsi'nako, 49
Ts'its'tsi'nako in, 43
Fitz, Brewster, 1, 169n25, 177n5
flint knife, 33, 36, 79, 164n15
   amd Tayo's screw driver, 132
   and Tayo's broken bottle, 132, 174n17
   as used by Betonie, Pacayanyi, and Kaupata, 177–78n11
   in Red Antway, 112
   in Silko and Boas, 148, 149
   Kaupata's, 174n17
   Pacayanyi's, 174n17
   Pacayanyi's use of, 79
Floyd Lee
   and Kaupata, 29, 30, 33, 131
fly
   Big Fly Silko and Wyman, 158
   in Gunn, 66, 174n2
   Josiah's homily on, 89, 96
                  See also Green Fly
Francis, Lee, 167n10

G

Gallup, 81, 103
   and Betonie, 92–93, 165n11
   and Helen Jean, 170n3
   and Kaupata, 168n21
   and Laguna village, 92, 107
   as spirit trap, 92
   Tayo's birthplace, 33, 90–92
Gallup Ceremonial, 51, 52, 92, 176n1
Gaukapuchume, 102
gender
   liminalization of, 41, 44
gendering
   in Keresan language usage, 167n10
Grandma (Tayo's), 6, 7, 16, 18, 48, 63, 70, 90, 96, 100, 109
   and Ku'oosh, 176n1
   and Nautsityi, 90
grandma A'mooh. *See* Marmon, Marie Anaya
Grandmother Spider. *See* Ts'its'tsi'nako
Graulich, Melody, 1, 162n4
Great Star chantway
   hoops in, 177n3
   Snake in, 177n4
Green Fly, 13, 14, 17, 23, 75, 76

and Gunn's fly, 175n2
and Hummingbird, as agents of recovery, 83–97
and Hummingbird in Silko and Boas, 149–52, 151
and Tayo, 88
creation of, 86–87, 164n15
Gunn, John
   "hama-ha" in, 58–59
   "Ko-pot Ka-nat," 28, 36, 65, 66, 164n1, 174n2
Gunnadeyah ("destroyers"), 105, 107, 121, 125
   Emo, Harley, Leroy, and Pinkie as, 125
   in Silko, Boas, Gunn, and Lummis, 153–54
   origin of, 123–24
   variant spelling in Boas, Gunn, Parsons, and Silko, 179n5
Gyi´mi, 26, 41, 66, 164n19, 166n5

H

Haile, Father Berard, 109, 110, 113, 177n3
hama-ha, 86, 125
   and sunrise, 61, 63
   as storytelling frame phrase, 21, 58–59
   hama-ha stories, 13, 29, 46, 65, 89, 162n1
   in Allen, 59, 169n3
   in Gunn, 57–58
   in *Keresan Texts*, 163n7
Harley, 16, 62, 77, 78, 125, 131, 133, 134, 170n3
   betrayal of Tayo, 134
Helen Jean, 16, 170n3
   and Laura, 170n3
   in relation to Big Hoop ceremony, 170n3
heyaashi. *See shiwanna*
   variant spellings in Ortiz, Boas, and Kurath, 165n13
homology, 29–37 *passim*
   of character, 29
   of cultural context, 30
   of function, 30
   of motif, 31–36
   principle of, 29
   Silko and Betonie, 54

Index

hoop(s), 95, 177n3, 177n4
  and star pattern in Great Star chant, 169n23
  and transformation in witchery, 127, 128, 135
  Buzzard's motion as, 84
  first four pages of novel as, 14, 39–56
  hoop motif, 50–56
  in Allen, 168n19
  in Bell, Wyman, and Wheelright, 168–69 n.23
  in Betonie's ceremony, 110, 169n24
  in Betonie's ceremony and Arrowboy witchery, 129
  in Great Star chantway, 177n4
  McAllester on, 169n3
  transformation into snake, 179n7
  used by Arrowboy to kill Kochinninako, 179n7
  and transformative zones in Big Hoop ceremony, 116
    See also Big Hoop ceremony
Hopi, 122, 124, 178n1, 179n2
  frame elements, 163n4,
hozho (balance, beauty, harmony), 53, 83, 115, 178n15
Hummingbird, 14, 26, 75, 164n15
  absent in Gunn, 175n2
  and Auntie, 73
  and Green Fly, as agents of recovery, 73–74, 76, 83–97
  and Green Fly in Silko and Boas, 149–52
  and Josiah, 88
  and Robert, 90–91
  as messenger figure, 86
  in Boas, 23–24, 27, 67

I

Ictsityi, 43, 66, 70
  as male, 41–42
  in Boas, 41, 42
  in Parsons, 42
  in Stevenson, 41
  in White, 167n9
Iktoa'ak'o'ya. *See* Reed Woman
I-sto-a-ko-ya. *See* Reed Woman
Iyetiku (Corn Woman)
  in Gunn (I-ye-ti-ko), 65–67, 70, 174–75n2
  in Parsons, 42
  in Stirling, 167n8
  in White, 167n8

J

Jackpile mine, 7, 32, 117, 128
  and Emo, 36, 105, 180n11
  as site of witchery, 77, 95, 125, 134
  Tayo's quality of vision at, 129–30, 132, 175n10
Jaskoski, Helen, 1, 178n1, 179n2
José, 41, 76, 172n4, 178n14
Josiah, 78, 81
  and Hummingbird, 88
  and Night Swan, 88–89, 96
  and Robert as branching versions of Laguna male, 176n6
  and speckled cattle, 87, 125
  as traditionalist, 87
  homily on flies, 89–90, 96

K

kashare. *See* koshare
katsina, 27, 59, 61, 164n4, 170–71n4, 172n8
Kaupata, 4, 17, 24, 27–37 *passim*, 129, 131, 170n1
  and Emo, 36
  and Gallup, 168n21
  and vision, 129
  as ck'o'yo witch, 85, 131, 174n12
  in Benedict, 165–66n14
  in Boas, 165n14
  in Gunn, 36
  in Parsons, 164n4
  in Silko and Boas, 145–46
  in White, 164–65n4
  location of, in Silko, White, and Benedict, 165n10
  variant spellings in Gunn, Boas, Benedict, and Silko, 164n4
Kawaika (Laguna village), 5, 10, 26, 61, 83
Keresan Texts, 23, 42, 60, 118, 162–63n3

"The Emergence," 66–67, 166n4, 178n14
  frame phrases in, 21–22, 58
  "hama-ha" in, 58
  "Kaup`a.t´a," 28
  "Nau´ts'it‌ʸ‌'i," 166n4
  "Origin Legend," 23, 164n15
  "P'acaya·´nʸi," 23, 75, 147–48
  "The Hummingbird," 23, 66–67, 75, 83, 149–52, 164n15
  "The Witches and Arrow-Youth," 153–54
  "The Witches and the Youth," 179n6
  "Ts'its'ts'i·´na·´k'o," 166n4
  "Warriors," 100
  "White-House," 166n4
  witch transformation in, 135
Kesey, Ken, 31
Κoai´k`tc` ("sunrise"), 60, 61, 63
Kochinninako
  in Silko and Boas, 153–54
  See also Yellow Woman
Kokopelli, 40
K'oo'ko, 99–105 *passim*, 173n10, 173–74n11
  and U.S. government, 79
  as sister of warrior twins, 101
  in Boas(K'oo·´κο), 76
  in Opi ritual, 100–02
  in Stirling (Ko'oko), 102
  mother of Ck'o'yo medicine men, 104
koshare, 34, 173n8
  in Boas, 60
  moiety, 60
Ko´Tʸɛ, 26, 41, 76, 128, 166n4
  on Opi ritual, 100
Kroeber, Karl, 165n7
Kunnedeyah. *See* Gunnadeyah
Ku'oosh, 45, 48, 90, 100, 102–05, 124, 168n17
  and Betonie, 103
  and Nautsityi, 90
  and old Grandma, 176n1
  and Scalp Ceremony, 102–05
Kurath, Gertrude P., 165n13
kurena, 60, 61, 62, 101
  and sunrise, 60
  in Boas, 60
Kush-Kutret ("White House"), 81, 118, 119, 165n10, 178n15

L

Laguna (village), 6, 80, 117
  and Gallup, 92
  as home to Silko, 5, 8, 9, 10
  destabilization/diseasement of, 9, 92, 100
  in relation to Chuska Mountains, 94
  Marmons at, 6
  Mt. Taylor in relation to, 32
  Nautsityi's departure from, 74
  Nautsityi's return to, 73
  Pacayanyi's coming to, 75, 79–80
  Tayo's departure from, 16, 107, 114
  Tayo's return to, 47, 107, 113
Laguna Pueblo, 4
  and Cañoncito reservation, 125, 129
  and Dripping Springs, 136
  as contact zone, 5–6
  as new home to speckled cattle, 34
  landscape of, 18
  map of, 141–42
  oral tradition,
  sociopolitical schism at, 180n12
  Sterling's departure and return, 10
  villages of, 7
    See also Kawaika
Langen, Toby C. S., 179n2
Laura (Tayo's mother), 81, 89, 107, 161n9, 171n6
  and Auntie as branching versions of Laguna female, 176n6
  and Helen Jean, 170n3
  and Nautsityi, 70, 87
  and Reed Woman, 69–71
  and Yellow Woman, 73
  as katsina spirit, 71–73
  Auntie's story about, 74, 87
Leroy, 16, 77, 125, 132, 134, 170n3
Lincoln, Kenneth, 169n25
Little Sister (Tayo's mother). *See* Laura
Lummis, Charles F., 127, 130, 133, 179n4
  witch transformation in, 135

M

Marmon, Agnes Anaya, 172n6
Marmon, Henry C. ("Grampa Hank"), 7,

Index

172n6
Marmon, Lee, 6, 7, 163n7, 172n6
"A Laguna Portfolio," 161n10, 162n1
Marmon, Marie Anaya, 6, 7, 162n1, 172n6
Marmon, Mrs. Walter G., 42, 76, 172n6, 176n2
Marmon, Robert, 6, 42, 172n6
Marmon, Susan Reyes, 6, 7, 162n1, 163n7, 177n5
Marmon, Virginia, 5
Marmon, Walter G., 6, 42, 166n5, 172n6
Martin, Pedro, 26, 66, 84
Maseewi, 74, 80
    and Tayo, 78–80
    as generic term for warrior, 172n7
    failure of vision, 77
    in Boas, 173n10
    in Opi ritual, 100–02
    in Silko and Boas, 147–48, 149
    variant spellings of, 167n8
McAllester, David P., 168n23, 169n3
Mesita, 6, 7, 16, 107, 170n3
Miller, Jay, 166n3
Mitchell, Carol, 169n25
Momaday, Scott, 1, 8, 11, 109, 171n1, 172n3
    Bear in, 177n4
    use of Jemez frame elements, 163n4, 170n8
Mooney, James, 122
Moore, David, 174n14, 179–80n9
Mountain Lion, 81, 97, 132, 164n15
    and cloud motion, 35
    and Emo, 86
    and Pacayanyi, 86
    and Ts'eh, 96, 176n1
    in Silko and Boas, 147–48
    Tayo's identity with, 174n17, 180n10
Mountainway
    and Bear medicine, 108
Mt. Taylor, 59, 94, 95, 117, 130
    and Bear, 7, 9, 109
    and Kaupata, 29–36
    and Malpais formation, 166n14
    and Mountain Lion, 96–97
    and star pattern, 32
    and Ts'eh, 96–97
    as "White House," 165n10
    fence on, 4, 131
    Night Swan's affinity for, 88
Mullett, G. M., 166n2

N

NAGPRA, 3
Natonabah, Andrew, 178n15
Nautsityi, 14, 16, 23, 43, 75–97 *passim*, 118
    and Corn Woman, 67, 70, 173n8
    and drought, 108
    and Laura, 87
    and Night Swan, 88–89
    and old Buzzard, 90
    and old Grandma, 90
    and old Ku'oosh, 90
    and Tayo, 94
    and Ts'eh, 96
    and Ts'its'tsi'nako, 96
    departure of, in Silko and Boas, 149
    in Boas, 24, 41, 42
    in Parsons, 42
    in Stevenson, 41
    in Stirling, 167n9
    in White, 167n9
    See also Corn Mother
Navajo ethnographic pretexts, 107–17
Neihardt, John G., 50, 168n19
Nelson, Elizabeth Hoffman, 161n15
Nelson, Malcolm, 161n15
Nelson, Robert M., 163n4, 164n3, 165n5, 169n2, 175n6, 181n16
Night Swan, 16, 34, 87, 88, 90, 96
    and Nautsityi, 88–89
    as female principlen1, 175n5

O

Old Buzzard, 18
Oñate, Juan de, 133
Opi (Scalp Society, Scalp Society member), 100–02
    in Boas, 100
    in Gunn, 100
    Maseewi and, 100–02
oracy, 2, 161n3
oral tradition, 3, 4, 13, 17, 18, 20–21, 23, 25–26, 27, 28, 31, 33, 36, 41, 50, 59, 60, 61, 62, 63, 65, 67, 80, 89, 100, 117, 118, 125, 127, 135, 136
    Ceremony's roots in, 1, 2
Ortiz, Simon, 163n12, 165n13

Ou'yu'ye'wi, 74
Our Mother. *See* Nautsityi, *See* Nau'ts'ity'i
Owens, Louis, 162n2, 168n16

P-Q

Pacayanyi, 14, 26, 75, 105, 108
   abuse of Bear medicine, 79–80
   and Army recruiter, 78–79, 80, 81
   and Coyote, 108, 112
   and departure motif, 75–82
   and Emo, 25
   and Ma'see'wi as relatives, 81
   and Mountain Lion, 86
   and Tayo, 80–82
   and vision, 77
   and witchery, 85
   as bearer of disease, 23, 173n8
   as son of Ck'o'yo, 164n15, 172n4
   in Boas (P'acaya·´nⁱi), 24, 27, 76, 128
   in Gunn (Po-chi-an-ny), 76
   in Parsons (Bacheani), 76
   in Silko and Boas, 147–48
   in Stevenson(Po´shaiyänne), 75
   in Stirling (Pishuni), 172n8
   variant spellings in Gunn, Parsons, Boas, and Stirling, 173n8
   variant spellings in Gunn, 172n5
Paguate, 6, 7, 11
Paraje, 6
Parrot (macaw), 87, 88, 175n5
Parsons, Elsie Clews, 21, 23, 26, 42, 67, 76
   as transcriber of *Keresan Texts*, 163n6
   Kaupata in, 164n4
   Notes on Ceremonialism at Laguna, 21, 42, 163n10, 164n4
   on Opi ritual, 176n9
Pa'to'ch (Butte), 136
   and Ts'eh, 117, 130
Pedro Martín, 41
Pinkie, 77, 125, 132
Pollen Boy, 53, 56, 111, 116
   in Silko and Wyman, 158
polyvocality, 46
Pratt, Mary Louise, 161n7

R

recovery, 66
   and *dis*-covery, 128
   and whiteness in Big Hoop ceremony, 115
   homology between Laguna and Navajo stories, 113
   in bear-child story, 108–09
   in Big Hoop ceremony, 108–17
   in Native prophecies, 122
   of Nautsityi in nine-part backbone story, 83–97
   of (pan-)Indian identity, 124
   of speckled cattle and stormclouds, 31–35
   Tayo's, 168n22
   See also departure-recovery motif
Recovery Chant (in Red Ántway), 111–14
Red Antway, 17, 27, 110, 111, 155–59, 168n23, 177n3
   and Laguna Scalp Ceremony, 104
   Bear medicine in, 177n3
   "Bear's Prayer," 112, 158, 177n3
   "cutting song," 111
   "Hoop Prayer," 158–59
   scalp ceremony in, 112
   "Thunder Prayer," 110–13 *passim*, 159
   unraveling songs in, 113
Reed Woman, 13, 16, 65–71, 72, 73, 75, 77, 81, 91, 94, 104, 108, 127, 171n6
   and Rocky, 69
   and Tayo, 68
   and tobacco, 179n4
   in Gunn, 65–67
   in Silko and Gunn, 145
Robert, 6, 32, 42, 52, 71, 91, 92, 103, 181n17
   and Hummingbird, 90–91
   and Josiah as branching versions of Laguna male, 176n6
Rocky, 68, 69, 78, 79, 81, 86, 89, 171n6
   and drought, 104
   and Emo, 85
   and Ou'yu'ye'we, 78
   and Red Woman, 69
   Tayo's deerhunt with, 85
Roemer, Kenneth, 161n1, 165n8
Rosen, Kenneth, 8
Ruppert, James, 122

Index

S

Salyer, Gregory, 1
San José River, 5, 6, 80, 181n15
Scalp Ceremony, 99–105
   and Enemyway, 104
   and Red Antway, 104, 112
   in Parsons, 176n9
   in Wyman, 177n10
Scalp Society, 99–102
   origin story in Stirling, 101
Scarberry-García, Susan, 1, 171n1
Seama, 6, 179n2
Seboyeta, 7
Sekaquaptewa, Helen, 163n4
shiwanna (Cloud People), 4, 24, 33, 35, 62
   heyaashi, 34
   in Allen, 169n6
   in Boas, 34
   in Swan, 34
   variant spellings in Boas, Parsons, Swan, and Kurath, 165n12
Shush, 52, 53, 110, 114, 115, 156–57, 159, 177n8
Silko, Leslie Marmon
   Almanac of the Dead, 9, 10, 37, 122, 161n15
      macaw in, 175n5
      snake in, 162n3
   "Arrowboy and the Witches," 9, 181n14
   The Delicacy and Strength of Lace, 8, 181n15
   "Estoymuut and the Gunnadeyah," 135–37, 136
   "The Fourth World," 162n3
   Gardens in the Dunes, 10
      macaw in, 175n5
   "Interior and Exterior Landscapes," 161n11
   Laguna Woman, 8
   "Landscape, History, and the Pueblo Imagination," 161n11
   "The Man to Send Rain Clouds," 6, 8, 161n8
   "Running on the Edge of the Rainbow," 11, 161n9, 161n13
   Sacred Water, 175n10
   Stolen Rain, 136
   Storyteller, 2, 5, 9, 28, 47
      "Aunt Susie had certain phrases," 168n14
      "Estoy-eh-moot and the Kunideeyahs," 9, 134–35, 153–54, 155
      "Lullaby," 8
      "One Time," 21, 23, 75
      Mt. Taylor in, 9
      "Skeleton Fixer," 163n12
      "Story From Bear Country," 109, 168n21
      "Storytelling," 161n8
      "The Two Sisters," 168n14, 179n4
      "Up North," 28
   Yellow Woman and a Beauty of the Spirit, 11, 162n4
      "An Essay on Rocks," 109
      "Notes on *Almanac of the Dead*," 169n4
      "Stone Avenue Mural," 162n3
sipapu (Emergence Place), 52, 55, 78,
   in Gunn ("Ship-op"), 65, 66, 67, 170n1
   in Stirling, 167n9, 172n8
Skeleton-fixer (Badger), 135
Snake
   at Dripping Springs, 162n3, 180n10
   hoop transformation into, 179n7
   in *Almanac of the Dead*, 162n3
   in Navajo Great Star chant, 168–69n23
   Tayo's identity with, 180n10
speckled cattle, 4, 11, 30, 33, 89, 125
   and Dripping Springs, 136
   and stormclouds, 33–36, 87
   and Tayo, 87
   and Tayo as "special breed," 87
   and Tayo as hybrids, 34
   Betonie's vision of, 94
Spencer, Katherine, 108
Spider Grandmother. *See* Ts'its'tsi'nako
star pattern, 31–33, 34, 117
   Betonie's, 166n1
   Betonie's vision of, 94
   "Big Star" pattern, 32
   Kaupata's eyes, 35
   Kaupata's eyes in Silko and Boas, 148
   Orion and Pleiades, 32, 148
   sketched by Betonie, 94
   star riddle, 32, 148
Stchi-mu-ne-moot, 66, 73, 174n2
Stevenson, Mathilda Coxe, 41, 75, 166n3, 172n3
Stirling, Matthew W., 101, 102, 167n9,

172n8, 173n8
stolen rain. *See* stormclouds, *shiwanna*
stormclouds
   and speckled cattle, 29, 30, 33–36, 87
   and Tayo, 87
   in Boas, 165n4
   in Kaupata story, 4, 24, 94, 165n10
   in nine-part backbone story, 73, 95
   in Silko and Boas, 154
                    See also shiwanna
Sun Man, 4, 14, 17, 24, 27–37 *passim*, 77, 87, 94, 129, 130, 132
sunrise, 37, 53, 81, 116, 117, 133
   and katsinas, 5
   and return motif, 71, 73
   and San José River crossing, 10, 35, 161n9
   and Tayo's re-entry, 95, 171n5
   as bracket term, 61
   as formal bracket 58–59
   as prayer, 61–62
   as setting, 57–58
   in Boas, 60, 170n7
   in Momaday, 170n8
   in Stirling, 167n9
   sunrise series, 14, 57–63
   text (p. 4) in hoop series, 49–50, 55, 57–59
                    See also emergence
Swan, Edith, 34, 88, 89, 90, 96, 113, 165n9
   on backbone motif, 163n13

T-U

Tedlock, Dennis, 45, 167n13
Thelma. *See* Auntie
Thorson, James, 1
Thought Woman. *See* Ts'its'tsi'nako
tobacco
   and Betonie, 175n8
   and Caterpillar, 83, 93–94
   and Green Fly, as new forms of life, 91
   and Reed Woman, 66–67, 91, 94, 179n4
   and Ts'eh, 94–95
   in Opi ritual, 101
   in Silko and Boas, 151–52
transformation, 17, 39, 45, 121
   animal transformation in witchery, 128–29

hoop to snake, 179n7
   in "Story From Bear Country," 109, 168n21
   in Arrowboy fragment, 127–37 *passim*
   in Arrowboy fragment, 128–32
   in Bear-child story, 108–09
   in Great Star chant, 169n23, 177n4
   in hunter-to-Coyote story, 109–17
   in recovery ceremonies and in witchery, 181n17
   of audience to storyteller, 42–43
   of the connotation of "sunrise," 57
   of hunter to Coyote in Silko and Wyman, 155–56, 157
   of K'oo'ko's appearance, 76, 173n11
   of narrative mode, 54–56
   of plot from departure to recovery, 73
   of storytelling voice, 56
   of Tayo, 83
   of Tayo from Green Fly to Hummingbird, 88–89
   of witches in Boas and Lummis, 135
   of word to world, 43
   recovery from ck'o'yo medicine, 82
   stories, as brackets, 107
   Tayo, from Mountain Lion to Snake, 180n10
   transformative zones in Big Hoop ceremony, 51, 116
Ts'eh, 34, 35
   and Caterpillar, 94
   and Dripping Springs, 133, 136
   and Mountain Lion, 96
   and Nautsityi, 96
   and Pa'toch Butte, 117, 130
   and tobacco, 94
   and Yellow Woman, 134
Ts'its'tsi'nako, 23, 29, 39, 42, 47, 49, 82, 94, 125, 130, 132
   and Nautsityi, 96
   Arrowboy's helper, 128
   as first word of novel, 40
   as storyteller, 40–43
   as ultimate protagonist in the novel, 121
   in Boas, 41, 42
   in "Estoymuut and the Gunnadeyah," 136
   in First World, 43, 118–19
   in Gunn, 41
   in Stevenson, 41–42, 166n3
   in Stirling, 167n9

S as, 47
Tyler, Hamilton, 175n4, 175n5
typography, 45, 46, 61
 and voice, 45–47
 in the witchery narrative, 46
 Silko's use of italic and quotation marks, 178n1

V

vision
 and Ck'o'yo witchery, 32, 33
 and hoop/transformation motif, 128–32
 and Kaupata's trickery, 129
 as inoculation against ck'o'yo witchery, 132
 as inoculation against witchery, 179–80n9, 180n9
 during Jackpile mine episode, 180n11
 Kaupata's trickery, 77
 Maseewi's failure of, 77
 Pacayanyi's trickery, 77–78
 Tayo's acquisition of, 130
 Tayo's vision of Ts'eh at Dripping Springs, 180n10
 Tayo's vision of witchery, 125
voice, 30, 39, 46, 49, 50, 100
 and typography, 45–47
 authorial, 23
 embedded and embedding, 121
 embedded and embedding, 39–50 *passim*
 in "Story From Bear Country," 109
 of witchery, 134, 79, 100
 Silko's use of italic and quotation marks, 178n1
 storyteller's, 27, 42, 45, 55–56
 transformation of storytelling voice, 56
 Ts'its'tsi'nako's, 40

W-X

Walam Olum, 162n2
Warrior Twins. *See* Maseewi
 as agents of recovery, 83
 Tayo and Rocky as, 78

Waters, Frank, 122
Welch, James, 51, 168n20
Weso, Thomas, 175n8, 175n10
Wheelwright, Mary C., 168n23, 177n4
white
 as color of First World, 118–19, 175n7
 as source of disease, 123
 in Keresan tradition, 117–19
White, Leslie A, 164–65n4, 165n10, 167n9, 178n14
Whitman, Walt, 67
Wiget, Andrew, 163n4, 165n7
witchery, 15
 as disease, 123, 123
 Tayo's acquired ability to resist, 131–32
witchery, 121–25, 127–37
  See also Pacayanyi, Kaupata, Emo, Gunnadeyah, Ck'o'yo
Wolf
 and witchery, 180n11
Wovoka, 122
Wright, James, 8, 181n15
Wyman, Leland, 27, 108, 109, 163n3, 168n23, 177n10
 "Bear's Prayer," 110
 Scalp Ceremony in, 177n10
  See also Red Anyway

Y

Yellow Woman, 10, 17, 170n3
 and Ts'eh, 134
 as wife of Arrowboy, 128–36 *passim*, 128
 betrayal of Arrowboy, 134
 Helen Jean as, 170n3
 in Allen, 170n2
 in *Almanac of the Dead*, 161n15
 Laura as, 72, 174n17
 motif, 5
  See also Kochinninako

Z

Zamir, Shamoon, 162n16
Zia (Pueblo), 41, 75, 161n2, 167n9, 172n7

www.ingramcontent.com/pod-product-compliance
Ingram Content Group UK Ltd.
Pitfield, Milton Keynes, MK11 3LW, UK
UKHW021312180426
11947UKWH00015B/1184